Covid and . . .

Covid and...
How to Do Rhetoric in a Pandemic

Edited by
Emily Winderman,
Allison L. Rowland,
Jennifer Malkowski

MICHIGAN STATE UNIVERSITY PRESS | *East Lansing*

Copyright © 2023 by Michigan State University

Michigan State University Press
East Lansing, Michigan 48823-5245

Library of Congress Cataloging-in-Publication Data
Names: Winderman, Emily, editor. | Rowland, Allison L., editor. | Malkowski, Jennifer A., editor.
Title: Covid and . . . : how to do rhetoric in a pandemic / edited by Emily Winderman, Allison L. Rowland, and Jennifer Malkowski.
Description: East Lansing : Michigan State University, [2023] | Includes bibliographical references.
Identifiers: LCCN 2022049105 | ISBN 9781611864618 (paperback) | ISBN 9781609177355 (pdf) | ISBN 9781628955019 (epub)
Subjects: LCSH: Rhetoric—Social aspects—United States—History—21st century. | Rhetoric—Political aspects—United States—History—21st century. | COVID-19 Pandemic, 2020—Influence. | LCGFT: Essays.
Classification: LCC P301.5.S63 C68 2023 | DDC 362.1962/4144—dc23/eng/20230303
LC record available at https://lccn.loc.gov/2022049105

Cover design by Erin Kirk
Cover art is *Miasmic Rise*, by Sarah Knobel, used with permission.

Visit Michigan State University Press at *www.msupress.org*

Contents

vii   Acknowledgments
ix   Introduction: An Agenda for Pandemic Rhetoric, *Allison L. Rowland, Emily Winderman, and Jennifer Malkowski*

PART 1. **Pre-existing and Chronic**

3   Covid and Racialized Myths: Pre-existing Conditions and the Invisible Traces of White Supremacy, *Raquel M. Robvais*
21   Covid and Environmental Atmospheres: Pulmonary Publics and Our Shared Air, *Sara DiCaglio*
37   Covid and Science Denialism: The Rhetorical Foundations of US Anti-Masking Discourse, *Kurt Zemlicka*
57   Covid and Vaccine Hesitancy: Tracing the Tuskegee-Covid Straw Man Fallacy as a History Presently Unfolding, *Veronica Joyner and Heidi Y. Lawrence*

PART 2. **Essential and Disposable**

79   Covid and Essential Workers: Medical Crises and the Rhetorical Strategies of Disposability, *Marina Levina*
97   Covid and Being a Doctor: Physicians' Published Narratives as Crisis Archive, *Molly Margaret Kessler, Michael Aylward, and Bernard Trappey*
123   Covid and Fatphobia: How Rhetorics of Disposability Render Fat Bodies Unworthy of Care and Life, *Hailey Nicole Otis*
147   Covid and Intersex: In/Essential Medical Management, *Celeste E. Orr*

PART 3. Remedy and Resistance

- 169 Covid and Shared Black Health: Rethinking Nonviolence in the Dual Pandemics, *DiArron M.*
- 191 Covid and Masking: Race, Dress, and Addressivity, *Angela Nurse and Diane Keeling*
- 209 Covid and Disability: Tactical Responses to Normative Vaccine Communication in Appalachia, *Julie Gerdes, Priyanka Ganguly, and Luana Shafer*
- 235 Covid and Doubt: An Emergent Structure of Feeling, *Jeffrey A. Bennett*

- 255 Contributors

Acknowledgments

WE DEDICATE THIS BOOK TO THOSE LOST IN THE PANDEMIC AND TO THOSE grieving a lost loved one. May their memories generate much-needed structural change in public health, medicine, and rhetorical practice. This volume also honors those living with long Covid—we recognize your struggle.

For the alchemically groovy and spiritually nourishing collaborative energy we have created as a trio, the editors are grateful to each other. For their fierce political projects, heart-stopping sentences, and willingness to produce marvelous chapters on an expedited timeline, we thank the contributors to this volume. While we have designed the chassis and gathered everyone along for the ride, their work is the engine that propels this volume. Even as we critique it from the inside, we are grateful for the field of rhetoric of health and medicine and the colleagues who labor under its aegis. In turn, we are grateful for scholars—many of whom we have never met—in the fields of public health, health communication, sociology, and medicine, whose thinking helped us broaden our approaches and stage a transdisciplinary conversation in the introduction to this volume.

We appreciate the time and talents of two colleagues who have made both visible and invisible contributions to this volume. Atilla Hallsby helped to generate the first iteration of the rhetoric-as-fascia model that you will find in our book's introduction during the end-of-semester crunch time in December 2021—just in time for our initial draft submission. Jenell Johnson has our admiration for her many talents, which include her intellectual leadership in our field and the gift of the gorgeous, finalized rhetoric-as-fascia illustration.

We thank Catherine Cocks, our editor at Michigan State University Press, for inspiring us with an early vision for this project before we had one ourselves. We thank our respective institutions for sustaining our scholarly work.

Emily is grateful for her partner, Atilla Hallsby, and son Isidore Felix, for their unending love. Allie is grateful for her partner, Denny, kiddos Rocky and Rosie, secure housing conditions, and reliable and loving daycare from Miss Bri Atkins. And a big thank you from Jenny to her home and heart, Steve, Elka, and Wells, who deliver love and calm when all is uncertain.

Introduction

An Agenda for Pandemic Rhetoric

Allison L. Rowland, Emily Winderman, and Jennifer Malkowski

IN JULY 2020, DINÉ KEEPER OF TRADITIONS SUNNY DOOLEY TOLD *SCIENTIFIC American*, "We have every social ill you can think of, and Covid has made these vulnerabilities more apparent. I look at it as a monster that is feasting on us—because we have built the perfect human for it to invade."[1] Two factors collided to create this "feast": Diné health and living conditions (contaminated groundwater; crowded housing; high rates of alcoholism, chronic stress, heart disease, diabetes, and cancer) and the material qualities of SARS-CoV-2 (aerosol transmission; tendency to damage chronically inflamed bodies). Structural conditions rooted in settler colonialism, racism, and dispossession rendered the Diné more vulnerable to Covid deaths. Dooley's simile of Covid-as-monster distills pandemic horror into an encounter of primal survival. For the editors of this book, the Covid monster is the least fearsome part of Dooley's testimony. Instead, it is Dooley's latter clause that chills us to the bone: "*we have built* the perfect human for [Covid] to invade." This volume centers the material-rhetorical enactments of structural harms—the living conditions that we have built—to show how rhetorical scholars can contribute amid an uncertain and dire situation.

While the Diné's vulnerabilities are unique, they are far from the only inhabitants of the United States whose living conditions, formed by long histories of oppression, left them disproportionately exposed to Covid harms. Dooley's monster personifies what Rupa Marya and Raj Patel call the *exposome*, or the "sum of lifetime exposures to nongenetic drivers of health and illness, from conception to death."[2] Influenced by Indigenous knowledge, Marya and Patel expand Christopher Wild's notion of the exposome that referred to environmental drivers of health to include social drivers of health (such as, for example, exposure to racism).[3] Their holistic understanding of the exposome locates the causal origin of disease in "the multidimensional spaces around and beyond the individual human body—its histories, ecologies, narratives, and dynamics of power."[4] We extend their ideas by considering the importance of public rhetoric in the exposome, unearthing a nascent tenet within the field of rhetoric of health and medicine central to the essays in this collection: infectious diseases enter communities pre-saturated with circulating meanings and are marked by inequitable distributions of vulnerability.

No matter the metric used to assess national pandemic responses, the United States is the developed country with one of the most abysmal responses to Covid, what historian Jackson Lears called "peculiarly catastrophic," noting that "for once, Americans can truly claim to be exceptional."[5] Just as Covid ravages chronically inflamed bodies by triggering autoimmune physiological responses, this collection investigates how US pandemic rhetoric functions as a "colonial project turned inward,"[6] as it triggers an autoimmune response within an already inflamed body politic. By focusing our efforts on the United States, contributors to this volume invoke a situated sensemaking to foreground what rhetoricians can offer—a close examination of emplaced experiences, histories, discourses, texts, affects, persuasive appeals and silences used to reveal, understand, and address the entwined material and symbolic features of pandemic public life. This focus should not trivialize the inherent global nature of pandemics or the myriad ways that the violent colonial ambitions of the United States harm people living elsewhere. While critical-rhetorical pandemic analysis must retain transnational sensibilities, Huiling Ding reminds us how "the context-dependent and locally determined nature of medical knowledge . . . is developed in response to local exigencies and material conditions."[7] In the case of Covid, American exceptionalism has proven more than just ethnocentric and myopic. American exceptionalism has been deadly—especially for historically resource-deprived communities within the United States.

Pandemics are supposed to "blow through distinctions and level all before it. This one did the opposite."[8] Across the United States, Black, Latinx, Indigenous, and poor people suffered higher rates of Covid incidents and age-adjusted death than their white or wealthy counterparts. The average life expectancy in the United States fell by 1.3 years, and the anticipated rates for Black people (2.1 years) and Latinx people (3.1 years) are worse.[9] Frontline workers, originally applauded for their heroism, now manage heightened risks with fewer resources. The service sector, including child and elder care and food industries, staffed disproportionately by women of color, continues to be underpaid while suddenly also becoming high risk. A class divide yawned open and temporary supports like eviction moratoria and unemployment pay have expired. Even after the reforms of the Affordable Care Act, millions of Americans remain un- or underinsured. For its racial and socioeconomic erasures, we reject the choral refrain of *we are all in this together*.[10]

Fueled by incompetent leadership, algorithm-driven misinformation, shortages of medical and personal protective equipment, a for-profit healthcare system, and the twin endemic diseases of settler coloniality and white supremacy, the United States fumbled hard. To this list, Lears would add: "the hollowing out of the public sector through draconian austerity measures, the shrinkage of any notion of a common good, the intensifying vacuity of debate between two political parties both committed to the upward transfer of wealth, and the militarization of police forces designed to contain discontent among the poorest, mostly black and brown, citizens."[11]

Ironically, in what can only be viewed in the sting of hindsight, in 2019, just months before the first case of Covid was identified in Wuhan, an international panel of experts ranked the United States as the nation most capable of preventing and mitigating epidemics and pandemics, scoring 83.5 out of 100.[12] Like many scientists and public health experts, the Global Health Security Index evidenced American exceptionalism in part because it underestimated the extent to which circulating public meanings were poised to undermine pandemic relief efforts in the United States. It failed to consider our national rhetorical climate's impact on the exposome. Covid entered an already burdened rhetorical ecology of health and then thrived upon a set of entrenched and distinctly US flaws.

Pandemic Rhetorical Studies

This book evinces the power of public rhetoric as indissociable from disease outcomes. Who could possibly contest, for example, that former president Trump's explicit denial of the severity of Covid, and the way this denialist rhetoric was amplified and informed by predatory algorithms and rightwing media outlets, affected the way the disease spread through the United States? Or who would deny that casting a face covering as a political statement versus a public health measure influenced masking behaviors? Finally, who would challenge that the scapegoating of Chinese nationals and Asian Americans generated anti-Asian violence when SARS-CoV-2 was labeled the "kung flu"? When it comes to matters of public health, rhetoric matters. While rhetoricians and communication scholars have long understood the power of rhetoric, the Covid pandemic has inspired a newly invested consciousness concerning the rhetorical underpinnings of public health and disease.

This book's subtitle echoes Paula Treichler's 1999 *How to Have Theory in an Epidemic: Cultural Chronicles of AIDS*. Treichler defended theory-building while asking that we "acknowledge the urgency of the AIDS crisis and try to satisfy its relentless demand for immediate action." More than twenty years later, we find ourselves in another crisis whose relentless demand warrants the tragic promotion from *epidemic* to *pandemic*. While Treichler made the compelling case for *theory* in an *epidemic*, the chapters collected here make the case for *rhetorical studies* in a *pandemic*. Treichler's oft-quoted phrase "epidemic of signification" is accompanied by the insight that we must go beyond the meanings that are generated in a pandemic and ask "precise questions about the conditions under which meanings proliferate."[13] The essays in this volume attend to the conditions under which Covid meanings proliferate and mark this practice as a priority for *pandemic rhetoric*—the study of discourse *about* pandemics and analysis of the material and discursive connections produced *by* pandemics.

In answering our book title's framing question: *how do we do rhetoric in a pandemic?*, we join scholars Shaunak Sastry and Ambar Basu who have also been inspired by Treichler to offer ways "to interpret the maelstrom of meanings that circulate" during pandemic times.[14] Rather than answer our central question with procedure or methodology, we offer a series of heuristics showcased in the chapters to follow that are grounded at the theoretical nexus of decolonial studies; anti-racist public health; critical health communication; and critical/cultural studies to inform the rhetoric of health and medicine. Our heuristics seek to provide scholars and scholar-activists across disciplinary boundaries company for thinking-with as we make sense of pandemic rhetoric.

Our first heuristic is that pandemic rhetorical studies is best served by an approach centering the material-rhetorical ecologies of health, with an understanding that all health and disease must be understood within the exposome. This approach attends to the way meanings rhetorically circulate and percolate. In turn, this enables our second guiding heuristic: a rhetorically attuned reading of the *structural* and *social* determinants of health wherein rhetoric is not considered as occurring temporally after the effects of structural/social determinants of health, but rather as the very fascia that connects and holds these factors in place as part of the exposome itself. Our third heuristic holds that doing rhetoric in a pandemic is an *in medias res* venture; plunged into the thick of the action, pandemic rhetoric must create and analyze partial archives. The essays in this volume respond to one or more of these prompts, collectively making the case for pandemic rhetorical studies to contend with the material-discursive folds of structural violence.

Heuristic 1: Rhetorical Ecologies of Health

In a landmark essay in rhetorical studies, Jenny Edbauer (Rice) complicated previous models of the rhetorical situation by claiming that "rhetoric emerges already infected by the viral intensities that are circulating in the social field."[15] We press the utility of this assertion into pandemic rhetoric by also claiming the chiasmic reversal to be true: viruses emerge already infected by the material-rhetorical intensities that are circulating in the social field. Contributors to this volume question how public discourse about disease transforms our symbolic and material worlds. To do so, we focus on the rhetorical ecologies of health, or "scholarship that attends to the processes through which health-related ideas, assumptions, and arguments have been communicated by and in relationship with the technical sphere, public or mainstream audiences, counter-publics, and vernacular or lay constituencies."[16] Two terms offer insight into how rhetoric moves: *circulation* traces ideas and discourses chronologically whereas *percolation* traces ideas that seep up through the sediment in chronologically disjointed or surprising ways.[17]

Circulation conceptually bridges rhetorical studies with the public health term used to define pandemic boundaries. Epidemiologists and infectious disease experts study how pathogens *circulate* through populations via contagion. In her prescient *Pandemics and the Media*, Marina Levina observes that disease management requires "proper accounting for circumstances, causalities, and circulations, which form contagion as a medical and narrative problem."[18] Far before we had modern understandings of bacteria, viruses, and other microbial life, fourteenth-century uses of the word *contagion* denoted "the circulation of ideas and attitudes."[19] Just as publics come into being by nature of material-discursive circulations, so do epidemics and pandemics. According to the CDC, an *epidemic* refers to "an increase, often sudden, in the number of cases of a disease above what is normally expected in that population in that area," whereas *pandemic* "refers to an epidemic that has spread over several countries or continents, usually affecting a large number of people."[20] The defining features of a pandemic rely on circulation: wide geographic extension, disease movement, high attack rates and explosiveness, minimal population immunity, novelty, infectiousness, contagiousness, and severity.[21]

Empires are adept at using disease rhetoric to aggregate power and resources. That the official distinction between *epidemic* and *pandemic* partially relies on the constructed boundaries of nation-states reveals the stakes of contemporary disease rhetoric in territorializing empires. If Jeff Bennett's assertion is correct that the term *epidemic* strategically justifies state intervention and regulation, then by extension *pandemic* bolsters authoritative governance structures even more.[22] Concretizing these observations in the context of the 2003 SARS epidemic, Ding writes: "Focusing on circulation-related risks, global risk politics attempts to supervise transnational flows of people . . . to prevent novel viruses from crossing national borders" and becoming *pandemic*.[23] Discourse about pathogenic microbes has long been used to structure our national peripheries by generating investments in the imperial state as protector of life.[24]

Heuristic 2: Rhetoric-as-Fascia in the Exposome

To understand the exposome of contemporary Covid in the United States, we need to account for more than what the World Health Organization calls the *social determinants of health* [SDOH]. Defined as nonmedical factors that influence health outcomes, SDOH are "the conditions in which people are born, grow, work, live, and age."[25] Because the SDOH model offers limited explanatory value regarding the *root causes* of health outcomes, it must be understood alongside the *structural* determinants of health, defined as the

> policies, institutions, and practices that define the distribution (or maldistribution) of SDOH. These structures and systems date back to the founding of [the United

States] and its economy on principles of racial, class, and gender hierarchy. They shape the distribution of power and resources across the population, engendering health inequities along racial, class, and gender lines.[26]

Many of the structural determinants of health that Joia Crear-Perry and colleagues supply to explain Black maternal health outcomes in the United States apply to Covid outcomes as well: histories of enslavement, punitive migration and citizenship policies, the Thirteenth Amendment's pipeline to mass incarceration, Jim Crow segregation, and housing segregation resulting from redlining, the government-backed denial of mortgages to Black people.[27] In turn, these structural determinants of health influence many of the social determinants of health downstream from them. In the case of Covid outcomes, these SDOH include exposure to air pollution and other toxins, access to healthcare and health insurance, food stability, occupation (white collar versus "essential" work, for example), and housing conditions. What's more, Black people in the United States confront daily acts of overt and micro-aggressive racism that result in a higher allostatic load, evidence of the toll that chronic stress takes on the body.[28] Accounting for the structural and social determinants of health in the Covid exposome allows racism to be named and prioritized as a foundational exigency.

An explanation of the Covid exposome would not be complete without accounting for how rhetoric works within and through the structural-social determinants of health. To engage a corporeal-material metaphor, we hold that rhetoric is the fascia that wraps, interweaves, and articulates the structural and social determinants to each other and to individual bodies. The fascial system enables a productive way to visualize how central public rhetoric is as a cultural force within the matrix of structures and individual bodies that animate it. While rhetoric has a long history of being described as connective tissue,[29] the physiological definition of fascia provides further resonance for this metaphor. Fascia names the connective tissue that holds muscles and ligaments to bones. *Fascia* entered English medical discourse in 1615, described as "more like a membrane than a tendon."[30] An "organ of communication" that sends messages to the nervous system and throughout the body, the fascial system's deep interconnectedness functions as a "tensional network" that changes density and fibrous arrangement depending on body movement.[31]

Rhetoric-as-fascia underscores the integrative, interdependent, and connective relationship among rhetoric, culture, and the structural-social determinants of health that comprise the exposome. Just as Plato subordinated rhetoric to philosophy, fascia has occupied a subordinated position within human anatomy: "From a gross anatomical standpoint, fascia seems to have mainly been perceived as a relatively unimportant body part."[32] Only in the past fifty years have Western researchers acknowledged the fascial system's centrality to corporeal function and movement. As the largest system in the body, the fascial system alone touches all of the other systems.[33] Like rhetoric, it is precisely fascia's omnipresence and interconnectedness that "frustrates the common ambition of researchers to divide it into a discrete number of subunits, which can be classified and separately described."[34] The classic visual rendering of human anatomy with color enhancements and "idealized depictions absent of fat and fascia," and the common dissection practice to cut away and discard fascia *trains* students to assume fascia is of no consequence.[35] Like rhetoric, the fascial system must be understood ecologically in dynamic relation to denser structures.

Fascial *dysfunction* also holds insight into how we might envision the interstitial work of rhetorical action within the exposome. Through patterns of repetitive movement or injury, layers of fascia can stick together, harden, and create further dysfunction throughout the anatomical chain. The connection between repetition, stickiness, and movement harkens to the work of Sara Ahmed, who tracked how "different 'figures' get stuck together, and how sticking is dependent on past histories of association that often 'work' through concealment."[36] The repetition of regressive rhetorical patterns stick and sediment in the form of colonial and racist structures. For example, participation in the "Covid sensorium"—an affective pedagogy that instructs individuals how to identify and avoid illness based upon sensory engagement—strengthens harmful structures through repetitive motion in stereotypes depicting Black and Asian people as vectors of disease.[37] Our emphasis on how rhetoric-as-fascia condition structural violence is not intended to dismiss or trivialize the agency of individuals. We are better able to argue for the centrality of rhetoric as it permeates the entire exposome and enables and prohibits material exigencies to move.[38]

Regarding individual agency, our rhetoric-as-fascia model complements the culture-centered approach (CCA) to health communication. Rather than engage the tired project of attempting to persuade marginalized people to change their behaviors, CCA prioritizes "listening to voices of marginalized communities [and] constructing discursive spaces which interrogate [their] erasures."[39] Its tripartite model of structure–culture–agency acts as a "sensitizing framework" to acknowledge how "members of marginalized communities continually interact with the structures within which they live, simultaneously working within these structures and participating in avenues

Introduction | xvii

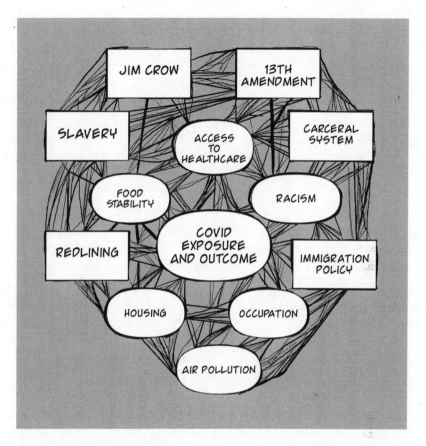

Rhetoric-as-fascia model. The structural determinants (in boxes) and the social determinants (in ovals) are adapted from Joia Crear-Perry et al., "Social and Structural Determinants of Health Inequities in Maternal Health," *Journal of Women's Health* 30, no. 2 (2021): 230–35, 231; and Ruqaiijah Yearby, "Structural Racism and Health Disparities: Reconfiguring the Social Determinants of Health Framework to Include the Root Cause," *Journal of Law, Medicine, and Ethics* 48, no. 3 (2020). Art by Dr. Jenell Johnson.

that seek to change them."[40] Our emphasis on the *recalcitrance* of structure and public discourse's fascial force is an orthogonal political project to CCA's emphasis on the locally situated knowledge of marginalized people.

In the model depicted in the figure, rhetoric-as-fascia is represented with stylized webbed lines that simultaneously connect, support, and lubricate the links of the exposome. In this depiction, fascial rhetoric is much more than the inconsequential filler between, for example, the structural determinants of slavery and redlining and the social determinants of crowded housing conditions that affect Covid vulnerability. Instead, public rhetoric conditions and justifies these connections. For example, in the leading chapter of this book, Raquel M. Robvais identifies how Black people with pre-existing conditions are blamed for their Covid vulnerability. As this myth rhetorically circulates, it cements structures of the exposome.

Our visual model of the Covid exposome depicts rhetoric-as-fascia *connecting* the structural determinants of health (in boxes) with social determinants of health (in ovals) for Black people in the United States, though our model is partial rather than complete. The elements of the exposome would change depending on the population and time frame. A Covid exposome focused on Indigenous people in the United States would include, for example, white settler colonialism and dispossession as structures. This visual model is a still shot of a dynamic unfolding process.

Our model visually depicts rhetoric in constitutive relation to the exposome. The lines represent rhetorical connections among larger, denser structural formations that shape how an individual is likely to encounter Covid. Many visual models depicting structural or social determinants of health entirely elide rhetoric, public discourse, or circulating meaning. For the models attempting to account for something like public discourse, they refer to *media messages* or *stigma* as afterthoughts relegated to an outer periphery and cast as discrete, rather than constitutive, elements.[41] Our fascial model intervenes in the *arhetorical* way that most public health models illustrate the relationship between structural/social determinants of health and particular diseases.

Heuristic 3: Create and Analyze Partial Archives

This edited volume is a partial archive of the unfolding pandemic within the United States through the lenses of our contributing authors.[42] We mean both senses of *partial*; as part of a larger whole and as taking a position. Archives should be understood "not as a passive receptacle for historical documents and their 'truths,' or a benign research space, but rather as a dynamic site of rhetorical power."[43] This power is doubled-edged, "both wielding a sword for oppression and a site of power and empowerment."[44] Despite the possibilities that this volume holds for enacting violence through the experiences and case studies that remain absent, we follow Matthew Houdek's hope that an archive might create "a memory-centered space for such critical dialogue, deliberation, and debate."[45] As such, this book constitutes and joins a partial Covid archive.[46]

While US deaths offer an impoverished account of pandemic magnitude and suffering, they provide crucial context for the timeline of this edited collection. When we made initial contact with our editor in December of 2020, just over three hundred thousand people had died of Covid in the United States. We had a contract signed by March 2021, just as the first wave of vaccinations became available and the US death toll crept to 550,000. We placed a call for chapter proposals in CommNotes and other relevant venues the following month. As our contributors embarked on a first round of chapter revisions, the Delta variant propelled a fourth wave that crested in September 2021 at about 680,000 US deaths.[47] When this volume went out for review, the death tally surpassed eight hundred thousand as omicron advanced. The press's editorial board approved the manuscript in May 2022, nearly the same week that the United States hit the staggering one million mark. We submitted the final manuscript in August 2022, as infection rates soared because of the BA.4 and BA.5 omicron subvariants and we slouched toward a deformed version of normal. In the production stage in December 2022, our copyeditors questioned verb tense inconsistencies throughout the book. Is the pandemic in the present or the past? Do we suffer or have we suffered? Pandemic status seems remarkably unhinged from the hundreds of Covid deaths in the United States every day.

We pause our tallying to note that Covid deaths are undercounted and that death numbers cannot account for all Covid-propelled cumulative harm, injury, trauma, or debility.[48] On May 24, 2020, the *New York Times* exemplified the impossibility to account for the magnitude of grief in an article called "U.S. Deaths Near 100,000: An Incalculable Loss." Publishing the names and a few notable words about just one thousand people—a 1 percent sample—this partial but powerful aggregation came nowhere close to honoring pandemic loss or the disproportionate emotional-viral-load of racialized grief. For example, Lila A. Fenwick, the first Black woman to graduate from Harvard Law, was reduced to a singular datum amid a sea of grief. Quantitative representations fail to consider the cumulative emotional-viral-load of racialized grief as an uneven outcome of structural violence.[49]

The viscerally crucial act of breathing spans what Kimberly D. Manning calls the "time of two pandemics"—Covid and anti-black police brutality.[50] Just one day after the *New York Times* aggregated the "incalculable loss" of 100,000 lives, Derek Chauvin knelt on the neck of George Floyd for 9 minutes and 29 seconds. While Floyd was one of many Black men lynched by the police in 2020, the video of his murder launched a series of national and global uprisings.[51] Read retroactively, his words "Please, I can't breathe," gesture toward the amplified weight that Covid placed on the necks of Black people.[52] Such suffocative weight evidences lynching and violent racial formations not confined to the Covid era. As Ersula Ore and Matthew Houdek historicize: "The rhetorical anachronization of Black life figures blackness as outside the purview of white civil society's responsibility, recognition, and grievability, leaving the Black subject in a space-time wherein breathing becomes constrained."[53] The public failure to protect George Floyd preceded his lynching and his positive Covid status.[54] We emphasize his Covid status not to shunt blame from Derek Chauvin or the police state (as some have attempted), but rather to hold ourselves and our social systems accountable for structural violence.

This book simultaneously builds and analyzes an archive of Covid trauma. In addition to mass death on a national and global scale, over one million children in the world have lost a primary caregiver, with wide racial disparities distributing the emotional load unevenly.[55] For the millions of us who have survived Covid infections, it has become a mass debilitating event, with somewhere between 10 to 30 percent of us suffering from the constellation of symptoms that patients call long Covid.[56] Rejecting the understanding of trauma solely from a medical frame, Ann Cvetkovich notes, "as a name for socially situated political violence, trauma forges overt connections between politics and emotion."[57] Because "trauma challenges common understandings of what constitutes an archive," it can exceed the capacities to speak, represent, and remember. "Marked by forgetting and dissociation," trauma places pressure on archives traditionally understood and affords the possibility of new forms of remembering.

To build an archive and disavow the disembodied scholar myth, we received permission from our contributors to share a partially anonymized sampling of major life events that they experienced over the course of the pandemic. Within our group of twenty-one contributors and editors, we defended dissertations, published books, moved to new homes, started new positions, joined justice movements, received promotions, embodied new habits, and adopted pets. We lost loved ones to Covid and other conditions. We provided care for others who were sick or dying. We lived with disabilities, injuries, chronic pain, and autoimmune diseases. One contributor's homeland was invaded. One of us temporarily moved away from home to work in a Covid-only hospital. Many major life events entwine with social reproduction and the Covid-compounded care crisis, such as fertility treatments, pregnancies, miscarriages, at least four newborn babies, and hundreds of aggregate workhours vanished to lost childcare. These so-called personal events slammed up against politics when *Roe v. Wade* was overturned in June 2022, viscerally underscoring the horror of compulsory pregnancy in a country with impeded life chances for Black birthing parents and their babies.[58] Covid has gone through us like thread through a needle. Everything we do is stitched with its color.[59]

Covid and Rhetoric: How This Book Is Organized

From the beginning of our editorial collaboration, we were committed to the syntax of *Covid and...* for our book title to draw out the fascial connections between Covid and rhetoric. Intended to emphasize that pandemic rhetorics are always *in conjunction* with other elements of the exposome, *Covid and...* gathers its name from the Black feminist theories of intersectionality that demand critics trace interlocking, and thus compounding forms of oppression.[60] Each of the three parts of the book are pairs that employ the word *and* as strategic connective: Pre-existing and Chronic; Essential and Disposable; Remedy and Resistance. Within these parts, each chapter pairs Covid *and* another issue, exploiting the deceptive simplicity of the polysyndetic monosyllable *and*. Each pairing both conjoins (as in *weds*) but also relates (as in *compares*.) Given that "the linkage of elements within a text [creates] certain effects in the audience," each pair unlocks a set of meanings about the other.[61]

Just as our guiding heuristics may set an agenda for pandemic rhetoric, we curated this collection based upon an epistemologically and methodologically promiscuous vision of what we think pandemic rhetorical studies could encompass. Contributors engage collaborations that create strong intellectual fascia among sociologists, physicians, and public health officials. Important to the health of any field, contributors span career ranks and institutional relations ranging from early career graduate students to contingently employed scholars to full professors. It is an honor to platform the field-building contributions that these scholars make to rhetorics of health and medicine.

Part 1: Pre-Existing and Chronic

A signifier with a shifty rhetorical history, the term *pre-existing conditions* circulated in medical fields as early as the 1940s, but was not well known until it emerged in the context of medical insurance companies' underwriting practices.[62] Before the Affordable Care Act's protection of pre-existing conditions (signed in 2010, effective in 2014), US health insurance companies had the legal capacity to deny coverage based on an astonishingly long list of health issues, including AIDS/HIV, alcohol and drug abuse, cancer, depression, dementia, diabetes, epilepsy, heart disease, "obesity," paraplegia, pregnancy, and stroke. Nearly one-third of non-elderly US adults had at least one declinable condition prior to ACA protections.[63] It is no accident that these conditions track closely with both structural and social determinants of health. Exclusionary pre-existing condition policies mechanized health insurance as a mode of capitalist extraction. Colloquially, as people heard about one death after another, the common refrain was "Did they have a pre-existing condition?" Not only was the question insensitive, but it also proves that capitalist health structures train our thinking.

Like *pre-existing conditions*, the term *chronic conditions* percolated during the pandemic to identify those most at risk for severe outcomes and to hierarchize medical resource management when hospitals activated crisis standards of care. The banal day-to-day management of chronic illness suggests a *gradualism*, an ongoing slow violence and debility.[64] In a discussion of crip time, Kristen Cole writes that rhetorics of chronicity "obscure cultural and systemic sources of (dis)ablism, including the fact that striving for normalcy is in and of itself an experience of chronicity, and disregard experiences of chronicity that disrupt the boundaries of normative/immune-typical time."[65] There is no relief—no break—from the chronic. The pandemic at once contracts and dilates experiences of chronicity, marking new progressions based upon that which has been pre-existing.

Collectively, the chapters in this part move beyond tendencies to tether the terms *pre-existing* and *chronic* to individual bodies. The lead essay by Raquel M. Robvais pairs Covid with racialized myths to interrogate how the structural violence that forms Black vulnerability to Covid is diverted into blame for Black people. As a result, public discourse in the United States constructs Blackness as a congenital defect, a pre-existing condition of its own. In addition to targeting Black bodies as inherently problematic, these racialized myths enable white innocence. Racialized myths demand that Black bodies testify against themselves and contribute to the rhetorical fascia that structure the exposome.

Sara DiCaglio's chapter theorizes the Covid-induced shift in how we think about the air that we breathe, nudging us toward pulmonary publics wherein air, community, and health are atmospherically entangled. Crucial to this intervention are the uneven ways air pollution—a leading cause of inflammation and therefore Covid vulnerability—is racialized. Our relations to atmospheres—which extend beyond pollutants to include temperature, humidity, and allergens—are at once rhetorically governed and structurally violent.

Kurt Zemlicka's essay pairs Covid with science denialism to historically contextualize anti-masking discourses in the United States. By tracing the rhetorical heritage of two distinct denialist discourses that preexisted the current pandemic—the bottom-up discourse of digital communities forming identities around denialist rhetorics regarding vaccines and the top-down discourse of climate change denialism coming largely from carbon-heavy industries and the politicians they support—Zemlicka explains how these discourses converged during the pandemic in anti-masking discourses. These historical excavations demonstrate what Zemlicka coins *stochastic denialism*, a form of science denialism with unpredictable individual arguments that serves a predictable overall identity-forming purpose.

This part is anchored by an essay from Veronica Joyner and Heidi Y. Lawrence who dispute the oversimplified "Tuskegee" frame that arises repeatedly as a synecdochic shorthand for medical racism and mistrust. (Following their lead, we put "Tuskegee" in quotes as a reminder that the abusive syphilis study was conducted not by the HBCU Tuskegee University, but rather the US government.) For Joyner and Lawrence, the predominant "Tuskegee" framing mischaracterizes Black mistrust and constrains possible solutions.

Part 2: Essential and Disposable

At first blush, the terms juxtaposed in the book's middle part seem like obvious antonyms: surely that which is *essential* cannot also be *disposable*. As Allison Rowland warns us regarding discourses that appear status-raising,[66] zoerhetorical claims of essentiality are complex, insofar as they *appear* to promote or acknowledge the status of a particular group—say, grocery store workers—while the underlying *function* is to justify the continued staffing of a grocery store despite dangerous conditions. Naming disposability as a rhetorical mechanism of racialization, Lisa Flores emphasizes that disposability "garner[s] force through the work that [it does] in public life."[67] Claims of essentiality and disposability are fundamentally evaluative and entrench hierarchies. Each of the chapters in this part complicates essentiality, disposability, or the relationship between the two.

Marina Levina's chapter "Covid and Essential Workers: Medical Crises and the Rhetorical Strategies of Disposability," demonstrates how the percolation of the pandemic-era phrase *essential worker* lubricates the machinations of capitalist exploitation, ultimately enacting what she calls a "sacrificial violence" on workers in fields dominated by women and Black and Brown people. It is precisely their rhetorical construction as essential that makes their disposability palatable. A narrative of care and moral obligation further constrains these workers and precludes us from apprehending their precarity.

In the next chapter, rhetoric scholar Molly Margaret Kessler collaborates with practicing physicians and medical school faculty Bernard Trappey and Michael Aylward to examine a complementary fold of the essential worker experience: the published personal narratives of physicians treating Covid. Foregrounding the emotionally wrought testimonies of doctors on the frontlines realizes this book's intention of creating a partial archive. If Levina's essential workers are dehumanized by heroism narratives that depict them at once as essential *and* disposable, then Kessler, Trappey, and Aylward document physicians pushing back against this objectification by centering their own experiences. As they conclude, access to publishing one's personal account in a reputable medical journal is a privilege enjoyed by a tiny minority of healthcare workers.

In further articulation with disposability, Hailey Nicole Otis explores how medicalized fatphobia renders fat bodies disposable in Covid public health messaging, popular social media discourses, and state-level crisis care guidelines. Fat people are simultaneously scapegoated for the pandemic itself, just as their suffering and deaths are trivialized. The topoi for fat disposability Otis offers in this essay—positioning a vulnerable group as a drain on resources; promoting logics of personal responsibility; scapegoating; and trivializing death, harm, and suffering—are generative for disposability rhetorics far beyond fatness.

In a politically similar yet conceptually distinct engagement with the essential, Celeste E. Orr's chapter navigates the culture of silence surrounding the routine intersex medical management of young children and offers a path by which the pandemic-era suspension of "nonessential" intersex surgeries unwittingly supports the arguments that intersex scholars and activists have been making all along. This chapter is laudable in that it locates, in the unfolding of the Covid pandemic, a rare opportunity in which the harness of compulsory dyadism might be shrugged off.

Part 3: Remedy and Resistance

In an April 2021 editorial in the journal *Nature*, the authors declared, "To *remedy* health disparities, more scientists must 'get political.'"[68] In it, they decried that despite over a century of knowing that marginalized and low-income people suffer the worst health outcomes during a pandemic, there remains considerable resistance to ameliorating these underlying conditions. Exhorting scientists to "get political" by contributing white papers, distilling the needs of grassroots community groups, and becoming involved in the political process, the editorial nonetheless enumerated the barriers to doing so. As scholars invested in the rhetoric of science, we know that the relationship among scientists, politics, and public health are a complex dance. A lack of funding for issues involving systemic change and rejection from politicians to engage with the technical expertise of researchers present two ways that remedial efforts are resisted. This is one example of the ecological relationship we see between the concepts of *remedy* and *resistance*.

As frameworks, remedy and resistance attend to how attempts to mitigate and resolve pandemics are entrenched in circulating material inequities that percolate in moments of disaster and must be understood at their respective intersections of history and oppression. When it comes to communicable pathogens that initially emerge on a relatively small scale, public health often encourages containment to prevent mass circulation. As V. Jo Hsu confirms, despite the inherent interdependence that characterizes any pandemic, containment logics are a "rhetorical project that must confine diseases to particular bodies before excising them from the body politic."[69] These ritualized exorcisms give privileged people a false sense of security. Containment is an example of how diseases become opportunities for nations to enact an *alienizing logic* "premised on exerting extreme forms of state violence against any of those, citizen or migrant, who do not conform to the state's white supremacist, anti-black, ableist, heteropatriarchal, capitalist norms."[70] Given that white ethnonationalist and anti-immigrant movements in the United States have gained ground during the pandemic,[71] borders and their containment matter as one facet of attempted Covid "remedy." In turn, this alienizing logic conditions Covid's epidemiological trajectories. Containment is just one example of attempts at remedy/resistance that must be understood in terms of long, intersectional histories of settler colonialism, racism, and oppression. Contributors attend to the complex relationships between remedy and resistance during the pandemic. Remedy can encounter resistance for many reasons—but resistance itself can be a remedy.

Exemplifying the ameliorating possibilities of resistance, this part opens with DiArron M.'s analysis of Atlanta mayor Keisha Lance Bottoms's press conference amid uprisings following the lynchings of George Floyd, Ahmaud Arbery, and Breonna Taylor. Framing the study within the dual pandemics of anti-blackness and Covid, M. draws upon Molefi Kete Asante's Afrocentricity to frame the concept of *shared Black health*. Situating uprisings as a vaccination for anti-blackness, M. demonstrates how the press conference's exhortations for uprisers to "go home" ultimately "police the collective Black body," and diminish the ameliorative power of the uprising. By framing participants as immature, violent, and ineffective; appealing to Atlanta's progressivism; and redirecting uprisers toward nonviolence, the press conference misremembers the civil rights movement.

Noting how "masks cannot be understood separately from the bodies that wear them," Angela Nurse and Diane Keeling examine early pandemic representations of Black men's masking deliberation. Within the context of the two pandemics of Covid and anti-black racism, their study investigates how Black men navigate self-protection from both police brutality and the virus. Offering the framework of *the swirl* that interrogates how histories of violence are pulled into a particular moment's decision, Nurse and Keeling illuminate the rhetorical labor Black men shoulder in navigating those histories. By attending to the materiality of dress in rhetorical theories of addressivity, Nurse and Keeling complicate resistance to masking.

Julie Gerdes, Priyanka Ganguly, and Luana Shafer pair interviews with disabled people living in Appalachian communities with critical-rhetorical analysis of vaccine promotion materials that their participants were regionally likely to encounter. They found that vaccine promotion communications from public health offices tended to be complicit in ableism and alienized disabled people as a result. In addition to showing the value of mixed methods, their contribution also demonstrates the value of rhetorical inquiry for practitioners as they collaborate with a local public health office.

Closing out the volume with the lingering sense of nonclosure that is sure to characterize Covid rhetoric for years to come, Jeffrey A. Bennett grapples with *doubt* as an emergent pandemic structure of feeling. Situating doubt as simultaneously a "constitutive outside" of rhetorical situations, a dehumanizing aspect of racialized doctor-patient interactions, and "an essential element of medical practice," Bennett argues that choice discourses undergird the proliferation of this structure of feeling. Doubt, then, encourages resistance to pandemic remedy. Interrogating vaccine discourses, breakthrough infections, and mainstream fixation on queer culture, he offers a sobering conclusion: "The lasting uncertainty that has exacted itself into our daily lives is sure to impose itself for years to come and, as a result, we must learn to more efficiently manage our relationship to doubt in an era of radical indeterminacy."

Conclusion: The Future Is Covid And

The United States has learned the hard way that the meaning-making practices associated with public health hold profound consequences for the duration and intensity of pandemics. Although many public health officials would agree that things like executive denial, disinformation, and distrust influence the spread of the disease as much as physical features of Covid, the power of public rhetoric is rarely named as such, except by scholars like those in this volume. Equipped with theories and methods that help make sense of how and why talk matters, rhetoricians and their collaborators are well poised to inform the fraught contexts in which public health happens. Collectively, contributors to this volume illustrate what rhetoricians notice that other scholars do not: how to address constraints involved with doing rhetorical work during/for/about emerging situations, and why, ultimately, pandemic rhetoric matters. In doing so, this volume illustrates how public discourse surrounding Covid reveals, complicates, and acts as a stressor upon each of the systemic and structural issues that our authors explore.

Given that variants of SARS-CoV-2 will be with us for years ahead, we live in the gray zone between pandemicity and *endemicity*—the latter signifying when a disease becomes a "constant presence" in the background, as unremarkable as the common cold.[72] Constructed both rhetorically and epidemiologically, endemicity is also a function of public discourse. Left-leaning news organizations foregrounded the pandemic; right-leaning news organizations backgrounded the pandemic, depicting Covid as endemic. Even the *New York Times* has shuffled toward endemicity as their stylistic amplification decreased from COVID-19 to Covid 19 to Covid. As ongoing rhetorical negotiations that shape how disease is experienced (and experienced *unevenly*), endemicity and pandemicity require attention and archiving. The future is Covid *and*.

We opened this book with Sunny Dooley's stirring image of a feasting monster and relish Dooley's gesture to think beyond Covid itself. In the end—isn't this true of all horror stories?—it is not the monster that is so fearsome but rather the vulnerabilities some humans impose on other humans. We cannot attend to disease without attending to rhetoric's relation to power dynamics. We hope this volume provides a cornerstone, a gathering place, and a set of priorities for coordinating projects dedicated to addressing pandemic rhetoric in theory and practice.

NOTES

1. Sunny Dooley, "Coronavirus Is Attacking the Navajo 'Because We Have Built the Perfect Human for It to Invade,'" *Scientific American*, July 8, 2020.
2. Rupa Marya and Raj Patel, *Inflamed: Deep Medicine and the Anatomy of Injustice* (New York: Farrar, Straus and Giroux, 2021), 32.
3. Christopher Wild, "Complementing the Genome with an 'Exposome': The Outstanding Challenge of Environmental Exposure Measurement in Molecular Epidemiology," *Cancer Epidemiology Biomarkers & Prevention* 14, no. 8 (2005): 1847–50.
4. Marya and Patel, *Inflamed*, 13.
5. Jackson Lears, "Editor's Note: One Hundred Seconds," *Raritan* 40, no. 1 (2020).
6. David L. Eng, "Colonial Object Relations," *Social Text* 34, no. 1 (2016): 2.
7. Huiling Ding, *Rhetoric of a Global Epidemic: Transcultural Communication about SARS* (Carbondale: Southern Illinois University Press, 2014), 253.
8. Louise Erdrich, *The Sentence* (New York: HarperCollins), 184.
9. Theresa Andrasfay and Noreen Goldman, "Reductions in 2020 US Life Expectancy Due to COVID-19 and the Disproportionate Impact on the Black and Latino Populations," *Proceedings of the National Academy of Sciences* 118, no. 5 (2021): e2014746118.
10. Eric King Watts, "The Primal Scene of COVID-19: 'We're All in this Together,'" *Rhetoric, Politics & Culture* 1, no. 1 (2021): 1–26; Kalemba Kizito and Andrew Carter, "Denied Access: COVID-19, the Epidermal Border and Black Health Disparities," *Communication and Critical/Cultural Studies* 19, no. 2 (2022): 127–33.
11. Lears, "One Hundred."
12. Global Health Security Index, 2020 Report. www.ghsindex.org.
13. Paula Treichler, *How to Have Theory in an Epidemic* (Durham, NC: Duke University

Press), 1, 316.
14. Shaunak Sastry and Ambar Basu, "How to Have (Critical) Method in a Pandemic: Outlining a Culture-Centered Approach to Health Discourse Analysis," *Frontiers in Communication* 5 no. 585954 (2020): 2.
15. Jenny Edbauer, "Unframing Models of Public Distribution: From Rhetorical Situation to Rhetorical Ecologies," *Rhetoric Society Quarterly* 35 no. 4 (2005): 14.
16. Robin E. Jensen, "An Ecological Turn in Rhetoric of Health Scholarship: Attending to the Historical Flow and Percolation of Ideas, Assumptions, and Arguments," *Communication Quarterly* 63, no. 5 (2015): 523.
17. Robin E. Jensen, *Infertility: Tracing the History of a Transformative Term* (University Park: Penn State University Press, 2017).
18. Marina Levina, *Pandemics in the Media* (New York: Peter Lang), 82.
19. Priscilla Wald, *Contagious* (Durham, NC: Duke University Press, 2008), 12.
20. Centers for Disease Control and Prevention (CDC), "Lesson One: Introduction to Epidemiology," *Principles of Epidemiology in Public Health Practice*, 3rd ed., May 18, 2012.
21. David Morens, Gregory Folkers, and Anthony Fauci, "What Is a Pandemic?," *Journal of Infectious Diseases* 200, no. 7 (2009), 1018–21. The third author went on to serve as chief medical advisor to presidents Donald Trump and Joe Biden.
22. Jeff Bennett, *Managing Diabetes: The Cultural Politics of Disease* (New York: New York University Press, 2019).
23. Ding, *Rhetoric of a Global Epidemic*, 247.
24. Neel Ahuja, *Bioinsecurities: Disease Interventions, Empire, and the Government of Species* (Durham, NC: Duke University Press, 2016); Lisa Keränen, "Concocting Viral Apocalypse: Catastrophic Risk and the Production of Bio(in)security," *Western Journal of Communication*, 75, no. 5 (2011).
25. "Social Determinants of Health," World Health Organization, www.who.int.
26. Joia Crear-Perry et al., "Social and Structural Determinants of Health Inequities in Maternal Health," *Journal of Women's Health* 30, no. 2 (2021): 230–35, 231.
27. Crear-Perry et al., "Social," 231. See also "Web of Causation," Restoring Our Own Through Transformation (ROOTT), 2016, https://www.roottrj.org/web-causation; and Ruqaiijah Yearby, "Structural Racism and Health Disparities: Reconfiguring the Social Determinants of Health Framework to Include the Root Cause," *Journal of Law, Medicine, and Ethics* 48, no. 3 (2020).
28. Hailey N. Miller et al., "The Impact of Discrimination on Allostatic Load in Adults: An Integrative Review of Literature," *Journal of Psychosomatic Research* 146 (2021): 110434.
29. Marc Fumaroli defines rhetoric as the "connective tissue peculiar to civil society." As

quoted in Andrea A. Lunsford, Kirt Wilson, and Rosa Eberly's "Introduction: Rhetorics and Roadmaps," in *The Sage Handbook of Rhetorical Studies*, ed. Andrea Lunsford, Kirt Wilson, and Rosa Eberly (London: Sage, 2008): xi–xxix.

30. Sue Adstrom and Helen Nicholson, "A History of Fascia," *Clinical Anatomy* 32 (2019): 867.
31. Robert Schleip "Fascia as an Organ of Communication," in *Fascia: The Tensional Network of the Human Body*, ed. Teoksessa R. Schleip, T. W. Findley, L. Chaitow, and P. A. Huijing (China: Elsevier, 2013): 77–79.
32. Adstrom and Nicholson, "History of Fascia," 867.
33. Schleip, "Fascia as an Organ."
34. "About Fascia," The Fascia Research Congress, https://fasciacongress.org.
35. T. Kenny Fountain, *Rhetoric in the Flesh: Trained Vision, Technical Expertise, and the Gross Anatomy Lab* (New York: Routledge, 2014), 75.
36. Sara Ahmed, *The Cultural Politics of Emotion* (Edinburgh: Edinburgh University Press, 2004).
37. Emily Winderman and Robert Mejia, "The Covid Sensorium and Its Victims, Vectors, and Violators," *Communication and Critical/Cultural Studies* 19, no. 1 (2022).
38. Heidi Y. Lawrence, *Vaccine Rhetorics* (Columbus: Ohio State University Press, 2020).
39. Mohan J. Dutta, *Communicating Health: A Culture-Centered Approach* (Cambridge: Polity Press, 2008), 5.
40. Sastry and Basu. "How to Have," 4. Dutta, *Communicating Health*, 9.
41. For example, see "Mental Health and Well Being Ecological Model," Center for Leadership Education in Maternal & Child Public Health, https://mch.umn.edu/resources/mhecomodel/.
42. For a comprehensive day-by-day "global chronology" of key moments from November 17, 2019's "first unconfirmed case of COVID-19," to November 8, 2020's 1.25 million confirmed deaths worldwide, see J. Michael Ryan, "Timeline of COVID-19," in *COVID-19 Volume I: Global Pandemic, Societal Responses, Ideological Solutions*, ed. J. Michael Ryan (New York: Routledge, 2021), xiii–xxxii. Ryan situates this timeline as partial, noting the impossibility of forming a timeline that could be meaningful to all communities.
43. Charles Morris, "The Archival Turn in Rhetorical Studies; Or, the Archive's Rhetorical (Re)turn," *Rhetoric & Public Affairs* 9, no. 1 (2006): 113–15.
44. Matthew Houdek, "The Rhetorical Force of 'Global Archival Memory': (Re)Situating Archives Along the Global Memoryscape," *Journal of International and Intercultural Communication* 9, no. 3 (2016): 204.
45. Houdek, "Global Archival Memory," 219.

46. Archiving the Covid pandemic began early in the United States. *QED: A Journal in LGBTQ Worldmaking, Cultural Studies,* and *Philosophy & Rhetoric* published special issues. Some scholars situated the onset of the pandemic within structural violence (e.g. Raka Shome, "The Long and Deadly Road: The Covid Pandemic and Indian Migrants," *Cultural Studies* 35, no. 2/3 [2021]: 319–35). Others processed experiences of compounded precarity (e.g., Marlon Bailey, "Black Queerness and the Cruel Irony of the COVID-19 Pandemic," *QED* 7 no. 3 [2020]: 174–78).
47. "Trends in Number of COVID-19 Cases and Deaths in the US Reported to CDC, by State/Territory," CDC, https://covid.cdc.gov/covid-data-tracker.
48. Josh Katz, Denise Lu, and Margot Sanger-Katz, "574,000 More U.S. Deaths Than Normal Since Covid-19 Struck," *New York Times*, March 24, 2021.
49. Avril Maddrell, "Bereavement, Grief, and Consolation: Emotional-Affective Geographies of Loss during Covid-19," *Dialogues in Human Geography* 10, no. 2 (2020): 107–11.
50. Kimberly Manning, "When Grief and Crises Intersect: Perspectives of a Black Physician in the Time of Two Pandemics," *Journal of Hospital Medicine* 15, no. 9 (2020): 566–67.
51. We follow Ersula Ore's use of the term *lynching*. See *Lynching: Violence, Rhetoric, and American Identity* (Jackson: University Press of Mississippi, 2019).
52. Rachel R. Hardeman, Eduardo M. Medina, and Rhea Boyd, "Stolen Breaths," *New England Journal of Medicine* 383, no. 3 (2020): 197–99.
53. Ersula Ore and Matthew Houdek, "Lynching in Times of Suffocation: Toward a Spatiotemporal Politics of Breathing," *Women's Studies in Communication* 43, no. 4 (2020): 443–58.
54. Hardeman, Medina, and Boyd, "Stolen Breaths."
55. Daniel Victor, "Over 120,000 American Children Have Lost a Parent or Caregiver to Covid-19, Study Says," *New York Times*, October 7, 2021.
56. Knvul Sheikh and Pam Belluck, "What We Know About Long Covid So Far," *New York Times*, May 21, 2022.
57. Ann Cvetkovich, *An Archive of Feelings* (Durham, NC: Duke University Press, 2003), 3.
58. Dána-Ain Davis, *Reproductive Injustice: Racism, Pregnancy, and Premature Birth* (New York: New York University Press, 2019).
59. We paraphrase from W. S. Merwin's "Separation," in *The Second Four Books of Poems* (Port Townsend, WA: Copper Canyon Press, 1993).
60. Kimberlé Crenshaw, *On Intersectionality: Essential Writings* (New York: New Press, 2017); Patricia Hill Collins, *Intersectionality as Critical Social Theory* (Durham, NC: Duke University Press, 2019). In our fields, we read Bernadette Calafell, "The Future of Feminist Scholarship: Beyond the Politics of Inclusion," *Women's Studies in Communication* 37,

no. 3 (2014); Karma Chávez, *Queer Migration Politics: Activist Rhetoric and Coalitional Possibilities* (Carbondale: University of Illinois Press, 2013); Hailey Nicole Otis, "Intersectional Rhetoric: Where Intersectionality as Analytic Sensibility and Embodied Rhetorical Praxis Converge," *Quarterly Journal of Speech* 105, no. 4 (2019): 369–89.

61. Nathan Stormer, "Articulation: A Working Paper on Rhetoric and *Taxis*," *Quarterly Journal of Speech* 90, no. 3 (2004): 260.
62. *Oxford English Dictionary*, s.v. "pre-existing conditions."
63. "Pre-Existing Condition Prevalence for Individuals and Families," Kaiser Family Foundation, www.kff.org.
64. Lora Arduser and Jeffrey Bennett, "The Rhetoric of Chronicity," *Rhetoric of Health & Medicine* 5, no. 2 (2022): 123–29.
65. Kristen Cole, "Selling a Cure for Chronicity: A Layered Narrative Analysis of Direct-to-Consumer Humira® Advertisements," *Rhetoric of Health & Medicine* 5, no. 2 (2022): 214.
66. Allison Rowland, *Zoetropes and the Politics of Humanhood* (Columbus: Ohio State University Press, 2020).
67. Lisa Flores, *Deportable and Disposable: Public Rhetoric and the Making of the "Illegal" Immigrant* (University Park: Penn State University Press, 2020).
68. "Editorial: To Remedy Health Disparities, More Scientists Must 'Get Political,'" *Nature* 592, no. 660 (2021).
69. V. Jo Hsu, "Containment and Interdependence: Epidemic Logics in Asian American Racialization," *QED: Journal of GLBTQ Worldmaking* 7, no. 3 (2020): 125.
70. Karma Chávez, *The Borders of AIDS: Race, Quarantine and Resistance* (Seattle: University of Washington Press, 2021), 166.
71. Michael Lechuga and Antonio Tomas De La Garza, "Forum: Border Rhetorics," *Communication and Critical/Cultural Studies* 18, no. 1 (2021): 37–40.
72. CDC, "Lesson One."

PART 1

Pre-existing and Chronic

Covid and Racialized Myths

Pre-existing Conditions and the Invisible Traces of White Supremacy

Raquel M. Robvais

IN 1943, IT WAS WIDELY BELIEVED THAT AFRICAN AMERICANS WERE NOT FIT for military service because they were susceptible to syphilis. Across political and scientific circles, this susceptibility was attributed to genetics. Dr. Robert Fullilove, an American public health researcher and civil rights activist, resisted that notion and, in the *Journal of the American Medical Association*, turned attention to the structural dynamics that influenced the status of African American bodies: "The Negro is discriminated against economically and educationally; it would be difficult to find conditions more favorable to the development of crime, carelessness and social ostracism than the poverty and ignorance engendered by the wage and education differentials that too often the lot of the Negro."[1] Concluding that Black "bodies were recruited to testify against themselves" to support systems of subordination and marginalization, Fullilove's argument resisted the white supremacist reduction of African American bodies to malformed material spaces prone to diseases.[2] While Fullilove's recognition of the structural determinants of disease is, perhaps, more widely understood and accepted nowadays, the remnants of past racist explanations for disease outbreak and casualty persist.

In a volume about Covid, I open with syphilis and blame, the Black body and a pre-existing condition to illustrate an important historical continuity. While the diseases may be different, discourse about the two are strikingly similar. Each narrates assumptions and arguments woven throughout history, concluding that African Americans are biologically different, and that these differences foster inferiority, defects, and disease susceptibility. In other words, *Blackness* is a preexisting condition. Under these circumstances, any discrepancies among Black, Brown, and white Covid mortality rates enfold into the creases of a well-worn script of racialized medical myths. This chapter centers the durability of the myths that race is biology, that human difference justifies hierarchy, and that Blackness is often interpreted as a disease condition.

This chapter tracks how myths of white innocence collide with myths of "blackness [as] a congenital defect" in Covid discourse.[3] Doing so reveals how disease discourse underscores an all too familiar repetitive cycle of shaming a body through blame, of naming nature as the cause, and of obfuscating the work of whiteness in the process. As Melissa Harris-Perry reminds us, there is rhetorical power in shaming to maintain regressive social order and create identities: "Though we seldom think of it this way, racism is the act of shaming others based on their identity. Blackness in America is marked by shame."[4] The habits of whiteness that are foundational to blaming and shaming gestures toward the performance of superiority and subjugation that course through history, undergirding ideologies of human difference, in discreet references to Black bodies as defective, are in need of correction.[5] These acts of rhetorical significance enable the innocence of whiteness, preventing its implication in how and why Black bodies are harmed by Covid. Labeling this practice as a crime with no claim to innocence, James Baldwin indicted, "neither I, nor time, nor history will ever forgive them... they have destroyed and are destroying hundreds of thousands of lives and do know it and do not want to know it. But it is not permissible that the authors of devastation should also be innocent. It is the innocence which constitutes the crime."[6] Baldwin's words both historically ground and illuminate the current intersection of whiteness, blame, and Covid discourse as they retell a story that creates pre-existing conditions that then create categories of superior and inferior bodies for the maintenance of whiteness.

Drawing from Sara Ahmed's concept of *use*—the reoccurrence of the same story told in different ways—I examine how the habits of whiteness have manifested in two circulating racialized myths that mark and wedge Black bodies into a contentious Covid predicament. Assembling an archive of mainstream corporate news sources from March 2020 to August 2021, I trace a doubled movement of racialized myths: Black folk are immune *from* Covid and Black folk are susceptible *to* Covid. In doing so, I explore the rhetorical heft of "pre-existing conditions." A seemingly benign phrase, "pre-existing conditions" reflects, inflects, *and infects* disease rhetoric to reinforce difference and hierarchy in/for matters of public health across Covid discourse. Ultimately, Covid discourse draws our attention—once again—to how "racial and natural essences are forged in the crucible of politics," a practice that codifies whiteness as invisible and superior and Blackness as vulnerable and blameworthy.[7]

I begin by explaining the power of use as the deliberate employment of language to construct and constrain. I then examine the historical mapping of racialized myths that shore up the belief in immunity and vulnerability of Black bodies during the Covid pandemic. I conclude by revealing how the past and present are sutured by the ways of whiteness, supporting the argument that Covid articulates old stories in new ways.

The Power of Use

Circulation is vital to parsing the material representations of racialized myths because the process sustains a language that orients ways of being in this world. To this point, Thomas Rickert writes, "Rhetoric is ontological, and material things, as they circulate in their specific ways become a site for conjoining and disclosing the world. To study circulation is to study how the world and the things in it, as they move and assemble, bring their own light—and their own pulsions."[8] The use and circulation of these racialized myths gain currency and maintain traction through a lineage of symbolic gestures, woven into practices because they have become habits. In *Habits of Whiteness*, Terrance Macmullan informs us of the subtlety and utility of habits as they "become sedimented in a person's behavior because they enable him [sic] to find equilibrium within the surrounding environment."[9] As orchestrated ways of being, habits often unwittingly lead us along, not drawing much attention to their use or meaning. The repetition of use—the perpetual acts of racialized narratives—foster habits that cause us to recall the social construction of how inept and insufficient the Black body is ascribed to be, assigning the blame to pre-existing conditions and not structures of inequity.

In *What's the Use? On the Uses of Use*, Sara Ahmed extends the common understanding of *use* as more than whether something is in or out of circulation. Instead, "Use is a technique for shaping worlds and bodies."[10] Use has a history, it does things and requires a response. We are beholden to its introductory ways, marking starting lines as it guides us along the way. This purview reveals to us that, "Use is treated as a generative or life principle, that is, as a principle that shapes the very forms of life."[11] Not only are we appreciative for the life use reveals, but we are also mindful of how lack of use is a signatory for death. Another way to look at use is to see how uselessness also tells a story and performs an intent. It is through assumptions of uselessness that disposability occurs. It is because of perceptions of uselessness that supremacy and hierarchies abound. Because "use can be treated as a record of a life," we can elucidate past and present reporting to learn how certain bodies have been used to support myths to sustain human difference. Knowing "institutions are shaped by such uses of use," we are able to point to systemic structures of inequity that permit the continuity of disease categories. Use is symbolic; it creates meaning and coordinates actions: "Use implies more than a habitual practice; it also is an activity that leaves traces (more or less). These traces can become outlines for something: invitations to do something, to proceed in a certain direction."[12] Use is, thus, a harbinger of things to come because it circulates a pattern of beliefs.

Without circulation, use is idle. It is the circulation of myths that rarify social inscriptions; it is the circulation of stories that project hegemonic assertions upon bodies of color, it is through circulation that habits of whiteness are produced, and norms are established. Our habits inform how we read and how we understand. As Nathan Crick reminds us, "Habits are neither mere repetitions nor thoughtless actions; they are methodical ways of acting in response to certain problems or tasks that involve physical as well as mental process."[13] Their use and governance gives us a sense of the familiar and routine. "They build upon coordinated actions that originate in need or desire and end in consummatory satisfaction."[14] This realization provides us with a clearer understanding of the rhetorical and ontological nature of use as it brings into being a body that becomes needful to naturalize race. Tracking the use and circulation of the trope "pre-existing conditions" in Covid discourse bears witness to habits of white supremacy that invite us to deny universal human qualities to Black bodies. What's unique about this text, this collection of ideas is that we are all talking about a new disease with an old past. We are giving space to examine Covid discourse and its creation of language and discrimination. Unfortunately, this new virus is the replication of an old record; pointing to the perpetual fractures and fissures that are found in the implementation of the creeds of this nation.

Historical Traces

Covid discourse represents a continuation of history, a reiteration of white supremacy in disguised characterizations. Whiteness judges the Black body and inscribes upon it myths of inferiority. History has facilitated myths to constitute organs and systems, tissues and cells with an identity befitting to the white gaze. In other words, history reveals how, during slavery and Jim Crow "southern physicians, in particular, invested Blackness with medical meaning and how white medical authority remained contingent on the identification of Black physiological peculiarities."[15] This is not simply a historical phenomenon but a present reality.

Whether the context is syphilis as reason for rejection from military service, tuberculosis as the sign for defective lung capacity, or the perceived thickness of Black skin to thwart Black pain, these arguments advance race science and maintain whiteness as superior to Blackness. To nestle these notions in nature, to normalize this discourse is to sustain the durability of race as the reason for preexisting conditions. Race then becomes the reason for a deficient body, degeneration occurs because the Black body is perceived as inferior. Race offers natural traits and tendencies that are birthed in Blackness, unique birthmarks that neither time nor medical intervention can remove. To this point Angela Saini writes, "Race is the counter-argument. Race is at its heart the belief that we are born different, deep inside our bodies, perhaps even in character and intellect, as well as in outward appearance. It's the notion that groups of people have certain innate qualities that not only are visible at the surface of their skins but also run down into their innate capacities, that perhaps even help define the passage of progress, the success and failure of the nation's our ancestors came from."[16] Thomas Jefferson embodies this ancestral heritage as he reminds us of our past; as a progenitor of the racialization of humans and the myth of human difference, as the perpetuator of untruthful myths. Jefferson is our guide to understanding how stories of difference became sedimented in society. His beliefs for human hierarchy and natural difference are established in *Notes on The State of Virginia*: "To our reproach it must be said, that though for a century and a half we have had under our eyes the races of black and of red men, they have never been viewed by us as subjects of natural history."[17] For Jefferson, race is born in nature and subsequently provides a particular understanding of physiological traits. However, he was not alone in crafting myths of human difference as they permeated the ideologies of the time. Subsequently, these convenient myths carry on from generation to generation. We wear them and walk around with them; they tell us who we are and how we get along. They cannot function alone but need science and society to warrant and maintain their relevance. Addressing the usefulness of science to facilitate racialized myths, Angela Saini writes, "But the stories we're raised on—the tales, myths, legends, beliefs, even the old scientific orthodoxies—are how we frame everything we learn. The stories are our culture. They are the minds we inhabit."[18]

Myths, then, are not simply stories about people, places and things. They are power statements that organize people, places, and things. They create identities of people, places, and things. They have the potential to persuade us and assign meaning. They forward a reality that conveniently and covertly rewinds us to the past. Myths are the work of a set of racialized practices that organize bodies and orchestrate identities. We owe to Thomas Jefferson, Samuel Cartwright, and Josiah Nott, the birthing of a set of beliefs that bequeath to us assumptions of human hierarchy that facilitate systems of power ultimately reflecting the context of our lives. This is the history, James Baldwin contends, that sticks to us, that saturates us, that centers us, that controls.

Baldwin unravels the strands of an American identity of innocence and purity that "puts oneself together," that "imagines oneself to be" the white problem:[19] "White man, hear me! History, as nearly no one seems to know, is not merely something to be read. And it does not refer merely, or even principally, to the past. On the contrary, the great force of history comes from the fact that we carry it within us, are unconsciously controlled by it in many ways, and history is literally present in all that we do."[20] Baldwin's utterances urge us toward the glaring gestures of history, the way it shapes our sentences, gives us a language, and puts us in our place. History memorializes our pain and keeps it in clear view; it leaves traces of racial terror that determine our comings and goings. Baldwin reckons with history's animations and iterations, knowing that America must do the same in order to rid itself of guilt. "It could scarcely be otherwise, since it is to history that we owe our frames of reference, our identities, and our aspirations. And it is with great pain and terror that one begins to realize this."[21]

Interrupting the work of history demands acknowledgment of the starting materials that brought it into being. We must go beyond a tacit nod to the practices of racism that legitimize race, to deciphering the stories that seek to persuade us that we are inherently different. Moving forward, we will witness how history repeats and recycles myths of Black immunity and vulnerability. Whether in the yellow fever pandemic of the eighteenth century or the Covid pandemic of the twenty-first century, racialized myths are the substance of supremacist logics, allowing us to visualize its power at work as we "analyze, interpret, evaluate and argue how whiteness haunts our supposedly 'postracial' society."[22] Through these hauntings, it will become evident that Covid discourse is a piece of a larger puzzle, one that essentializes race as the product of human difference, the means by which scientific knowledge is known, and the way we come to value each other's lives.

Racialized Immunity

Covid is not the first acquaintance with supposed Black immunity. In *Medicalizing Blackness*, Rana Hogarth recalls the perpetuation of presumptions that Blacks were immune to yellow fever during the outbreak in Philadelphia in the late eighteenth century. The relative absence of yellow fever in the Black communities was regarded as an inherent immunity. Use of the racialized claim provided a way of telling stories, inferring the work of something else. Use was a way of centering the claim, while pointing to the body. Hogarth takes us to the work of use in the yellow fever pandemic. "The rationale for Black people's seemingly low mortality was grounded in the assertion that as a race, Black people were innately immune to yellow fever ... this logic held that Black and white bodies were inherently distinct because of the way each race experienced disease, and the reason why each race suffered differently from disease had to do with their different racial constitutions."[23] As a sign, Black immunity tells us that "something is in use."[24] The notion of Blackness as a pre-existing condition does the work of whiteness during the yellow fever epidemic, it presumes the peculiarity of Black physiology in Covid explaining resilience to disease.

At the onset of Covid, rumors spread that Black people were immune to the virus, that their physiology was a sufficient barrier to the barrage of toxins that were killing others. Their assumed cellular difference was enough to cordon off the Black body from the ravages of coronavirus. This was not just a passing rumor among a few but rather a conversation had by Black folk in the community, throughout the nation in different venues, and on different levels. The perpetual use of the proposed conspiracy theory of Black immunity serves the purpose of erasing Black suffering and the disposability of Black bodies. Rhetorics of disposability are pervasive throughout Covid discourse as they give rise to logics supporting the marginalization and dehumanization of Black and brown bodies. Authors throughout this volume articulate precisely how scheme is perpetrated. The use of the conspiracy theory of Black immunity lays the foundation for a story told through Covid, one that measures the realization of white supremacy's assertiveness, that monumentalizes white supremacist habits, that ultimately suspends rational thought of human equality. From Baltimore and basketball players to actors and others came a collective pushback against the perpetuation of these rumors, knowing that their circulation supported shared beliefs of human difference. The *Baltimore Sun* reported on the pervasiveness of the myth of Black immunity:

> There's this myth that Black people cannot get the coronavirus ... What began as a lie, a myth, a joke, has seeped very deeply into the Black community. In Baltimore, where three of five residents are Black, efforts are underway to combat the misconception. City leaders are printing flyers to spread in poor neighborhoods. We're actually discussing it, what are the ways we can target our messaging to dispel those myths and rumors?[25]

More specifically, it was believed "that melanin, the dark pigment in the skin of Black people, is a natural antidote to the virus."[26] The actor Idris Elba confronted the fallacy with facts in a twitter video, "My people—black people, black people—please, please understand that coronavirus ... you can get it all right? There are so many stupid ridiculous conspiracy theories about black people not being able to get it ... The disease does not discriminate."[27] Gregory Townsend, a retired health services administrator, reiterated how this particular myth of immunity mirrored the fallacy during slavery that Black bodies were superhuman: "And you know, initially there was a sense of euphoria, heightened sense of pride because now we can do something that nobody else can do. We're superhuman Black people that can ward off this illness. Other folks are gonna die, but Black people are going to live."[28] These erroneous thought patterns saturated social media during the early stages of Covid. This myth demonstrated how Blackness was perceived as the pre-existing condition to prevent the body from being a host to Covid. Blackness offers a seemingly more sequestered way of vocalizing that difference in physiology decreases difference in susceptibility. The recycling of this myth on social platforms does rhetorical work in persuading and pronouncing how Black bodies are determined in time and in various circumstances. Use, says Ahmed, leaves an impression; it is an intimate as well as a social sphere distributed between persons and things.[29] George Yancy considers the consequences of the use of myths that perform racialized duties. Mythologizing Blackness as a disease quality concludes that the "corporeal integrity of my Black body undergoes an onslaught as the white imaginary, which centuries of white hegemony have structured and shaped, ruminates over dark flesh and vomits me out in a form not in accordance with how I see myself."[30] This occurs not just in the formation of myths of immunity but also in accordance with myths of vulnerability, stories that blame and accuse.

Racialized Vulnerability

The infection and death of African Americans from Covid is unequal to the suffering of white people. Even with the different variants, as the pandemic has surged, disparities in health care have remained consistent. Subsequently, Black life in the United State, has been erased and often not accounted for. Along with the inordinate loss of Black life is talk about the cause, the pre-existing conditions, the comorbidities, all of which could infer that these bodies are more susceptible to the virus than others. Repetition and reiteration of these claims inform us of how "use also leaves an impression."[31] These indentations become patterns perpetuating a myth of Blackness as a disease property. Diabetes, hypertension, kidney disease, and respiratory distress are welcome mats for Covid to walk upon and into a host of its choice. Attention to these maladies often takes attention away from the structures or systems of inequality that invite them, emphasizing more focus on ideals regarding the bodies that carry diabetes and hypertension and less words about how they got there. The infirmed bodies then are witnesses to a "slow violence."[32] They show and tell us about a "violence that occurs gradually and out of sight, a violence of delayed destruction that is dispersed across time and space, an attritional violence that is typically not viewed as violence at all."[33] The violence to the Black body is often the blame that the same body absorbs and is accustomed to. Blaming one often absolves the other, allowing for the deflection of guilt or even denying the possibility of it. To blame is to assert judgment, to empower one or the other. It is the foreshadowing of shame, the premonition of penalty for wrongdoing or way of existence. This continued use empowers blame and gives it a sense of normalization, to where blame is expected and even looked for. "There is a kind of transfer" with use, says Ahmed, a bequeath of responsibility and judgment. Reliance on the racialized myths requires this to be so.[34]

In an NPR interview, Senator Bill Cassidy offers an example of the rhetorical means of pre-existing conditions as cover for the conclusions of whiteness. When asked about the disproportionate impact of Covid on African Americans, Cassidy highlights Black physiology as essential to the cause.

But if you're going to look at the fundamental reason, African Americans are 60% more likely to have diabetes. Now, if you look at the NIH website, that would say that's for obesity, for genetic reasons, perhaps other things. The virus likes to hit what is called an ACE receptor. Now if you have diabetes, obesity, hypertension, then African Americans are going to have more of those receptors inherent in their having the diabetes, the hypertension, the obesity. So, there's a physiologic reason which explains this.[35]

Blame of the diseased body draws attention from structural to hegemonic domains of power as Cassidy casually nods to the responsibility of the state but concretizes the behavior of African Americans in their culpability to death from Covid. Cassidy then guides us to the historical myths that condemn Black bodies within the space of the white gaze. In doing so, Cassidy's claim disguises a container for white supremacist logic and its hegemonic norms. Furthermore, he manages the expectations of the Black body's ability to do anything but succumb to its perceived inherent and disabled physiology. Cassidy's reliance on racialized myths underscores how "use can be a way of being in touch with things."[36] Never far from the grasp of white supremacist logic, racialized myth concretized inferiority, "articulating inclusion and difference in American ways of life."[37]

In tandem with Cassidy, Rod Dreher of the American Conservative proposes that the culinary pallet of African Americans could offer cause for comorbidities in the "extent Black folks all over the country still eat the traditional soul food diet, with lots of grease, salt, pork, sugar, and carbs."[38] Robert Winn, director of VCU Massey Cancer center, explains how his research identifies genetic causation to African American susceptibility:

> The frequency with which we observed this genetic variation among African Americans is likely responsible in some manner for the severity of COVID-19 comorbidities and mortality in the same population. Our findings provide a strong argument for the use of existing blood pressure and heart failure medications as effective clinical strategies to reduce serious complications and improve outcomes in COVID-19 patients.[39]

Harkening back to the racialized myth that opened this chapter, genetic variation once again explains the high rate of Covid among African Americans. Each of these claims has been recycled and reused. It is through use that they gain capital; it is through circulation that they gain use. Each of these notes ways of persuasion that pivot to myths of racial difference, drawing on pre-existing conditions as cause. They take us back to a kind of rationale that justifies blame of the Black body, that warrants a critical white gaze. Blaming food, blaming bodies, blaming habits obfuscates the responsibility and culpability of systems and structures of disparity and oppression. It removes the potential of white guilt while employing new strategies to sustain white innocence. This performance of blame helps us to differentiate between social and structural determinants of health inequities. Dr. Joia Crear-Perry and colleagues identify the sturdiness and historical durability of the structural: "These structures and systems date back to the founding of this nation and its economy on principles of racial, class and gender hierarchy. They shape the distribution of power and resources across the population, engendering health inequities along racial, class, and gender lines and intersections."[40] While social determinants are visible, structural forces are left invisible and often obscured, giving rise to historical injustices without recourse and with little recognition. Cassidy and Dreher's reiteration of racialized myths express what this volume's introduction addresses as the substitution of blame for the obfuscation of structural and social determinants of health. The normalization of this performance is sedimented into the daily spaces of our lives without much notice or fanfare. Whiteness then is the privileged position to innocently disassociate from the scene while being guilty of the crime.

Innocence communicates a context and reiterates a history that allows it to characterize certain bodies as blamable whether it is rational or not. The use of innocence as an intervention "brings things to mind"; things like arguments and assumptions, that make up the myths to preserve blame and confer shame.[41] Blame on African Americans for the Covid surge in his state by Texas lieutenant governor Dan Patrick represents the rhetorical use of this trope to script a narrative grounded in racialized myths instead of the callous disregard of health policies in his state. During an interview on Fox News, Patrick explained: "The Covid is spreading, particularly most of the numbers are with the unvaccinated, and the Democrats like to blame Republicans on that... Well, the biggest group in most states are African Americans who have not been vaccinated. Last time I checked, over 90 percent of them vote for Democrats in their major cities and major counties, so it's up to the Democrats to get... as many people vaccinated."[42] Eliding the history of Black medical coercion that Veronica Joyner and Heidi Y. Lawrence trace in their chapter in this volume, Patrick traffics in what Charles Mills records as an "epistemology of ignorance" or an intentional performance of not knowing to preserve white innocence. Patrick embodies a white supremacist system subsumed in "false belief and the absence of true belief."[43] Ignorance perpetuates myths that take the form of scientific truths and, as Ahmed asserts "offers a way of telling stories about things."[44]

The appropriation of medical discourse to advance myths supporting Blackness as a disease category as an essentialized way of being emerges in the comments of Dr. Frank McGeorge as he explains why the Covid death rate is so high for African Americans. After acknowledging the disparity in death of African Americans, the presence of risk factors such as heart disease and diabetes, McGeorge opines that research in the genetic makeup of such populations should be conducted to detect whether the cause lies there: "Another avenue being investigated is whether there could be genetic or physiological factors that could make certain races more susceptible to Sars-Covid. Everything from different numbers to certain types of receptors to the way certain races respond to the massive inflammation induced as Covid-19 worsens are being looked at."[45] As these perceptions circulate, they normalize hegemonic ideals by "manipulating ideology and culture."[46] They purport that there is always something fixable about Black bodies, something in need of work—a missing cell, a defective gene, an incomplete system, a flawed physique. These are the starting materials that cast myths as the actualization of a larger narrative. Covid discourse appropriates blame to deflect from systemic structures of inequality, to marginalize and shame. This reiterates what Harris-Perry identifies as a dereliction of the nations to its citizens. "A state that shames its citizens violates the foundational social contract of liberal democracies: government's commitment to respect individual dignity."[47] As we have witnessed in Covid discourse, shame and blame have served as useful tools to build societal barriers that maintain separation.

The malleability of arguments of difference and assumptions of inferiority, the recuperation of racialized myths about certain bodies are useful measures to assert the supremacy of whiteness. Consequently then, we see how use gives us the tools of "arranging worlds as well as ourselves" through these stories and the practice of these habits.[48] Without use, whiteness is stagnant and still; with use, whiteness makes meaning and maintains its hierarchies.

Conclusion

In 1899, W. E. B. Du Bois published *The Philadelphia Negro*, a comprehensive sociological study that identified structural impediments to the wellbeing of those living within Philadelphia's Seventh Ward.[49] A scientific rebuttal to his contemporaries that asserted the Seventh Ward citizens were created inferior and subject to a commensurate life, Du Bois's meticulous record of systemic injustices and structural racism contextualized lives subject to disease, poverty, lack of suitable education, and poor housing as structural factors. As Lawrence Bobo writes, "Du Bois eschewed interpreting the hardship in which most Black Philadelphians lived as a reflection of basic Black capabilities. Instead, Du Bois crafted a historically grounded analysis of Blacks, whose circumstances had clear social or environmental roots."[50] To be sure, Du Bois's exposé cataloged patterns of prejudice designed to keep Black citizens in place. Attending to the past and present, Du Bois's reasonings reckoned with white supremacist actions and attitudes toward the Negros. Du Bois's conclusion was straightforward: Black citizens of the Seventh Ward were disadvantaged because of structural systems of racism. Their bodies were subject to environmental injustices that left traces and markers of debilitation, demise, and ultimately death. Du Bois's conclusions also reveal how racism needs scapegoats, it searches for ways to hide and normalize, to defer and deny. It was true then; it is true now. Covid shows us how.

In the time of Covid, racialized myths of Black immunity and vulnerability through pre-existing conditions circulate human difference, projecting race upon cells, organs, systems, and bodies. They make inferences and assumptions, causes and conclusions, resulting in human hierarchy. These flexible myths categorize and compensate for human use and habits, practices that occur without thinking, without looking, and without knowing. Ultimately, racialized myths point to the notion of defect in some bodies and perfection in others, thereby maintaining that certain bodies are flawed. The circulation of use gives us patterns and paradigms, to persuade us toward habits that move us toward societal norms that reify whiteness. Habits are generative places of discovery where we find whiteness at work, particularly in matters of the wellbeing and maintenance of Black bodies. Even more revelatory is the interconnectedness of habits and whiteness. When viewed as a manifestation of habits, whiteness becomes more accessible to advocate for change and more amenable to critical inquiry. The invisibility of whiteness gives it the ability to assimilate into the annals of historical myths that call for the regularity of use with racialized medical algorithms in the perpetual reading of Black bodies as irregular and insufficient. This reading is often justified, as whiteness equates race with biology; the work of race is to inform us of the biological essence of beings, the natural qualities that are fixed and thus presumed. Consequently, when race is employed, there is little need for queries or critiques.

The *Philadelphia Negro* was a refutation of scientific racism, of the belief that Black bodies were diseased, inherently different, and consequently inferior. Covid as a case study offers us an old argument in new packaging. Regardless of how the assumptions are accessorized, despite the passing of time, we witness the persistent belief that race is biology, and the Black body is largely to blame. We witness the obfuscation of whiteness and thus the insistence of pre-existing conditions that determine the nature of Black being and the durability of Black bodies. These conclusions count on science and societal norms to give them credence, to keep them within current discourse, to give them cover from criticism.

Whether our discussion centers on diseases of the past or the present, we find a similar refrain that has affirmed the notion of whiteness as superior and Blackness as a disease marker. Because these habits of whiteness have become so ingrained in the fabric of American society, very little about the disparity in care, the blame in cause, and subsequent shaming into personal responsibility with Covid is new and surprising to most African Americans. These anti-blackness sentiments permeate Covid discourse, as DiArron M. will argue later in this volume, reminding us that Black suffering is inextricably woven into the fabric of the American narrative. Patrice Peck speaks with a collective voice in her article "The Virus Is Showing Black People What They Knew All Along":

> For centuries, Black people have spoken about the struggles we face, pointing to root causes like poverty, housing segregation, unemployment, and environmental degradation. And for centuries, those concerns have largely gone ignored. The same thing has happened with the pandemic. Long before any data confirmed our worst fears, Black people knew that the coronavirus would disproportionately devastate our already vulnerable communities.[51]

This new disease circulates in an old discourse, unraveling throughout time as we have witnessed presidents and politicians, scientists and physicians, news reporters and researchers all contribute to the cause of racialized myths. The fodder they formulate becomes the stuff we believe about each other regardless of evidence that proves otherwise. It is a rhetorical history that requires us to "understand how those symbols and systems of symbols may have suasory potential and persuasive effect."[52]

Marginalized communities are familiar with myths of immunity to myths of vulnerability; it is nothing to become acquainted with, but instead a manner of existence to live by. DuBois's research, refutations of syphilis susceptibility, along with the steady drumbeat of other voices to decry historical myths of human difference have not been sufficient to warn America that "the value placed on the color of the skin is always and everywhere and forever a delusion."[53] Covid discourse offers reasons that Black bodies were unlikely to contract the virus and that these same bodies were likely to die from the virus. This mishmash of myths extends invitations for senators and citizens alike to explain the objectification of the Black body and judgments aligned against its very existence. As the United States was becoming acquainted with Covid, the pernicious myth of Black immunity against the virus meandered throughout society, recuperating racialized folklore that race is biology, that human difference justifies hierarchy, and that Blackness is often interpreted as a disease condition. These acts of rhetorical significance enable the innocence of whiteness, preventing its implication in how Black bodies are harmed by Covid and why. In this chapter, we witness how the Black body is used against itself, to argue that it is the cause of unparalleled Covid death. The body created in racialized folklore informs our understanding of a body beset by disease, bringing along with it a language of subjugation, dehumanizing assumptions, and cultural meanings that have circulated from slavery until the present.

NOTES

1. Robert E. Fullilove Jr., "Syphilis and the Negro," *JAMA* 122 (1943): 764.
2. Sarah E. Chinn, *Technology and The Logic of American Racism: A Cultural History of the Body as Evidence* (London: Continuum, 2000), 7.
3. George Yancy, *Black Bodies, White Gazes: The Continuing Significance of Race* (Lanham, MD: Rowman & Littlefield, 2008), 4–5.
4. Melissa Harris-Perry, *Sister Citizen: Shame, Stereotypes, and Black Women in America* (New Haven, CT: Yale University Press, 2011), 108.
5. Terrance Macmullan, *Habits of Whiteness: A Pragmatist Reconstruction* (Bloomington: Indiana University Press, 2009), 76.
6. James Baldwin, *Collected Essays* (New York: The Library of America, 1998), 292.
7. Donald S. Moore, Jake Kosek, and Anand Pandian, eds., *Race, Nature, and The Politics of Difference* (Durham, NC: Duke University Press, 2003), 4.
8. Thomas Rickert, "Circulation-Signification-Ontology," in *Circulation, Writing, and Rhetoric*, ed. Laurie Gries and Collin Gifford (Louisville: Utah State University Press, 2018), 306.

9. Macmullan, *Habits of Whiteness*, 76.
10. Sara Ahmed, *What's the Use? On the Uses of Use* (Durham, NC: Duke University Press, 2019), 12.
11. Ahmed, *What's the Use?*, 69.
12. Ahmed, *What's the Use?*, 12, 22, 45, 69.
13. Nathan Crick, *Democracy & Rhetoric: John Dewey on the Arts of Becoming*, (Columbia: University of South Carolina Press, 2010), 48.
14. Crick, *Democracy & Rhetoric*, 98.
15. Rana A. Hogarth, *Medicalizing Blackness: Making Racial Difference in The Atlantic World, 1780–1840* (Chapel Hill: University of North Carolina Press, 2017), 11.
16. Angela Saini, *Superior: The Return of Race Science* (Boston: Beacon Press, 2019), xiii.
17. Thomas Jefferson, "Laws (Query XIV) (1781–1782)," in *The Nature of Difference: Sciences of Race in the United States from Jefferson to Genomics*, ed. Evelynn M. Hammonds and Rebecca M. Herzig (Cambridge: MIT Press, 2008), 28.
18. Saini, *Superior*, 24.
19. James Baldwin, *The Cross of Redemption: Uncollected Writings* (New York: Vintage Books, 2010), 89.
20. James Baldwin, *Collected Essays*, (New York: The Library of America, 1998), 722.
21. Baldwin, *Collected Essays*, 723.
22. Tammie M. Kennedy, Joyce Irene Middleton, and Krista Ratcliffe, *Rhetorics of Whiteness: Postracial Hauntings in Popular Culture* (Carbondale: Southern Illinois University Press, 2017), 11.
23. Hogarth, *Medicalizing Blackness*, 18–19.
24. Ahmed, *What's the Use?*, 27.
25. Tim Prudente, "Coronavirus Fights Shifts to Baltimore's Poor Neighborhoods as City Leaders Battle Mistrust," *Baltimore Sun*, April 11, 2020.
26. Dahleen Glanton, "Let's Stop the Spread—of the Myth Black People are Immune to the Coronavirus," *Chicago Tribune*, March 18, 2020.
27. Glanton, "Let's Stop the Spread."
28. Nick Patterson, "The Rumor: Black Americans Are Not Affected as Much by the Coronavirus Pandemic," *Birmingham Watch*, April 20, 2020.
29. Ahmed, *What's the Use?*, 7.
30. Yancy, *Black Bodies*, 2.
31. Ahmed, *What's the Use?*, 7.
32. Rob Nixon, *Slow Violence and the Environmentalism of the Poor*, (Cambridge, MA: Harvard University Press, 2011), 2.

33. Nixon, *Slow Violence*, 2.
34. Ahmed, *What's the Use?*, 22.
35. James Doubek, "Louisiana Sen. Cassidy Addresses Racial Disparities in Coronavirus Deaths," *WBUR News*, April 7, 2020.
36. Ahmed, *What's the Use?*, 21.
37. Anne Pollock, *Medicating Race* (Durham, NC: Duke University Press, 2012), 14.
38. Rod Dreher, "Class, Race, Coronavirus and Cuisine," *American Conservative*, April 8, 2020.
39. Massey Cancer Center Staff, "A Genetic Variation Could Help Explain the High Rate of Covid-19 Among African Americans," *VCU News*, October 15, 2020.
40. Joia Crear-Perry et al., "Social and Structural Determinants of Health Inequities in Maternal Health," *Journal of Women's Health* 30, no. 2 (2021).
41. Ahmed, *What's the Use?*, 6.
42. Dareh Gregorian, "Texas Lt. Gov. Dan Patrick Blames Covid Surge on 'African Americans Who Have Not Been Vaccinated,'" *NBC News*, August 20, 2021.
43. Shannon Sullivan and Nancy Tuana, *Race and Epistemologies of Ignorance* (Albany: State University of New York Press, 2007), 16.
44. Ahmed, *What's the Use?*, 22.
45. "Why Is Coronavirus (COVID-19) Death Rate So High for African Americans?," *Detroit Local 4 News*, April 7, 2020, https://www.youtube.com/watch?v=KWkbwcSkLyQ.
46. Patricia Hill Collins, *Black Feminist Thought* (New York: Routledge Press, 2009), 274.
47. Harris-Perry, *Sister Citizen*, 107.
48. Ahmed, *What's the Use?*, 26.
49. Henry Louis Gates Jr., "The Black Letters on the Sign: W.E.B. Du Bois and the Canon," in *The Oxford W.E.B. Du Bois: The Philadelphia Negro A Social Study*, ed. Henry Louis Gates Jr. (Oxford: Oxford University Press, 2007), xv.
50. Gates, "Black Letter," xxvii.
51. Patrice Peck, "The Virus Is Showing Black People What They Knew All Along: Covid-19 Doesn't Discriminate by Race, Yet It Has Still Laid Bare the Brutality of Racism in the United States," *Atlantic*, December 22, 2020.
52. Kathleen J. Turner, *Doing Rhetorical History: Concepts and Cases* (Tuscaloosa: University of Alabama Press, 1998), 2.
53. Baldwin, *Collected Essays*, 346.

Covid and Environmental Atmospheres

Pulmonary Publics and Our Shared Air

Sara DiCaglio

BREATHING IS AMONG OUR MOST BASIC AND VITAL BODILY FUNCTIONS. Whether we are paying attention, in goes the oxygen, out goes the carbon dioxide; life continues. But, of course, breathing is more complicated than all that. Air—even the fresh, pure kind of our imaginations—is not made up only of oxygen, and our collective in and out brings with it a great deal more than just what we need to live. And yet we must do it, again, and again, and again, and again.

In twenty-first-century America, we are instructed to breathe in and out to relax ourselves, to follow wellness programs sent by our corporate workplaces; breathing, it sometimes seems, is the solution for every problem. Breathing is presented as an individual action in plentily available fresh air; when there are breakdowns in the availability of that air or the ability to breathe, they are either framed as anomalous or largely ignored. But breathing has required new attention during the Covid pandemic. From early reports of Covid as a spate of pneumonias with unknown causes to public health interventions around viral particles, the pandemic has forced us to confront the closeness of our collective atmospheres. The model of breath as an individual action has never been enough in a world of structural violence, but the pandemic has made the inadequacies of the individual breath particularly visible. Because Covid travels through aerosol particles, public health rhetoric has needed to convince its audience to reconsider what it breathes in: to understand that its breaths and atmospheres entangle with the breaths and atmospheres of others, and that such entanglement has tangible effects on the health of the individual and the community. This attention to invisible relations is necessary to convince the audience of the necessity to mask, to distance, and to otherwise work to "flatten the curve" so that we might all continue to breathe together.

The effectiveness of such public health communication has been mixed, to put it mildly. But the need for such appeals, as well as the need to communicate the atmospheric entanglement of air, health, and community, is not isolated to Covid. The global pandemic has played out alongside various other environmental disasters and inequities—wildfires in Australia and California, ongoing inequities in asthma rates and access to clean air, etc. Just as the Covid pandemic has had unequal effects on members of marginalized groups, who often have been unable to socially distance themselves from the viral atmospheres of others, so too do other atmospheric pre-existing conditions have unequal effects. Indeed, the very right to breathe at all is also unequal, as the cries of "I can't breathe" that came from Eric Garner, Elijah McClain, George Floyd, and other Black Americans who died at the hands of police illustrate.[1] Moreover, such moments illustrate the inability or unwillingness of one party to believe the words of another, to recognize or respond to language about breath.

Taking these various atmospheric inequities as its background, this chapter considers Covid as an environmental issue, with "environment" here defined as the ecological, political, and structural forms that affect our interrelations with the material world. To do so, I examine what I call *atmospheric relations*: interactions related to the intake and exhalation of air and whatever might come along with it. For the sake of feasibility and focus, this project centers on the American context, though these inequities are only intensified on a global scale, and though air's lack of respect for boundaries, national or otherwise, is a vital part of understanding atmospheres. With the inequity of atmospheric exposure comes the need for improved *atmospheric rhetorics*, which I define as a kind of ambient rhetoric attuned to the ways we communicate about and conceptualize the air.[2] The rise in visible atmospheric pollutants, as in the fallout from fires, or otherwise noteworthy pollutants or alterations, as in Covid, is just one aspect contributing to this need. Other atmospheric relations may also relay themselves to the public in one way or another: this area is abject, filled with scent or smog or refuse; this area is dangerous, filled with smoke, fire approaching.

To trace the ways that the pandemic's specific atmospheric relations are situated within the broader context of atmospheric rhetorics, we might think about Covid through an ecological view of rhetoric, in which the interconnected web of rhetorical attention and relations comes into focus, as the editors of this volume discuss in their introduction. Following Robin Jensen, among others, I proceed from an understanding that an ecological view of rhetoric is necessary for understanding the strange relations and "percolations" within rhetorics of health and medicine.[3] In this chapter, I consider one strand of Covid-related public health messaging, the "Don't Share Your Air" campaigns. Building on Jenell Johnson's theory of *visceral publics*, I introduce *pulmonary publics* as a way of understanding the unevenness and invisibility of our shared air—air that we are always already sharing, but that is both unevenly apparent and inequitable. Pulmonary publics are defined by their relation to breath as well as their inherent partiality. Through a rhetorical analysis of these public health campaigns as well as a discussion of pulmonary publics surrounding masking, I highlight a shared model of atmospheric relations that, despite occasional nods toward the ecological and molecular complexity of air, repeatedly figures the air as inherently pure to suggest that relations with the air are matters of individual sensitivity. I argue that it is only through attention to the multiplicity of atmospheric relations—of the invisible molecular structures we breathe together—that we might develop an improved atmospheric rhetoric in a drive toward atmospheric justice.

Thinking Ecologically

Atmosphere and breath propel oral language, allow us to hear one another, carry the scents of the world to us. But we are largely inured to them, noticing them only when they change or alter in some way. We notice the wind, not the still air; we notice smog and smoke, not the absence thereof. We notice shifts in smells but lose track of scents as we spend more time with them. Moreover, on the level of the microscopic, we—the lay American public in our day to day lives—are particularly unaware of what is contained in the atmosphere.[4] Despite an obsession with the marketing of high-efficiency particulate air (HEPA) filters, particles remain largely out of sight, out of mind.

    Practices of surface cleaning remain more comforting: we can wash our hands and wipe our desks and know we have done something, even if we cannot tell whether we were successful. The hard surface below, the feeling of the wet wipe or rag in our hands, the practice of rubbing soap between our fingers—these haptic experiences feel clean. The lingering smell of cleaner and the cracks my hands developed early in the pandemic from washing so frequently are tangible markers of this practice. They are a part of a familiar rhetorical framework that emphasizes cleaning as a ritual and, importantly, suggests that it is surfaces and bodies, not the air, that need to be cleaned. Thus, cleansing actions or sensory markers related to cleaning function as enthymemes for cleanliness itself, regardless of whether they make a sanitary difference. This olfactory and haptic sense of cleanliness functions as another part of what Emily Winderman and Robert Mejia call the "Covid sensorium," the "socio-corporeal entanglement by which publics come to sense and know COVID-19."[5] Hygiene theater, as Derek Thompson refers to it, makes us feel like we and others have done our individual job.[6] But though we imagine cleaning practices to mark the absence of germs, they may or may not; we do not see what remains after the wiping and washing.

The tangible nature of cleanliness as a state accomplished by a series of sensory processes does not, however, translate to Covid as an aerosol disease. Visually, we cannot tell what remains in the air. This is also true in terms of the microbial scale of surface viruses and bacteria, but we trust that such germs may be wiped up in the practice of surface cleaning. Surface-cleaning rhetorics assume the body as a hard boundary and the exterior—embodied threats—as that which we touch or feel: droplets, desks, floors, spit. To contend with these threats is to do something wholly different than to think about aerosol relations, whose surfaces and relations happen within the body or within largely inaccessible sites such as air filtration systems.

To be won over by public health interventions such as masking and social distancing, we need to turn attention from the hard boundaries of surface cleaning to the more porous boundaries of our breath.[7] We must conceptualize breathing as a relation with others, one that we change and that is changed by those around us. As our understanding of the role of asymptomatic carriers in the spread of Covid grew, our logic had to shift from one of obvious illness—the air is only contaminated by rare and noticeable actions that clearly break the boundary between inside and outside—to one in which the air was more suspect, more potentially full of viral life, and in which that boundary was much more porous and indistinct.[8] This necessary perceptive shift runs up against what the editors of this volume might refer to as fascial dysfunctions: the model of atmospheric relations as contingent on individual or group susceptibility, and the model of individual acts of breathing as always beneficial.

One example of the framework of individual susceptibility can be seen in the public reporting of air quality indexes. The very language of these indexes focuses on the person who breathes rather than on the air itself. For example, the EPA's Air Quality Index (AQI) reports air quality in terms of lung sensitivity. A Yellow

(Moderate) day is described as follows: "Air quality is acceptable. However, there may be a risk for some people, particularly those who are unusually sensitive to air pollution." Similarly, the description of an Orange (Unhealthy for Sensitive Groups) reads: "Members of sensitive groups may experience health effects. The general public is less likely to be affected."[9] These indexes ultimately measure and report the amount of particulate matter within the air. However, the linguistic focus on the individual, marked in terms of "unusual sensitivity" and membership in a "sensitive group," obscures the object of that measurement and its relation to the atmosphere itself. The word "sensitive" itself is noteworthy; rather than documenting susceptibility or medical conditions themselves, this term connotes frailty, an individual choice or state that can and should be overcome. Such an individual risk-based analysis makes it easy to reframe pollution as issues of individual needs and weaknesses: the problem becomes not the pollutants but the sensitivity of the person breathing them in. The atmosphere and its contents are neutral here; it is the person who inhales, the one who has heightened sensitivity or, in the case of the pandemic, "underlying conditions," who needs to manage their own individual risk.

Communicating Atmospheres

Our collective reliance on the individual model of breath and its risks make communicating the shared nature of our breath difficult. In the public health campaigns I discuss in this section, public health entities attempted to communicate our entangled atmospheric relations through attention to our "shared air." However, as I argue here, doing so presented deep challenges due both to the individual models of breath and risk as well as to the tendency to communicate the air as a singular entity.

The "Don't Share Your Air" campaign from hospital systems in the State of California presents a useful case study for how atmospheric rhetorics during the pandemic attempted to overcome the invisibility of aerosol transfer.[10] In a video aimed at people considering gathering prior to the 2020 holidays, a series of frontline workers describe the overwhelming conditions hospitals face and the threat of them worsening. Toward the end of the public service announcement (PSA), they plead with viewers, "Don't be the person that gives Covid-19 to someone you love or know ... Don't share your air. Stay home."

The urgent message of this PSA hinges on this possessive: don't share *your* air. But what air is that? This air has presumably already been inhaled by the viewer. It is *your* air—air that is already potentially contaminated by the viewer, by *you*—that is not to be shared. Accordingly, the audience of this piece is framed as already contaminated; the message suggests that they, in fact, possess virally contagious air. The framing attention here is not on the inhalation but the exhalation, as the audience here is positioned as unconcerned with their own potential illness. It is their duty not to pass it on to anyone they love, anyone for whom such air might presumably pose more danger.

A similar message by the LA-based AIDS Health Foundation (AHF) appeared on transit and billboards in sixteen states in the late fall of 2020.[11] In it, the words "#Don'tShareAir" are written in large block letters, moving diagonally up and out of the mouth of a speaker. Around each letter are droplets, represented by small white, yellow, and neon green dots. The letters grow as they approach another face, not actively speaking, who is lightly dappled by the dots, which grow increasingly brightly colored as they grow closer to the listener on the right, who is covered with small dots. In the background, a subtle purple shaded pattern of large coronavirus images appears.

The audience of this billboard, like that of the previous PSA, consists of potentially already-contaminated, likely asymptomatic, carriers. Though the lips on the listening figure are slightly parted, reminding us of their role in the exchange of air, for the most part the image is unidirectional. The speaker's projection is aggressive, the droplets only increasing in apparent size and force as they move toward the receiver. The air itself is suspect in its nature, aggressing toward the entirety of the listener's face and orifices, outlining them in an abject neon of droplets and unknowns. The more moderately toned purples and blues that come off the speaker seem to represent a growing toxicity—that is, as the droplets grow closer to the speaker, they become more dangerous. Their level of danger is *proximal* rather than *inherent*, as the growing neon color makes an enthymemic argument about atmospheric toxicity.

The neon green has an abject quality. The color readily recalls representations of unknown, unnatural toxicity that were, among other things, ubiquitous in cartoons of the 1980s and 90s about the ecological risks of science: the toxic sludge of *Captain Planet*, the mysterious ooze of *Teenage Mutant Ninja Turtles*. Even in nature, neon is a warning sign, a sign of poison or some danger lurking below. Neon suggests something toxic at its core, calling to mind the rising of a swamp thing, an unnatural other hidden by uncontrollable growth. Such neon suggests an object that is also fundamentally unknowable. Whatever it may mark is bad and toxic, but what it is and what comprises it remains an unknown, unrepresentable other. We can only recognize and know the neon object as something *unnatural*, either synthesized in a lab or coming from alien origins. Being touched by such toxins, this pop cultural argument goes, creates incalculable change. Though not all that change infuses a figure with supervillain otherness (the Turtles retain their goodness, for instance), it may—and, regardless of their ethical position, such characters are *altered* by this toxicity, usually without any hope of returning to a pretoxic state. Through contact with these representative neon substances, in other words, figures are unquestionably and permanently othered.

Within the specific worlds of these ads, that toxicity operates primarily on the air itself as well as the body of the other. Here, air is the thing we seem to possess, and the interactive act of breathing near another makes that air more toxic. This framing is understandable, given the need for public health interventions that recognize the risks of asymptomatic transmission. Yet the very idea of #Don'tShareAir remains difficult due the nature of that air. The air is something we inevitably must share with humans and nonhumans alike—viruses, microbes, plant life. The models of air sharing central to these PSAs conflates the air itself with what it contains. The air itself becomes impossibly toxic through its exhalation and movement toward the other. The central atmospheric relation here is simple: there is the potentially contaminated audience, the air, and the other who might become contaminated through this air. But, as I argue below, the relation here hinges on multiple definitions and understandings of "air."

When we hear a phrase like "don't share air," we need to conceptualize several pieces of the phrase. First, there is the question of sharing—who is doing it, and with whom. Within the model of these PSAs, those involved in this relation include the audience, potentially already contaminated, and their loved one, who might become contaminated through their atmospheric relations. Unspoken here are the others involved in the exchange of breath: plant life providing CO_2, animal and human life around us, the ecological structures and molecules we inhale. The second half of the phrase "don't share air" returns us to the air itself: what do we understand as the thing being shared? When we think of air, oxygen quickly follows, imagined as a pure substance that adds to our body to rejuvenate it and keep it alive. However, as Samantha Frost notes, oxygen is "a trash carrier" that, rather than adding to the body, simply removes the bodily detritus which would get in the way of our life functions.[12] Oxygen is also far from the only component of air, which includes a vast array of other molecules, some of which we need for life and some of which are simply viruses or environmental pollutants or smells or other components along for the ride. Importantly, those neon green elements represent the viral entanglements within the air, highlighting the air's multiplicity. As such, these PSAs do vital work in reminding us that the air is neither pure nor simple; it is a relation, a true atmo-sphere.

While these ads do work to highlight the air's status as a vector and a composite of molecules, at the same time, a certain flattening occurs here. It is the air that we are not to share, not the particles within it; for the sake of simplifying their message, these campaigns relay "air" as a singular object. This object contains multiple aspects, including both oxygen and viral particles; however, we refer not to the component parts but to the whole, the air itself. To some extent, this flattening strategy is helpful: by making the air a singular object made up of many component parts, including viral particles, we can communicate the realities of asymptomatic and aerosol spread. There does not need to be an action—a symptom, a droplet, a sneeze, a clear breaking of a boundary—for there to be viral spread.

And yet, this image of the air as a singular object highlights the multiple pieces of the air only for long enough to recapture them into the whole, into the singular object. Allison Rowland's work on the microbiome clarifies how this reframing works; similar to what we see happening within the air here, she argues that through discourse shifts surrounding the microbiome, "the boundaries that constitute humanhood are upset, however briefly—only to powerfully reassert their domination again."[13] In other words, what seems like it should be paradigm shifting—in Rowland's example, the redefinition of the human to incorporate the microbial, and in ours, the reframing of the air through its aerosolized viral particles—is reincorporated into safer and more comfortable paradigms. In our atmospheric example, rather than thinking about masks and filtering strategies that might change the components of the air itself, we are presented with an air that is a singular object, that is singularly dangerous.

In the process, the air becomes a singular possession that one can avoid sharing, something one can opt into and out of. As a result, these campaigns take part in the familiar conceptualization of air as individual: something we can individually react to, something we can isolate ourselves within. The atmospheric rhetoric here expands into the environmental and ecological momentarily in its recognition of the multiple components of the air. But it does so only to reframe the emergent crisis of atmospheric relations into something more familiar, more individual. In these examples, we are briefly reminded that we exhale and inhale together something that is more than just air as we might conceive of it. But, as I discuss in my next section, the framework reasserted here suggests an individual model of atmospheric relations in which one can control their definition of the air they breathe.

Pulmonary Publics

Public health campaigns, like the ones discussed above, attempt to craft a public that understands threats to its boundaries. As such, they work to establish a manageable form of what Jenell Johnson refers to as a *visceral public*. Such publics, as Johnson notes, "emerge from discourse about boundaries, and they cohere by means of intense feeling."[14] While the publics Johnson consider arise largely on their own, public health messaging that actively builds manageable visceral publics deliberately harnesses fears surrounding bodily boundaries to establish the risks of our shared porosity. According to Johnson, such porosity is distributed not just through the body's boundary spaces, but through discrete events that make that porosity visible. As she writes, the visceral "concerns the surfaces and orifices—the skin, the mouth, the lungs, the alimentary tract—that link the inside to the outside and the body-as-subject to the body-as-object... Eating, drinking, having sex, giving birth, undergoing an injection: these are moments when the boundary between the body's interior and its exterior is not just encountered, it is produced."[15] These moments of boundary production bring our interrelation to our attention, allowing for the creation of visceral publics in response to perceived threats.

While visceral publics respond to the produced boundary between the body and what lies outside, what I refer to as *pulmonary publics* form around and through less immediately tangible openings. The visceral nature of the atmosphere—at least when it comes to things like viral spread—is more diffuse, more hidden than other forms of visceral threat such as the historical fluoride controversies of Johnson's article. Though the lungs appear on her list of orifices and surfaces, the list of boundary-producing acts lean more tangible to the actor than breathing. We may attend to or ignore our breath, but breathing occurs involuntarily, regardless of our active thought. Indeed, it requires active thought to hold one's breath, to *not* breathe. We might put our subconscious breaths closer in relation to digestion than to eating itself. Boundaries are created, and we may become aware of them if we choose to notice them or if something challenges our basic processes. But these occurrences might also continue without our attention, without our active knowledge, and pulmonary publics respond in multiple ways to that ambiguity.

For a public to form and defend boundaries it understands as threatened requires an inherent claim that the boundary is both worthy and capable of being defended. The public health messaging I discuss in my previous section, for instance, establishes air as a shared good. However, in its suggestion that one could simply *not* participate in certain atmospheric relations, the ads end up focusing back on the selective permeability of bodies—the idea that air could, in fact, just not be shared. Similarly, claims minimizing Covid, as in the case of anti-mask rhetoric and the general diminution of its threat, form visceral publics that are in some way shifted from the typical defense of embodied boundaries. These pulmonary publics are connected by their atmospheric relations—that is, by boundaries that are inescapably permeable and permeated. However, as a subset of visceral publics, these pulmonary publics are defined by their attention to breath and their required partiality—that is, because the air is unmistakably multiple, pulmonary publics inherently must choose to make cuts in what they focus on or ignore, on what the singular object of air might refer to.[16] In the case of the pandemic, pulmonary publics form to deny that their embodied boundaries can be permeated. Rather than viewing foreign threats to the boundary of the body as the threats of interest, this public coheres to reject the idea that such a boundary exists and is at risk.

This concept of the natural is itself porous, shifting according to the specific public's needs and desires. Anti-mask discourse, for instance, marked the mask as unnatural, registering concern about a vast array of possibilities related to its presence. According to this discourse, the mask might cause us to touch our faces more, picking up viruses; we might inhale higher levels of bacteria, causing bacterial pneumonia.[17] Individual levels of carbon dioxide would, according to this logic, be heightened, leading to deleterious health effects, and children who masked at school would never learn how facial expressions worked (despite the likely absence of mask wearing at home). Despite evidence to the contrary (doctors and other workers having long worn surgical masks and other respirators, social media posts by medical professionals of their blood oxygen levels after mask wearing, etc.), the rhetorical framing of the mask relied on enthymematic logic tied to commonplaces around naturalness: the mask is unnatural; it therefore must have negative effects (because natural things are innately better than unnatural). Moreover, the shadow of antivaccine, antidisability rhetoric—vaccines as a cause of autism, autism as the inability to read the faces of others, and thus masking as a potentially dangerous interference in the ability to read faces that picks up from both these misplaced beliefs—lurks in the background of this argument, subtly aligning it with the rampant eugenic logic of our age.[18]

Rejecting threats to boundaries necessitates the crafting of new boundaries that can contain potential risks, as seen above. Visceral publics and pulmonary publics alike form around a fear of the unknown, a fear of additives and toxicity that comes often from a racialized other.[19] As Emily Winderman et al. argue, visceral publics do not just focus on threats to one's own boundaries, but do so by othering certain bodies as inherently unbounded.[20] As they argue through their example of media framing of pregnant Brazilian women at risk of Zika collapsing the women into the air itself, bodies at risk are turned into bodily vectors. Through the very act of being at risk, these women *become* contaminants; through living in air that is visually represented as unclean and miasmatic, the women themselves become rhetorical vectors for passing illness to a variety of sources: their fetuses, most prominently, but also the white American viewer. In other words, the rhetorical framing of these women as inextricable from and one and the same as the contaminated air itself acts as a holding space for risk—women who are themselves at risk become the risk itself.[21]

Environmental Crises

Covid-related public health messaging presents the atmosphere as an individual object and relation, which, I have argued, connects to our broader understanding of atmospheric risks and air quality. Such understandings contribute to the development of pulmonary publics that deny their own atmospheric relations and offload embodied risk onto the bodies of others. But Covid is not isolated, even in its own moment.

While the Covid pandemic was just beginning in Wuhan, other atmospheric disasters were ongoing. The 2019–20 wildfire season in Australia burned more than forty-six million acres. A series of increasingly terrible fire seasons in California have similarly illustrated climate-related effects on atmospheric relations. These fires, clearly linked to the climate change crisis,[22] change the air in tangible ways. Like smog and other forms of pollution with visible particles, the very visual—and tactile, and olfactory—qualities of the atmosphere change during and due to fires, not just in the immediate area, but far beyond; for instance, the smoke plume from the Australian fires could be tracked for months as it circumnavigated the globe.

And it is not just in what we might traditionally consider the environment that we see the inequities and structural issues of atmospheric rhetorics. If an ecological attunement suggests attention to the wide variety of intersections we are situated within—persuasive, linguistic, political, biological, or otherwise—certainly structural racism is a part of that ecology. It is not just the inequities of what air is available to different populations, but also the way air is taken away—the final words of George Floyd and Eric Garner both relating to breathing, for instance. Eric Garner's asthma, too, can be connected to the environmental pre-existing conditions that lead to a higher rate of asthma in people of color, particularly those who live in urban environments;[23] the mortality rate for Black Americans, for instance, is about three times higher than that of white Americans.[24] And the tear gassing of crowds during 2020 protests for racial justice further illustrate the way that atmospheres can be transformed and controlled with unequal effects.

Contemporary appeals related to environmental atmospheres are, like Covid's relations, more focused on a form of denialism, denying the possibility of things being spread via the air, rather than a form of boundary setting. Such pulmonary publics are visible in resistance to the possibility of human-caused climate change, in appeals that blame increased fires on the absence of forest management, on the drive to carbon capture technologies in place of reduced output, on the rolling back of air pollution limits during the Trump administration. These problems become spun into a form of the natural, the controllable, and the optimizable. This tendency is perhaps more broadly true of responses to pollution within the twentieth and twenty-first centuries. The denial of climate change, ignoring the dangers of fracking and pipelines, and overlooking disasters such as the crisis of lead in the water in Flint, illustrate a tendency to look away from environmental discomfort. This looking-away occurs most prominently and most often when those affected belong to racially or otherwise marginalized communities.

Conclusion

This is a piece about Covid, yes, but the atmospheric relations we live with and within are not just viral. Atmospherics extend to temperatures, to allergens and pollutants, to humidity levels and air pressure, to our ability to access technologies to heat or cool our living spaces and bodies, to our access to CO_2 monitors alongside generators. As I have composed this piece, in the Pacific Northwest, temperatures broke record after record, climbing to previously unknown heights—109°F—and reminding me of our flipped experience earlier in the year in Texas, when freezing February temperatures and mismanaged power grids led to a week of blackouts, rolling for the lucky, constant for others. Then, as in the West's heat wave, atypical temperatures stressed infrastructure, and people died from the temperatures and their attempts to manage them, with carbon monoxide poisoning a too common occurrence. These are not all strictly questions of "air" as we might think of it—these are questions of temperature, bodily responses to weather changes, increasing pollution leading to increasing pulls on the power grids, leading to increasing pollution as well as a breakdown of that system. Moreover, these conditions might further change the physical conditions in which we breathe, pushing people into cooling centers near one another at a time when proximity and risk intertwine, or adding deadly and hard to detect carbon monoxide to domestic environments. Those of us reliant on technologies for sleep apnea or for respiration might be additionally burdened and threatened by these shifts. We might be warned away from unsafe environments made through these changes by the added smell we have come to associate with natural gas, or we might be unaware of such shifts due to the odorless qualities of something like carbon dioxide.

The pandemic reminds us that we are vectors for one another, for good or ill. Oversimplified debates over personal relations to the mask—does it protect the user or those around the user—leave the air a kind of personal bubble, a personal relation that is your own problem. How can we tell an atmospheric story when these are our models, when all things that might cross a body's boundary are so deeply visceral? Moreover, how might we think about the contaminants and everything else that crosses our body's boundaries every day?

As we close, we might ask who lives with access to which atmospheres, who is a part of which pulmonary publics. Local, national, and global questions of air quality, access to oxygen during the pandemic, the smoke of climate change–related fires, the stench of bodies that cannot be buried quickly enough or that lead to too many simultaneous cremations abound and interconnect. Our air—inevitably shared by all of us, contributed to in ways that are micro- and macroscopic—unites us, regardless of whether we want it to. Our pandemic moment demands attention to the inequities of atmospheres that persist during it, that predate it, and that threaten to continue long after this moment passes. It is only in tracking and accounting for those inequities that we might begin to determine how we might all begin to breathe a more just air together.

NOTES

1. For a discussion of this inequity and how "relearning to breathe in/as/through collective action, radical care, and mutual exchange might cultivate breathable futures," see Matthew Houdek and Ersula J. Ore, "Cultivating Otherwise Worlds and Breathable Futures," *Rhetoric, Politics & Culture* 1, no. 1 (2021): 85–95, 86. See also Rachel J. Hardeman,

Eduardo M. Medina, and Rhea W. Boyd, "Stolen Breaths," *New England Journal of Medicine* 383 (2020); and DiArron M.'s chapter in this volume.

2. Thomas Rickert, *Ambient Rhetoric: The Attunements of Rhetorical Being* (Pittsburgh: University of Pittsburgh Press, 2013).
3. Robin E. Jensen, *Infertility: Tracing the History of a Transformative Term* (University Park: Penn State University Press, 2016).
4. Due to the limitations and scope of this chapter, the atmospheric relations I am talking about here are those of approximately the past twenty or so years in the American context; they come after the Clean Air Act and a series of regulations and public health campaigns that led to a decline in smoking in public. In other words, we are talking about understanding atmospheres that have, in a limited but visible way, already been "cleaned."
5. Emily Winderman and Robert Mejia, "The COVID-19 Sensorium and Its Vectors, Victims, and Violators," *Communication and Critical/Cultural Studies* 19, no. 1 (2022): 22–29.
6. Derek Thompson, "Hygiene Theater Is a Huge Waste of Time," *Atlantic*, July 27, 2020.
7. For more on histories informing the droplet/aerosol division and Covid-19, see Katherine Randall, E. Thomas Ewing, Linsey Marr, Jose Jimenez, and Lydia Bourouiba, "How Did We Get Here: What Are Droplets and Aerosols and How Far Do They Go? A Historical Perspective on the Transmission of Respiratory Infectious Diseases," *Interface Focus*, 11, no. 6 (2021): 1–10.
8. Though recommendations about masking would remain patchy and contradictory through much of the early months of the pandemic—and though he himself would not be seen in a mask publicly until a visit to Walter Reed in July of 2020, and rarely from that point forward—then-president Donald Trump admitted in an early February 2020 interview with Bob Woodward that "the air, you just breathe the air. That's how it's passed." That interview would not be published until Woodward's book came out in September 2020. See Rachel Martin and Steve Inskeep, "Trump Tells Woodward He Deliberately Downplayed Coronavirus Threat," NPR, September 10, 2020.
9. U.S. EPA, "Air Quality Index (AQI) Basics," AirNow.gov.
10. "Don't Share Your Air," Kaiser Permanente, https://about.kaiserpermanente.org.
11. Ged Kenslea, "As COVID-19 Soars, AHF Urges 'Don't Share Air' in New Nat'l Billboard Campaign," AIDS Healthcare Foundation, https://www.aidshealth.org.
12. Samantha Frost, *Biocultural Creatures: Toward a New Theory of the Human* (Durham, NC: Duke University Press, 2016), 103.
13. Allison Rowland, *Zoetropes and the Politics of Humanhood* (Columbus: Ohio State University Press, 2020), 44.

14. Jenell Johnson, "'A Man's Mouth Is His Castle': The Midcentury Fluoridation Controversy and the Visceral Public," *Quarterly Journal of Speech* 102, no. 1 (2016): 1–20.
15. Johnson, "A Man's Mouth," 5.
16. I explore this partiality through what I call *atmospheric erasure* elsewhere. See Sara DiCaglio, "Breathing in a Pandemic: Covid-19's Atmospheric Erasures," *Configurations* 29, no. 4 (2021): 375–87.
17. For instance, in an interview with the *Wall Street Journal*, Donald Trump suggested that "[People] put their finger on the mask, and they take them off, and then they start touching their eyes and touching their nose and their mouth. And then they don't know how they caught [Covid]?" Donald Trump, interview by Michael Bender, *Wall Street Journal*, June 18, 2020. See also "Fact Check: No Evidence Mask Wearing Will Cause Bacterial Pneumonia," Reuters, February 22, 2021.
18. In the interest of brevity, I will just list here a few of the tendrils of this logic: the language of "underlying conditions" and "individual choice," the eugenic logic related to who lives and dies during the pandemic, etc. Kurt Zemlicka's contribution to this collection also offers more discussion of the relation between anti-vaccination discourse, anti-masking discourse, and science denialism.
19. See also Priscilla Wald, *Contagious: Cultures, Carriers, and the Outbreak Narrative* (Durham, NC: Duke University Press, 2008).
20. Emily Winderman, Robert Mejia, and Brandon Rogers, "'All Smell Is Disease': Miasma, Sensory Rhetoric, and the Sanitary-Bacteriologic of Visceral Public Health," *Rhetoric of Health & Medicine* 2, no. 2 (2019): 115–46.
21. See also Hsuan L. Hsu, *The Smell of Risk: Environmental Disparities and Olfactory Aesthetics* (New York: New York University Press, 2020); DiCaglio, "Breathing in a Pandemic."
22. Rebecca Miller, Katharine Mach, and Chris Field, "Climate Change Is Central to California's Wildfires," *Scientific American*, October 29, 2020.
23. Elsewhere in this collection, Raquel M. Robvais discusses the ways that these pre-existing conditions, structural at their heart, are used to uphold systems of white supremacy.
24. Melanie Carver, Sanaz Eftekhari, Hannah Jaffee, and Mo Mayrides, *Asthma Disparities in America: A Roadmap to Reducing Burden on Racial and Ethnic Minorities* (Arlington, VA: Asthma and Allergy Foundation of America, 2020).

Covid and Science Denialism

The Rhetorical Foundations of US Anti-Masking Discourse

Kurt Zemlicka

POPULAR MEDIA COVERAGE OF ANTI-MASKING DISCOURSE IN 2020 OFTEN focused on political polarization as a leading cause for the phenomenon, highlighting polling that showed a sharp partisan asymmetry in masking practices.[1] Many outlets argued that these attitudes were the result of then-president Donald Trump's comments and behavior, citing both his failure to wear masks in public and his anemic endorsement of CDC guidelines.[2] However, attributing this resistance primarily to Trump's behavior risks framing the issue as beginning and ending with Trump and his actions, often at the expense of exploring the rhetorical antecedents present in anti-masking discourse itself. Many of the tropes and arguments leveraged against both the efficacy of masks in slowing community transmission and the social impact of masking requirements are nearly identical to those used against a variety of proposed environmental and public health-based policies over the past several decades in American political discourse. Specifically, partisan anti-masking rhetoric contains many of the same beats as other discourses aimed at stalling regulatory measures by publicly questioning, politicizing, and ultimately denying the scientific research upon which those regulatory actions are based. Because of these similarities, partisan-based anti-masking itself can be understood within the rhetorical heritage of science denialism.

However, it also represents an evolution of that heritage. Anti-masking rhetoric throughout 2020 brought together two different rhetorical strands that previously existed in related, yet largely separate discourse communities. The first strand was driven by Republican politicians and influential figures in conservative media who spent the better part of a decade espousing skepticism over the existence of climate change. While this strategy was developed primarily to stall governmental regulation of carbon emissions, it became increasingly enmeshed within a broader political strategy of victimization and resentment aimed to motivate voter turnout. The second strand contained loosely affiliated, largely nonpartisan individuals in online spaces questioning the safety of vaccines and other scientific dogma, forming identities around feelings of persecution, marginalization, and a belief that scientific institutions were involved in conspiracies ranging from maximizing profit to social control. While these two discourse communities began to loosely associate prior to the pandemic, masking was the first time they coalesced around a singular issue. This chapter traces the rhetorical heritage of these two discourses to understand how Trump, along with the politics shaped by his presidency, merged two denialist strands together. The nature of that merger was one of codependence: conservative politicians and media figures utilized the tropes of climate skepticism to conflate the science of masking efficacy with questions related to masking policy, encouraging their audience to disregard expert advice in favor of nebulous concepts like choice and independence. Meanwhile, participants in online spaces deployed the same tropes used to question research related to, among other things, the MMR vaccine to frame anti-masking as an identity-making practice and form of resistance to larger cultural forces. The two strands signaled each other in a feedback loop that was *holistically* consistent in its opposition to masking while *individually* inconsistent in terms of content and strategy. The result was that partisan anti-masking discourse in 2020 functioned as a kind of *stochastic denialism*, a form of science denialism that, while unpredictable in terms of individual arguments about the research in question, served a predictable identity-forming function for its disparate discourse communities.

I proceed in two sections. In the first I will trace the rhetorical foundations of contemporary science denialism in the United States by examining the argumentative strategies and topoi in two discursive spaces in the decade prior to the pandemic. First, I look at how climate denialism, originally motivated by the economic concerns of the energy lobby seeking to forestall regulatory action on emissions became enmeshed within a broader Republican strategy playing on victimization and racial resentment to motivate voter turnout, effectively enlisting science denialism into the culture war. Second, I explore how the largely online-based anti-vaccine movement amplified feelings of victimization to forward conspiracy theories about pharmaceutical companies, fostering science denialism as an identity-forming practice. In the second section, I look at how the rhetoric of these two spaces coalesced over masking to foster a pattern of stochastic denialism. Importantly, not all anti-masking discourses exist within these two strands, and resistance to masking is not monolithic.[3] However, exploring the rhetoric of partisan anti-masking is nonetheless critical to understanding how this strand will continue to function well beyond the pandemic itself.

The Rhetorical Foundations of Contemporary Scientific Skepticism

While providing a comprehensive history of science denialism in the United States is well beyond the scope of this chapter, its recent manifestations contain some broad rhetorical consistencies that help explain its persistence. At its core, practitioners appear to be arguing against a scientific fact—knowledge produced by an institution that is tasked with creating the closest thing to objective truth in society. As such, the science denier seems to deny reality, and the natural impulse is to reiterate the existence of the denied science as if it were sufficient proof in and of itself. However, research demonstrates again and again that strategy is ineffective.[4] As Veronica Joyner and Heidi Y. Lawrence compellingly argue later in this volume, treating denialism as a deficit in knowledge whereby the denier merely does not understand the science in question oversimplifies both the problem and the perceived remedy. The denier is not purely ignorant of research on the topic, they actively resist the research's truth value. Both a lack of controversy *among scientists* on the topic, and the amount the research is communicated are functionally irrelevant. Denialism functions publicly, in a discursive sphere distinct from those governing scientific knowledge production. It invokes public argument and deliberation, whereas discourse between and among scientists, largely in the form of peer-reviewed articles and academic conferences, is often not for public consumption. The generic constraints that determine the status of something as a scientific fact differ between these two discursive spaces. Contemporary science denialism relies on conflating those differences, producing a model that has proven effective nearly to the point of intractability.

Science denialism misapplies the norms of public deliberation and debate to question the facticity of scientific research by framing it as a public issue. To understand why this is effective, it is important to look at how the public and scientific spheres of discourse handle truth. Scientists, especially those working within the natural and medical sciences, aim to produce necessary truths—knowledge about the world that cannot be otherwise and would exist independent of our ability to perceive it. While scientific facts, even ideally, must be constructed since they are produced by humans,[5] science nonetheless produces knowledge under this general framework. Conversely, truths subject to deliberation in the public sphere are contingent, meaning they could always be otherwise. As David Zarefsky notes, the goal of deliberation over contingent truths "is *phronesis*, practical wisdom about what we should do or how we should act."[6] While both scientific research and public issues require deliberation to settle disputes, the *goals* and *scope* of those deliberations differ depending on the kind of truth under discussion. Framing the truth value of scientific research as a public issue creates a demand to assess that research within the bounds of public deliberation. Refusing that demand is extremely difficult since, as Leah Ceccarelli explains, members of the scientific community that do so are often portrayed as either undemocratic or unable to defend their work.[7] Agreeing to debate is likewise problematic as the issue in question is evaluated *as if* it were a contingent truth. Once science deniers collapse the boundary between necessary and contingent truths, appeals to technical expertise are flattened alongside other aspects of *phronesis*, while appeals to democratic norms, free and open discussion, and common sense experience are used to short-circuit scientific and technical explanations.

To see how denialism mobilized public argument to destabilize nonexpert perceptions of scientific research in the years before the pandemic, I will focus briefly on how Republican rhetorics of climate denial evolved between the presidencies of George W. Bush and Trump. This period is an important precursor for anti-masking rhetoric for two reasons: first, climate denialism during this time is structurally representative of many contemporary denialist discourses, using nearly identical rhetorical strategies invoked by other deniers regardless of the specific research at hand. The specific science in question is less significant than the discourse community that denies it—the same community that would later embrace anti-masking and directly import many of the same rhetorical tropes. Second, climate skepticism shifted with the underlying politics of the Republican Party during this period. While it began as a tactic deployed by the energy lobby to stall emission regulations, it became enmeshed as a culture war issue in the broader Republican electoral strategy during the 2010 midterms, the 2016 presidential elections, and beyond.

Climate Skepticism, the Culture War, and the Conflation of Truth, 2007–16

By the end of George W. Bush's presidency, a bipartisan framework to curb domestic carbon emissions began to emerge. Republican presidential candidate John McCain campaigned on his credentials to combat climate change, arguing in a December 2007 speech that he was the better candidate to responsibly curb emissions.[8] Two years later, the Obama administration pressed Congress to pass cap-and-trade legislation amid bipartisan support in the House and Senate. During debate over the bill, conservative activists looked to inject climate skepticism back into the discussion as a tactic to stymie the bill's passage. Drawing on resources from oil-industry-funded academics and think tanks, they looked to discredit research on climate change by claiming that it was being manipulated by the scientific community.[9] Ultimately, the cap-and-trade bill failed to pass as Republicans looked to hinder any further Democratic legislation before the 2010 midterm elections. In the wake of the debates, climate denialism gained steam within the Republican Party and the 2010 *Citizens United* ruling allowed the oil industry to incentivize its entrenchment. The energy lobbying group Americans for Prosperity (AFP) spent vast sums of money during the midterm cycle aimed at electing candidates that would oppose new emission regulations. According to the *New York Times*, by the end of the 2010 cycle, "165 congressional members and candidates had signed [AFP's] 'No Climate Tax' pledge," and most won reelection.[10] Climate denialism became a de facto part of the Republican Party platform and with the election of Trump in 2016, it moved into the executive branch.

Republican denialism during this period exemplified the strategy of characterizing climate science *as if* it were a contingent truth. During his confirmation hearing to administer the EPA, Scott Pruitt lamented that the existence of climate change was a political issue where "civil discourse is absent."[11] His solution was to ensure that research regarding the anthropogenic impact on climate is "subject to continuing debate and dialogue" between scientists, policymakers, and industry experts.[12] By invoking the language of public deliberation and dialogue, Republican denialism of this type sought to shift the conversation away from the efficacy of the research in question to the necessity of open public deliberation. This recharacterization frames climate change like any other political issue, moving the core of the controversy further afield from the facticity of the research itself. For example, six months after his confirmation, Pruitt's EPA began an initiative to support a "back-and-forth critique of specific new reports on climate science."[13] Using the language of public deliberation, the program sought to review climate science "outside of the normal peer-review process" in the interest of "a fresh and transparent evaluation."[14] The (necessary) question of scientific research related to climate change is rhetorically reframed as one of several (contingent) issues related to climate policy. We see this clearly in an interview with initiative-participant Luke Popovich, a spokesperson for the National Mining Association, who told *Politico*, "We're not debating the 'accept or deny climate science.' We approach it as a policy issue: how do we deal with this issue, what is the most prudent and rational course for that."[15] The rhetoric of Republican climate denialism relies on collapsing the distinction between climate research and climate *policy*, thereby reinforcing the narrative that climate science is itself a *policy issue*.

While climate denialism may initially have been economically motivated, it inevitably took on aspects of the broader Republican political strategy at the time. The influx of campaign funding following *Citizens United* that incentivized readopting climate denialism coincided with the rise of the Tea Party during the 2010 midterm cycle. Republican electoral strategy increasingly relied on blending economic libertarianism with a rightwing populism that combined economic, cultural, and racial anxieties to amplify resentment toward America's shifting cultural landscape.[16] The Tea Party recontextualized arguments against regulation and small government within this broader matrix of resentment. Lisa Disch argues that a defining aspect of the Tea Party's populism relied on making distinctions between who deserved government benefits and who did not.[17] For example, the movement explicitly viewed the Affordable Care Act as irresponsible and unfair because it gave benefits to non-white citizens who were "lazy and undeserving," while programs like Social Security and Medicare were worthy entitlements because they were "earned through hard work."[18] As such, the movement simultaneously mobilized resentment and victimhood as a defense of white entitlement while effacing its own racial elements under the language of small government and deregulation. Darrel Wanzer characterizes this dynamic as "racial neoliberalism," in which the Tea Party was able to "mark Obama as a threatening, uncivilized, racialized Other without invoking the term 'race' and while hiding behind the justification of 'policy disagreements.'"[19]

This dynamic continued through the presidency of Trump, where, as Casey Kelly argues, the politics of victimhood further linked together emotions of resentment with political ideology and identity.[20] The mobilization of resentment simultaneously invoked and effaced racial identity, culminating in what Robert Terrill argues was Trump's "rejection of a specifically racial burden" that fostered a broader rejection of responsibility toward others.[21]

As denialism became part of the culture war, scientific research was folded into a narrative that framed expertise as another elitist institution fomenting unwanted social change. Arguments against the regulation of fossil fuels and against expanding the social safety net became conceptually equivalent as necessary to combat socialism and government overreach. In September 2013, a group of Republican Senators, led by Ted Cruz, gave a twenty-one-hour speech in the Senate opposing the Affordable Care Act. At one point during the speech, Oklahoma Senator Jim Inhofe asked for the floor to commiserate with Cruz, arguing, "I went through this [when] everyone thought global warming was coming... I was the bad guy because I stood and said: No, this isn't true."[22] He then encouraged Cruz to press on, saying, "[When] a person is right on a controversial issue, they are going to be the subject of a lot of criticism, a lot of cussing, a lot of name-calling, and a lot of violence."[23] Inhofe's seeming non sequitur is illustrative because it functionally collapses the distinction between climate denialism and arguments against the Affordable Care Act. Inhofe frames science denialism as a righteous act of speaking up on a "controversial issue." Not only does this conflate the necessary truth of climate research with the contingent truth of healthcare policy, but it also implies that Inhofe was subject to "violence" for speaking up. Once denialism became part of the culture war, the simple act of denial itself became a morally righteous act of speaking out in the face of persecution.

Anti-Vaxxers, Social Media, and Denialism as Identity, 2015–19

The further entrenchment of the Tea Party during the second Obama administration overlapped with the rise of social media as the primary avenue for the public to consume news and learn about science.[24] Social media played a substantial role in spreading science denialist discourse, and during this period multiple denialist communities formed on Facebook and Twitter over a variety of scientific "controversies." Paranoia about the motives of social institutions in general (and scientists themselves in particular) manifested in online discourses of denialism where users were encouraged to "do their own research" on various scientific issues, often channeling them toward information that would encourage and amplify their suspicions. Unlike climate denialism, many were not explicitly linked to partisan political ideologies. However, they relied on the tropes of victimization and resentment, thriving on platforms that incentivized outrage and conspiracy to drive user engagement.[25] The anti-vaccine movement, along with other, primarily online-based denialist discourses, represents a strand of scientific denialism distinct from climate skepticism. In contrast to climate skepticism's top-down structure that was propelled by partisan actors and media coverage, the anti-vaccine movement circulated via bottom-up online communities on Facebook and Twitter.

A defining characteristic of anti-MMR vaccine rhetoric during this time was an emphasis on personal experience and anecdotal evidence to devalue and dismiss scientific knowledge and expert rebuttals. A 2019 survey of online anti-vaccine networks by Naomi Smith and Tim Graham noted that users often portrayed themselves as victims who were devalued or dismissed by mainstream public and scientific institutions. Within these spaces, the content of denialism was less important than the act of denial itself, with the latter serving as its own identity-making practice. Smith and Graham note that anti-vaccine Facebook groups amplified the belief that women's experiences were "privileged as [a form] of knowledge as mothers were argued to be best placed to tell if their children were healthy or not."[26] For example, in a 2015 interview for PBS, prominent anti-vaccine activist Jenny McCarthy was asked if she could prove there was a link between the MMR vaccine and autism. She responded, "I've got evidence in [my son]. And I've got evidence in thousands and hundreds of thousands of parents all over the world."[27] This demonstrates the identity-forming aspects of this strand of denialism. McCarthy's identity and experience as a parent supersedes scientific expertise. As a result, refuting specific arguments for the safety of vaccines is not needed, one's identity as a denier is sufficient in and of itself.

While the anti-vaccine movement was not expressly partisan, its reliance on themes of resentment, victimization, and paranoia mirrored Republican electoral strategies in the years leading up to the pandemic, and eventually the movement became enmeshed in Republican politics. In 2015, the California State Assembly deliberated over a bill banning personal belief as a legal exemption for childhood vaccination. Renee DiResta and Gilad Lotan analyzed Twitter hashtags related to the bill and found that anti-vaccine groups shifted from hashtags and messaging that was explicitly anti-vaccine in favor of those invoking parental choice and personal freedom, the same language used by prominent Californian Tea Party activists on the platform.[28] One year later, Republican candidates for state legislature in Texas and California, ran on "vaccine choice" platforms.[29] Research on vaccine attitudes of voters in 2016 indicated a higher likelihood that skeptics voted for Trump.[30] Vaccine skeptics were also more likely to believe that they were at risk of broadly having their freedom taken away by government actors, another refrain of Republican electoral discourse at the time.[31] By 2019, two different strands of denialist discourse were loosely entwined within the Republican Party: a top-down climate denialism, pushed by conservative politicians and media figures that framed climate research as a contingent truth, and a bottom-up denialism exemplified by the anti-vaccine movement that leveraged denialism as an identity marker to affectively engage its audience. Both discourses were permeated by resentment and victimization, a distrust of social institutions and expertise, and concerns about personal freedom and liberty. With so much commonality, it was only a matter of time before the two strands merged on a singular issue.

Anti-Masking as Stochastic Denialism

In late February and early March 2020, scientists were still trying to understand SARS-Cov-2's primary vectors of transmission. At the time, news organizations and public health officials maintained that the virus spread primarily by respiratory droplets that were too heavy to remain airborne.[32] The prevailing narrative was that people became infected when those droplets either landed on someone or were transferred by touching infected surfaces, downplaying the theory that the virus spread through aerosolized inhalation, despite gaps in the research at the time.[33] Based partly on this theory of transmission and partly over concerns about saving the dwindling stockpile of face coverings for healthcare workers, the CDC and Surgeon General recommended against masking for the general public.[34] A month later, as more research pointed toward aerosolized transmission as the primary vector of spread, the CDC changed course and recommended that all Americans wear a face covering where social distancing measures were hard to achieve.[35] The CDC's attempts to quell uncertainty and project confidence by making definitive recommendations on incomplete science backfired. This uncertainty was mapped onto existing narratives about climate change by conservative news outlets, and science related to the pandemic was quickly politicized. In April, *Fox News* host Laura Ingraham argued, "They'll say this whole mask thing is settled science, just like they do with climate change. Of course it's not."[36] Conservative news outlets also jumped on the CDC's reversal to conflate scientific research on the virus as a contingent issue. In a segment responding to New York City's then-recently imposed mask mandate, Tucker Carlson interviewed self-identified "Covid contrarian" Alex Berenson, who argued that public health officials were "spending time haranguing us about masks and destroying the economy with lockdowns," conflating masking research with public health policy. Carlson responded, "It sounds like you're suggesting that some of the people espousing these measures—which are really warping and destroying, in some cases our society—know that they're really not necessary."[37] The CDC's early messaging fueled the perception that masking was a political issue and ultimately undercut the agency's future credibility on other aspects of the pandemic.[38] Throughout the summer and fall, a scientific consensus began to form both on aerosolized particles as the primary vector of transmission for Covid and the effectiveness of masking at slowing its spread.[39] But as scientific evidence for the benefits of mask wearing mounted, so too did attempts by denialists to frame the issue as a matter of policy instead of science. While research about a virus and disease that were unknown before November 2019 continued, science communicators struggled within a rhetorical landscape formed by years of political messaging that systematically devalued scientific institutions. Partisans were already primed to view policymaking based on scientific research like any other contingent political issue, refracted through the lens of resentment and victimization.

Over the summer, Trump offered contradictory remarks on masking. This ambiguity was the catalyst that united both top-down and bottom-up denialisms by focusing these underlying conditions on a singular object. His vague and contradictory messaging mirrored his rhetoric in the lead up to the violence at the Capitol in early 2021. Former assistant secretary at the Department of Homeland Security Juliette Kayyem, argued that Trump's refrain about the "stolen" 2020 presidential election led to "stochastic terrorism," a "method of political incitement that provokes random acts of extremist violence, in which the instigator uses rhetoric ambiguous enough to give himself and his allies plausible deniability for any resulting bloodshed."[40] Trump's comments on masking functioned in much the same way, sending supportive signals to anti-maskers without denouncing the practice altogether. Invoking stochastic terrorism is about more than maintaining plausible deniability, however. It also relates to the chaotic and disorganized way in which the violence occurs. According to Mark S. Hamm and Ramón Spaaij, this method of radicalization allows an actor to use mass media to indirectly provoke "acts of ideologically motivated violence that are statistically predictable but individually unpredictable."[41] Similarly, his inconsistent comments about masking made denialism much more likely, but the forms it would take and the topoi it would use were initially undetermined. Trump's vague objections offered a signal toward denialism without a clear reason, allowing deniers to fill in a justification. This ambiguity mobilized two different elements: politicians looking to gain favor in the upcoming general election and partisans looking to engage in the identity-making performative politics of Trumpism. Of course, these two groups are not insulated from each other, with politicians relying on electoral support from partisans, and partisans demanding that politicians enact their values. Here, the two loosely connected strands of denialism found common cause, with politicians enacting the top-down denialism of climate skepticism and partisans enacting identity-forming denialism online.

Top-Down Denialism and the Tropes of Climate Skepticism

Republican political figures responded to stochastic denialism by invoking many of the same rhetorical tactics they used in discussing climate change to situate masking within the broader culture war. In July, Georgia governor Brian Kemp sued the City of Atlanta over its mask mandate, citing an executive order that banned any local public health measures more restrictive than those passed at the state level. Kemp explained his rationale for the lawsuit in a tweet, arguing that it, "is on behalf of Atlanta business owners and their hardworking employees who . . . are doing their very best to put food on the table for their families while local elected officials shutter businesses and undermine economic growth."[42] That same month, Iowa governor Kim Reynolds argued that mandates were overly restrictive and instead encouraged Iowans to "practice personal responsibility" to mitigate the spread of the virus.[43] In South Dakota, Governor Kristi Noem argued that people who choose not to mask are making a "personal decision" and deserve respect.[44] Similar statements were made by Republican governors in Texas and Arizona.[45] Even in heavily Republican states *with* a mask mandate, local politicians rebuked the orders. In Indiana, Republican governor Eric Holcomb, who was running for reelection, faced an unexpected challenge from third-party Libertarian candidate Donald Rainwater, who campaigned entirely on his opposition to the state's mask mandate. By October, the Rainwater campaign raised more money than the Democratic candidate, leading a Democratic advisor to lament, "This rise in the Libertarian vote is because of these anti-maskers."[46]

This top-down denialism leverages the asymmetry of topoi resulting from conflating necessary and contingent truths. We see this in the recurrent arguments used by politicians to argue against mandates. In July, Trump spoke against a national mask mandate in an interview with *Fox News*, saying people should have a "certain freedom" in deciding to mask in public and his administration framed public health measures as a matter of states' rights.[47] This situated the debate within the broader contours of ongoing political confrontations at the state level since 2010, well before the pandemic. Following the midterm elections that year, Republicans gained control of many state governments, while major cities, even in conservative states, grew more liberal. This led to increasing conflict between state governments and municipalities. As David Graham notes, battles over preemption laws "had been playing out for years. States often blocked cities from banning plastic bags or fracking or sugary drinks. They've prevented the enactment of stricter gun rules, higher minimum wages, and paid sick leave ... COVID-19 is just another theater for this battle."[48] The topoi of "economic concerns," "individual liberty," and "personal responsibility" used in those debates were imposed on discourse over mask mandates as masking became yet more gristle for the culture war.

Bottom-Up Denialism and Anti-Masking as an Identity

At the same time, stochastic denialism manifested in a more diffuse, bottom-up manner, coming from individuals leveraging the same rhetorical mechanisms as the anti-vaccine movement. In interviews and on social media, people speaking out against masking often echoed claims by politicians, drawing on the change in federal guidelines to cast doubt on the effectiveness of masks. However, many saw the existence of uncertainty as evidence of conspiracy. In an interview with *Vox*, one anti-mask activist argued that mandates were a step in "getting people into compliance so that they can make vaccines mandatory as well," while others remarked that masking was part of a larger effort by the government to prepare the population to accept other forms of social control.[49] Likewise, videos of anti-maskers confronting employees over masking policies spread on social media, with agitators calling workers "Democratic pigs" and "fascists."[50] Others argued that masks were used to drum up fear in an attempt to "make the president look bad, so they can cause all the problems they are causing."[51]

Wearing a mask was portrayed as weak and feminine. As early as May 2020, reporting on Trump's view of masking indicated that he was hesitant to wear a face covering in public because he feared he looked weak.[52] Later that month, BrieAnna Frank, a reporter for the *Arizona Republic* and *USA Today*, live tweeted her coverage of a Trump appearance at a plant manufacturing PPE. She noted that a crowd of supporters began harassing her for masking, with one man exclaiming that wearing a mask was "submission. It's muzzling yourself, it looks weak—especially for men."[53] In the midst of the presidential campaign, conservative media personality Tomi Lahren tweeted that Democratic nominee Joe Biden "might as well carry a purse with [his] mask."[54] This fits within broader appeals throughout the Trump campaign and presidency. Paul Johnson notes that appeals to masculinity were an essential part of Trump's strategy, with him often portraying his supporters as victims of a feminized political establishment.[55] Masking itself mapped clearly onto this dynamic as it became another way the establishment sought to feminize men.[56] As the anti-vaccine movement demonstrated, identity-based categories, particularly when linked to feelings of victimhood, play a central role in driving conspiracy-based denialist discourses. Research by Carl Palmer and Rolfe Peterson found "that men and women who embrace masculine norms of toughness are equally likely to feel negative affective responses toward the idea of wearing masks, even after accounting for other predictors such as partisanship and ideology."[57] While the gender-identification between anti-masking and anti-vaccine discourses is reversed, the centrality of victimization is consistent, demonstrating its power as a motivator for denialism.

Another commonality between anti-vaccine and anti-masking discourse is an inherent distrust of expertise and the desire for alternative sources of information, often those that amplify conspiracy theories. Anti-maskers emphasized distrust in both mainstream news outlets and public health officials, arguing that they were actively attempting to deceive the public. In an interview with *Vox*, one mask opponent summarized this viewpoint, stating, "there's definitely some sort of an agenda here to initiate control upon the people and to make people more obedient and compliant, and see which people are going to comply with some directives."[58] In response, this person sought to do their own "independent investigations," and turned to YouTube, since that is "where alternative thinkers are going to do their thinking."[59] Importantly, the turn to social media for independent research drew the anti-vaccine movement into the anti-masking fold. For example, the viral, twenty-six-minute "Plandemic" video, which argued that Covid was part of a broader conspiracy by pharmaceutical companies to gain power and profit, circulated on Facebook through prominent anti-vaccine groups and political groups against shelter-in-place orders, generating over eight million views less than a week after its initial upload.[60] The blending of these communities imported many of the same anti-vaccine arguments to masking, with anecdotal evidence functioning as persuasive refutations of scientific research.[61] Some anti-maskers argued that they either did not know anyone with the coronavirus or knew someone who only had mild symptoms, which they justified as grounds that the pandemic was overblown, and mask mandates must therefore be about social control.[62]

Anti-Masking, Identity, and Performative Denialism

Any specific argument against masking seems less important than the identity-shaping aspects of denial itself. The simultaneous ambiguity of *reasons*, coupled with a unicity of *affect*, seems to be one of the defining characteristics of anti-masking's stochastic interplay in its bottom-up manifestation. Significantly, those affects focus on themes of individuality, especially the fear that individual liberty is threatened to enforce social responsibility. It decontextualizes risk by universalizing the denier's existing risk factors and risk tolerance. Instead of understanding how structural and systemic inequities contribute to the overall risk of Covid for different communities, anti-mask proponents often assume *their* risk level is *everyone's* risk level, and that the choice to mask only affects the wearer. In this way, anti-masking, fueled by the latent racialized elements underlying the politics of many of its proponents, can be understood within a context of privilege and whiteness. Raka Shome argues that whiteness often operates through a "rhetoric of deflection and evasiveness" that "adopts an individualized perspective... instead of a systemic one."[63] The same can be said about the individuation of freedom and responsibility inherent in both aspects of anti-masking's stochastic dipole. Perhaps this dynamic works in tandem with the repetitive cycle of blame and shame Raquel M. Robvais outlines earlier in this volume. Calls for personal responsibility go hand-in-hand with a refusal to understand public health as a collective problem requiring collective action. Anti-masking, and the structure of whiteness that enables it, seems to limit an understanding of freedom to something that only exists in terms of individual choice and not as something that can be communally fostered through systemic thinking and collective actions that benefit others. Viewing anti-masking as a conduit of whiteness helps explain why resentment motivates much of its dynamic. Shome notes that when whiteness is contested, even in a way that very marginally challenges its power, "it begins to mark itself as 'other,' as 'different,' as an identity in crisis and therefore having a particular location that, like minority locations, needs to be defended, salvaged, and protected."[64] This may be why the act of denial is more important than any particular argument against masking—masks themselves are just another casualty of a politics that renders everything part of a culture war, fomenting white resentment as a political identity in and of itself.

Stochastic denialism is in many ways more pernicious than its antecedents. Like climate denialism and the anti-vaccine movement, it leverages the tropes of public deliberation, democratic governance, personal experience, and truth telling to devalue scientific expertise. What differentiates it from its predecessors is that it has no concretized set of topoi and does not rely on any one argument. Instead, it relies on the performance of denialism itself to foster political identity. However, it nonetheless draws on discourses that preceded the pandemic, and as such, lessons learned in combating (even partially) climate denialism and anti-vaccine skepticism are still relevant. Denialism exists in its contemporary form because facts alone will not convince the denier and emphasizing the science in question cannot be the only strategy to combat it. In this way, the relationship between anti-making discourse and Trump is not one of causality, but *simultaneity*. If whiteness is indeed a conduit that underpins the stochastic nature of anti-masking discourse, then formulating strategies to counter it requires interrogating structures of inequity that enable it as an act of privilege. Understanding anti-masking's rhetorical lineage is therefore essential as denialism inevitably concretizes on a new scientific "controversy" in the future.

NOTES

1. Ruth Igielnik, "Most Americans Say They Regularly Wore a Mask in Stores During the Past Month; Fewer See Others Doing It," Pew Research Center, June 23, 2020. Anna North, "Why Masks Are (Still) Politicized in America," *Vox*, July 22, 2020.
2. Editorial Board, "Opinion: Don't Listen to Trump. Mask-Wearing Is Essential," *Washington Post*, June 23, 2020. Paul Krugman, "What Is It with Trump and Face Masks?," *New York Times*, July 17, 2020.
3. Angela Nurse and Diane Keeling's work later in this volume highlights how resistance to masking by Black men draws on a different rhetorical heritage.

4. Brendan Nyhan and Jason Reifler, "When Corrections Fail: The Persistence of Political Misperceptions," *Political Behavior* 32 (June 2010): 303–30.
5. Bruno Latour and Steve Woolgar, *Laboratory Life: The Construction of Scientific Facts* (Princeton, NJ: Princeton University Press, 1987).
6. David Zarefsky, "Reflections on Making the Case," in *Making the Case: Advocacy and Judgment in Public Argument*, ed. Kathryn M. Olson, Michael William Pfau, and Kirt H. Wilson (East Lansing: Michigan State University Press, 2012), 3.
7. Leah Ceccarelli, "Manufactured Scientific Controversy: Science, Rhetoric, and Public Debate," *Rhetoric and Public Affairs* 14, no. 2 (2011): 198.
8. Paul Guinnessy, "John McCain on Climate Change," *Physics Today*, January 2, 2008.
9. Andrew C. Revkin, "Hacked E-Mail Is New Fodder for Climate Dispute," *New York Times*, November 21, 2011.
10. Carol Davenport and Eric Lipton, "How G.O.P. Leaders Came to View Climate Change as Fake Science," *New York Times*, June 3, 2017.
11. U.S. Congress, Senate, Committee on Environment and Public Works, *Hearing on Nomination of Attorney General Scott Pruitt to Be Administration Head of the U.S. Environmental Protection Agency*, 115th Congress, January 18, 2017.
12. "Hearing on Nomination of Attorney General Scott Pruitt to be Administrator of the U.S. Environmental Protection Agency," U.S. Congress, https://www.govinfo.gov/content/pkg/CHRG-115shrg24034/html/CHRG-115shrg24034.htm.
13. Timothy Cama, "EPA Head Launching Initiative to 'Critique' Climate Science," *The Hill*, June 30, 2017.
14. Cama, "EPA Head."
15. Emily Holden, "Pruitt Climate Science Challenge Splits Conservative Allies," *Politico*, August 9, 2017.
16. Chip Berlet, "Reframing Populist Resentments in the Tea Party Movement," in *Steep: The Precipitous Rise of the Tea Party*, ed. Lawrence Rosenthal and Christine Trost (Berkeley: University of California Press, 2012).
17. Lisa Disch, "The Tea Party: A 'White Citizenship' Movement?," in Rosenthal and Trost, *Steep*, 134.
18. Disch, "Tea Party," 137.
19. Darrel Wanzer, "Barack Obama, the Tea Party, and the Threat of Race: On Racial Neoliberalism and Born Again Racism," *Communication, Culture & Critique*, 4 (2011): 26.
20. Casey Ryan Kelly, "Donald J. Trump and the Rhetoric of *Ressentiment*," *Quarterly Journal of Speech* 106, no. 1 (2020): 5.
21. Robert E. Terrill, "The Post-Racial and Post-Ethical Discourse of Donald J. Trump,"

Rhetoric and Public Affairs 20, no. 3 (2017): 499.
22. "Transcript: Sen. Ted Cruz's Marathon Speech Against Obamacare on Sept. 24," *Washington Post*, September 25, 2013.
23. "Ted Cruz's Marathon Speech."
24. Emma Frances Bloomfield and Denise Tillery, "The Circulation of Climate Change Denial Online: Rhetorical and Networking Strategies on Facebook," *Environmental Communication* 13, no. 1 (2019): 23–34.
25. Luke Munn, "Angry by Design: Toxic Communication and Technical Architectures," *Humanities and Social Science Communications* 7, no. 53 (2020): 1–11.
26. Naomi Smith and Tim Graham, "Mapping the Anti-Vaccination Movement on Facebook," *Information, Communication & Society* 22, no. 9 (2019): 1325.
27. "Jenny McCarthy: 'We're Not an Anti-Vaccine Movement . . . We're Pro-Safe Vaccine,'" *PBS Frontline*, March 23, 2015.
28. Renee Diresta and Gilad Lotan, "Anti-Vaxxers Are Using Twitter to Manipulate a Vaccine Bill," *Wired*, June 8, 2015.
29. Jessica Glenza, "Disgraced Anti-Vaxxer Andrew Wakefield Aims to Advance His Agenda in Texas Election," *Guardian*, February 26, 2018.
30. Matthew J. Hornsey et al., "Donald Trump and Vaccination: The Effect of Political Identity, Conspiracist Ideation and Presidential Tweets on Vaccine Hesitancy," *Journal of Experimental Social Psychology* 88 (2020): 1–8.
31. Matthew J. Hornsey, E. A. Harris, and K. S. Fielding, "The Psychological Roots of Anti-Vaccination Attitudes: A 24-Nation Investigation," *Health Physiology* 73, no. 4 (2018): 307–15.
32. Katrina Lamansky, "Coronavirus: How Basic Manners Can Help Prevent the Spread," *WQAD*, March 9, 2020.
33. Roxanne Khamsi, "They Say Coronavirus Isn't Airborne—But it's Definitely Borne by Air," *Wired*, March 14, 2020.
34. Centers For Disease Control and Prevention, Twitter Post, February 27, 2020, https://twitter.com/cdcgov/status/1233134710638825473; Jerome Adams, Twitter post, February 29, 2020, https://twitter.com/Surgeon_General/status/1233726563881029632.
35. Trisha Greenhalgh et al., "Face Masks for the Public During the Covid-19 Crisis," *BMJ* 369 (2020): 1–4. German Lopez, "The CDC Now Recommends Everyone Use Cloth Masks in Public," *Vox*, April 3, 2020.
36. Robert Mackey, "Trump Manages to Wear a Mask and Undercut Mask-Wearing at the Same Time," *The Intercept*, July 12, 2020.
37. Yael Halon, "Ex-NY Times Reporter Blasts Governors Over 'Infuriating' Lockdowns:

'They Are Fools and Haven't Read the Data,'" *Fox News*, May 5, 2020.
38. Zeynep Tufekci, "Why Telling People They Don't Need Masks Backfired," *New York Times*, March 17, 2020.
39. Derek K. Chu et al., "Physical Distancing, Face Masks, and Eye Protection to Prevent Person-to-person Transmission of Sars-Cov-2 and Covid-19: A Systematic Review and Meta-Analysis," *Lancet* 395, no. 10242 (2020): 1973–87.
40. Mark Follman, "National Security Experts Warn Trump 'Is Promoting Terrorism,'" *Mother Jones*, December 17, 2020.
41. Mark S. Hamm and Ramón Spaaij, *The Age of Lone Wolf Terrorism* (New York: Columbia University Press, 2017), 84.
42. Veronica Stracqualursi and Paul LeBlanc, "Georgia Governor Sues Atlanta Mayor Over City's Mask Mandate," *CNN*, July 16, 2020.
43. Kate Payne and Katarina Sostaric, "Iowa Governor Says Cities, Counties Can't Require Masks; Highlights 'Concerning' Covid-19 Increase," *Iowa Public Radio*, July 7, 2020.
44. Stephen Groves, "South Dakota's Noem Defends Forgoing Masks as Virus Surges," *AP News*, November 18, 2020.
45. David A. Graham, "The Battle for Local Control Is Now a Matter of Life and Death," *Atlantic*, July 26, 2020.
46. Adam Wren, "How Anti-Mask Politics Are Scrambling Indiana's Governor's Race," *Politico*, September 17, 2020.
47. "Coronavirus: Donald Trump Vows Not to Order Americans to Wear Masks," *BBC*, July 18, 2020.
48. Graham, "Battle for Local Control."
49. Emily Stewart, "Anti-Maskers Explain Themselves," *Vox*, August 7, 2020.
50. "Trader Joe's Shopper Caught on Camera Ranting, Calling People 'Democratic Pigs' After Being Told to Wear a Mask," *CBS Los Angeles*, June 27, 2020.
51. Stewart, "Anti-Maskers."
52. "Trump Tells Allies His Wearing a Mask Would 'Send the Wrong Message,' Make Him Look Ridiculous," *NBC News*, May 7, 2020.
53. BrieAnna J. Frank, Twitter post, May 5, 2020, https://twitter.com/brieannafrank/status/1257710908928745472?s=20.
54. Tomi Lahren, Twitter post, October 5, 2020, https://twitter.com/tomilahren/status/1313312828670046208.
55. Paul Elliott Johnson, "The Art of Masculine Victimhood: Donald Trump's Demagoguery," *Women's Studies in Communication* 40, no. 3 (2017): 230.
56. Jonathan M. Metzl, *Dying of Whiteness: How the Politics of Racist Resentment Is Killing*

America's Heartland (New York: Basic Books, 2020).
57. Carl L. Palmer and Rolfe D. Peterson, "Toxic Mask-Ulinity: The Link Between Masculine Toughness and Affective Reactions to Mask Wearing in the Covid-19 Era," *Politics and Gender* 16 (2020): 1049.
58. Stewart, "Anti-Maskers."
59. Stewart, "Anti-Maskers."
60. Sheera Frenkel, Ben Decker, and Davey Alba, "How the 'Plandemic' Movie and Its Falsehoods Spread Widely Online," *New York Times*, May 20, 2020.
61. Jack Goodman and Flora Carmichael, "Coronavirus: 'Deadly Masks' Claims Debunked," *BBC*, July 24, 2020.
62. Stewart, "Anti-Maskers."
63. Raka Shome, "Outing Whiteness," *Critical Studies in Media Communication* 17, no. 3 (2000): 367.
64. Shome, "Outing Whiteness," 386.

Covid and Vaccine Hesitancy

Tracing the Tuskegee-Covid Straw Man Fallacy as a History Presently Unfolding

Veronica Joyner and Heidi Y. Lawrence

AS THE REALITIES OF THE NOVEL CORONAVIRUS PANDEMIC HIT THE UNITED States, the possibility and promise of vaccines as time-tested, effective, and safe ways to prevent infectious disease emerged early in popular discourses, media, and the public imagination as a possible "way out" of the pandemic. Alongside that hopeful narrative of vaccination quickly emerged a counter-concern: what if people don't accept the vaccine? Covid has disproportionately affected communities of color, highlighting health disparities among Black and Indigenous people of color (BIPOC) in particular. Early hesitancy toward the vaccine by those very communities prompted a reckoning about the consequences of egregious exploitative practices in medicine. Old anxieties about the ways in which vaccine hesitancy, skepticism, and refusal jeopardize public health combined with "new" worries about the very particular reasons that those historically mistreated by medicine might be wary of a vaccine developed at "warp speed."

In this chapter, we examine how the media has articulated Covid vaccine hesitancy among Black Americans. First, we examine how the "problem" of vaccine refusal was reported in the media. We argue that the mainstream news media's specific focus on "Tuskegee" as an explanation for hesitancy elides the larger historical context of mistreatment of Black Americans by medicine, something we call the *Tuskegee-Covid straw man*. Instead of a long-standing reaction to a decidedly *past* misdeed, hesitancy among Black Americans results from a justified wariness of medicine and its capabilities, stemming from a wide history of abuses alongside a history presently unfolding, where medicine and science continue to be indifferent to the pain, suffering, and death of Black Americans.[1]

The "Tuskegee" framing mischaracterizes the nature of skepticism experienced by this group and constrains corresponding discursive solutions to resolving hesitancies. Understanding the history of how Black Americans have been treated by health and medical systems reveals a need for a different rhetorical approach to the exigencies of vaccine skepticism elided by reductionist paradigms. Such an approach requires a materialist understanding of rhetoric and demands that vaccine programs have as their goal not simply "shots in arms" but rather collaborative work with communities to achieve positive relationships and trust as the basis for health decisions about vaccines. Consequently, news media framing must move past deficit-based understandings about why people question vaccines. Instead, we argue, in a context of justified wariness of medicine and its capabilities as an institution, vaccine hesitancy, skepticism, and refusal can function as an act of collective self-preservation in response to historic mistreatment by the medical system.

Complexities, Deficits, and Straw Men: Media and Vaccine Controversy

Vaccine controversy—encompassing skepticisms, hesitancies, refusals, and "anti-vaccination" theories and groups—is a vast and complex social phenomenon demanding diverse answers. Research on vaccine controversy has long emphasized and examined this complexity. Historical research has established the trajectories of vaccine skepticisms from the first vaccinations in England in the late seventeenth century, to the specific articulations of vaccine controversy in the United States through to present day. Social science, health communication, cultural studies, and rhetoric have long parsed the rationales people have for questioning and refusing vaccines and posited the ways in which interventions might help to forestall or overcome those concerns.[2] Public health and medical literature has established how a range of factors, from social structures to health beliefs to access to low-cost, quality care, prevents certain groups from trusting vaccines and ultimately accepting them.[3] The complexity of the problem, however, is often elided in media representations and resulting popular views on vaccine skepticism, complicating public discourse. From news media, to fictional representations of "anti-vaxxers" on television, to social media memes, media constructions about vaccine controversies are often incomplete, one-sided, or inaccurate.

Scholars in rhetoric and social science observe two intersecting problems with responses to vaccine concerns reiterated in media discussions about vaccination.[4] First is the notion of deficit-based reasoning.[5] Deficit-based reasoning occurs when it is assumed that any rejection of science by the public comes from a place of deficit, or something that is lacking among that part of the public. The assumption is that members of a public reject the science because they do not *understand* the science, how it works, or its value. Deficit-based assumptions often lead to education or other necessarily fulfillment-focused responses, wherein the public simply needs the thing that is wrong with them to be answered or resolved, and then, once that is achieved, people will accept the science.[6]

The primacy and ubiquity of deficit-based reasoning pervades understanding of health belief, behavior, and decision-making. Public health scholars and practitioners have long attempted to create frameworks for understanding, predicting, and changing health beliefs. Foundational, though not solitary, among these is the Health Belief Model (HBM). Developed by Irwin Rosenstock in response to mid-twentieth century vaccination and other health campaigns that attempted to understand why people did and did not respond to public health interventions, the HBM asserts that people work in predictable ways to move toward positive experiences and away from negative ones, the latter of which includes, for Rosenstock, disease.[7] A number of factors could contribute to why one might move *away* from disease, such as fear of its seriousness, severity, and one's perceived susceptibility to the disease.[8] Within such a paradigm, deficit-based reasoning becomes reified in the basics of public health understanding like a key in a lock: if people are not sufficiently informed about a disease, they will not take actions to prevent it. Therefore, those deficits must be corrected for the intended health behavior to be enacted.

However, there is an additional, and perhaps more problematic, way in which the deficit model is used and perpetuated in messaging about science and medicine: the ways deficit-based understanding is used not just to form a foundation of *communication to* those who are hesitant—which is the primary audience conceived of in the HBM—but to report on *communication about* those who are hesitant presumably to an audience of confident listeners. Perceived in-group communication, among media and scientific experts that assumes a nondeficient, vaccine-supporting audience as its standard, employs deficit-based models for explaining why *others* are hesitant as well.

The second reductionist view of vaccine controversy is the straw man fallacy, which reduces the complexity of vaccine concern to a singular focus on the fraudulent claim that MMR is responsible for autism.[9] Mark Largent argues that the vast array of public concerns about vaccines are diverse and long-standing yet are streamlined into the MMR-autism straw man, a connection research shows few people truly believe or, even if they believe it, will have their faith in vaccines restored even if it is disproven.[10] Yet, for years, news media about vaccine controversy has reinforced the deficit-straw man fallacy of MMR-autism, in particular because it makes vaccine skepticism easily resolvable. The original study that posited a connection between MMR and autism has been retracted, the study deemed fraudulent, and has never been replicated or borne out in subsequent study. Setting up MMR-autism as the straw man creates a central rationale that is seemingly easily disproved through a deficit-based response, such as "correcting" beliefs about MMR and autism by merely educating the public. Brendan Nyhan's work suggests that trying to dispel the MMR-autism connection is uniquely subject to the backfire effect—wherein merely bringing up the idea helps the idea gain more stickiness, especially to its adherents.[11]

The straw man fallacy is a rhetorical tactic that purposefully weakens an argument in order to make it easier to refute. As Schumann et al. note:

> Straw man focus[es] on two essential aspects of the fallacy: first, the straw man distorts the original point of view, and second, it does so with the aim of refuting it. ... when committing the fallacy, the interlocutor reformulates the original content in a distorted and often exaggerated way. The straw man aims at creating the impression that the distorted argument is closely related to the original standpoint, where in reality the fallacy uses a new, fictitious position, as a basis for its attack.[12]

Key to the straw man fallacy is *weakening*—taking an argument and purposefully distorting its original configuration such that it becomes easier to refute; weakening is necessary to amplify the deficit and corresponding correction to fix the deficit. Stating that Black Americans have valid reasons past and present to distrust medical systems and their products is, in fact, a strong, valid rationale for being skeptical about vaccines; the corresponding answers to that argument cannot be deficit-based, but rather are more logically grounded in other, material, systemic acknowledgments and changes that must occur. In the absence of such conditions (or desires), straw man tactics offer an immediate, deficit-based answer to pushback. In this most specific case, the weakening happens via a synecdochal tactic, reducing *the whole* (a past and present of documented medical abuse, neglect, and mistreatment) to just *one part* (the specific case of "Tuskegee"). In this case, this factual weakening allows interlocutors to feign acknowledgment of past abuses while comfortably addressing the perceived deficits it creates by saying, "We are sorry for these egregious misdeeds, but *that time has passed.*" Of course, data and experience show that abuses of Black bodies by medicine and science did not begin or end with "Tuskegee," *and* present problems in medicine persist, with results that range from low-grade, ever-present aggressions in examination rooms to overt verbal and physical abuse, both of which lead to disparate outcomes for Black patients. Thus, the Tuskegee-Covid straw man makes the most sense, as we discuss further below, for broader, primarily *white* audiences, for purposes of explaining and refuting why Black Americans' skepticisms are past and thus invalid.

When combined, this deficit-straw man fallacy works to elide the complex network of vaccine concerns, reducing them to a singular problem-to-be-solved, with a built-in expectation that the concern can be easily fixed through finite interventions, education, explanations, or, in the case of "Tuskegee," apologies. The deficit-straw man fallacy works to make it seem like the reasons for the problem are simple, while the fallacy also deludes audiences—skeptical and confident alike—into thinking that the corresponding solution ought to be simple as well. We argue that the deficit-straw man fallacy also operates in a critical way *for an audience* particularly when dealing with topics related to science. Deficit-straw man fallacies are especially potent in controversies involving science because they are always already constructed as solvable for the audience to whom they are presented, which is crucially not the audience for whom persuasion is sought. The MMR-autism deficit-straw man fallacy is persuasive argumentative grounding for those who support vaccines; those who refuse or are skeptical about vaccines know their own hesitancies and those of their community and do not need arguments reframed to them in such a way. Arguments that use the MMR-autism straw man as their foundation are inherently unpersuasive to vaccine refusers, as they likely do not believe that the MMR vaccine causes autism, or at least this is not singularly responsible for their hesitancy.[13] Rather, such discourse is aimed toward those who support vaccines as a mechanism for explaining why some refuse vaccines in the face of irrefutable scientific evidence that they are safe, a way of establishing the pro-science in-group, hailed to agree with one another.[14]

Similarly, we argue that "Tuskegee-Covid" straw man functions as a deficit-straw man *for audiences that are not Black*. It is a way for white people and members of other groups who have privileged historical relationships to science and medicine to understand why someone else might distrust medicine. It purposefully constructs the argument as weak and solvable, with a ready-made set of apologetic rebuttals to refute the claim. Just as with MMR-autism, Tuskegee-Covid ignores why Black Americans might possess deep skepticisms about medicine. For many Black Americans, "Tuskegee," if it factors at all, is only one tessera in the mosaic of mistreatment that is far from past. Additional pieces of the picture include many other, more recent examples of abuse that extend beyond "Tuskegee," in addition to data that show Black women and babies dying at higher rates in hospitals, cases of untreated pain while in a physician's care, and a whole host of additional forms of mistreatment.[15] It is not just the past—it is the past alongside the present.

Given this context for public and media portrayal of vaccine skepticism, hesitancy, and refusal, it is no wonder then that the media continued to deploy the deficit-straw man fallacy in response to concerns about Covid vaccine acceptance. Early discussions about the pandemic's disparate effect on communities of color—and Black Americans in particular—quickly transitioned to questions about whether those who were at greater risk of Covid would accept a vaccine that could stop more deaths from occurring. The straw man that the media landed on—"Tuskegee" or "the Tuskegee Experiment"—recited the deficit-straw man fallacy, repeatedly connecting complex vaccine concerns to a singular historical abuse that happened to Black Americans. In this iteration, the argument is set up to be easily resolved if larger social and historical factors are simply ignored or apologized away. However, just as the MMR-autism straw man elides immense complexity of vaccine beliefs and is ultimately not aimed at convincing those who have questions about vaccines, so too does Tuskegee-Covid as it relates to widespread mistrust of medicine and its products, including vaccines, and ultimately does little to address the needs or concerns of those with hesitations.

Black Americans and the Past and Present of Medical Abuses

The institutionalized medical abuse of Black people in the United States is not a secret. It is simply one of those truths so painful and ubiquitous in its consequences that it seems easier to ignore, forget, or rhetorically reduce in the way we often do with "Tuskegee" itself. The "Tuskegee Experiment" ran from 1932 to 1972 and involved over six hundred subjects. During the Study, participants were denied access to treatment for syphilis so that researchers could study the natural progression of the disease. Participants were deceived about the nature of the Study, denied easily-accessible treatments, and the "results [were] disproportionately meager compared with known risks to human subjects involved."[16] Moreover, to use the term "Tuskegee Experiment," as many often do, is to tell two near-lies in one. First, as Susan M. Reverby outlines, our general nomenclature for Tuskegee tends toward "Tuskegee" or the "Tuskegee Experiment," relocates the focus of this crime away from the US Public Health Service (USPHS), which funded and conducted this "study," and instead leaves the legacy of naming with Tuskegee, which risks confusion with the Tuskegee University, a historically Black institution, and the Tuskegee Airmen, an entirely different project conducted by the US Air Force in Tuskegee in the 1940s.[17] Historians have thus moved toward a formal naming convention of "The U.S. Public Health Service Study at Tuskegee."[18] Yet as Reverby concludes (and our research confirms): "But in truth the word 'Tuskegee' is what circulates and what is known."[19] Retaining "Tuskegee" also elides the reason that Macon County, Alabama, was chosen as the site for the USPHS Syphilis Study to begin with. In reality, Macon County, Alabama, where Tuskegee sits, was chosen for its purportedly high rates of syphilis among Black men. This combined with prevailing racist notions within medicine that syphilis was more common in Black Americans due to failings of "morality and virtue," and that Black men were most dangerous as late phases of syphilis infection would likely lead to "increased insanity and crime."[20] We do not repeat these historical facts lightly. We do so because it is important to note that the very nature of the Study was racist at its core assumptions, never focused on care, and always existed to advance white supremacist goals through medicine, at the expense and suffering of Black men and women.

The second lie that the term "Tuskegee Experiment" tells lives in the word "experiment," which it was not, by any standards. Reverby argues thus: "In reality, it was never really an experiment in the sense of a drug, biologic, or device being tested. It was supposed to be a prospective (going forward in time) study of what the doctors called the 'natural history' of latent syphilis, even though the PHS created much of this 'natural history' through their actions."[21] In the conduct of the Study, the USPHS subjected participants to tests including spinal taps and other invasive procedures to establish the extent of syphilis infection at the outset of the Study, deceived participants about the "treatments" they were receiving, and knowingly withheld important, life-saving treatment that was widely available and that there was no medical reason to refuse. Even when some men pursued treatment for syphilis independent of the Study and obtained antibiotics, the concern of the lead researcher conducting the Study focused on study outcomes only, noting, "I hope that the availability of antibiotics has not interfered too much with this project."[22]

Although the USPHS Syphilis Study was undeniably heinous, what many Black Americans have experienced, and what scholars of medical history like Harriet Washington know all too well, is how pervasive and habitual these events really are. In *Medical Apartheid*, Washington recounts medicine's history of abuse against Black people.[23] As Washington recounts, the obstetrics and gynecology specialty was founded on the unwilling bodies of enslaved African women, a fact that has caused widespread criticism of its "father," J. Marion Simms, in recent years in particular. Also well-known is the case of Henrietta Lacks, whose cell line has been used extensively in medical testing and procedures in the decades following her initial treatment in 1951 at Johns Hopkins University without her consent, with no research oversight, and ultimately no direct benefit to the patient.[24] And of course the study is another example of horror, abuse, and mistreatment of Black bodies in the name of medical progress. But Washington also draws attention to other less reported on unethical medical experiments on Black bodies in the history of medicine. As recently as 1997, researchers injected Black children with fenfluramine, a chemical that later proved damaging to brain and heart functions.[25] The chemical was meant to help identify the chemical imbalance researchers claimed made poor Black children inherently more violent. Researchers recruited the study's sample population from the files of Black teens in the juvenile justice system, and then leveraged that connection to coerce parents into consenting to have their younger children participate in the study. In an earlier campaign (1950–70), the Army Chemical Corps in Fort Dietrich bred millions of mosquitos carrying various pathogens and set them loose in Carver Village, Florida, a Black neighborhood named after George Washington Carver.[26] This community of test subjects was chosen amid rampant racial unrest spurred by the Ku Klux Klan's attempts to eradicate the Black subdivision. The impetuses in both examples were tied to white supremacist ideas and agendas that characterized Black people as violent and threatening. These examples of medical abuse show that the rhetoric of white supremacy has been supported by and enacted through medical research and practice for hundreds of years. In the same way the rhetoric of medical care in eighteenth-century Europe adapted to maintain and support the economic needs of the Industrial Revolution,[27] the rhetoric of health in the United States pathologized Black bodies. Black bodies were deemed human enough to practice medical procedures on, but not human enough to be worthy of even the most basic human protections. This ideology, of course, also fueled the agricultural economy of the South in nineteenth-century America (and beyond).

Physician willingness to construct Black bodies as simultaneously deficient and near indefatigable became a tool for justifying their continued enslavement and securing an unprotected supply of human test subjects that would support the medical and technological advances that secured doctors' place in the social hierarchy.[28] This original sin, an unjust power dynamic that undergirds many Black Americans' relationship with health care, may go undertheorized or underreported, but those who experience that relationship firsthand continue to mitigate its effects through strategic cynicism, or even *suspicion* of the recommendations of health practitioners and officials about vaccines specifically.[29] Indeed, connections abound between this history of racism and health disparities today. As just a few examples: Black women have higher rates of maternal mortality, Black babies in neonatal intensive care units are more likely to receive substandard care than their white counterparts, and Black children are less likely to receive pain treatment in hospitals.[30] Statistics such as these add up to a continuation of these historic abuses, a *history presently unfolding*, in which these incidents of poor care are not just bad luck or finite problems to be fixed, but rather just medicine furthering its indifference to the lives and deaths of Black bodies.

In the context of this history, vaccine hesitancy among Black Americans is perfectly logical, forming a kind of collective self-preservation amid an indifferent system. Generational trauma that extends from having family members who were victims of the USPHS Syphilis Study, being the fourth generation of women in your family to have a hysterectomy and not really know why, and the grandmothers and grandfathers whose graves were robbed to be sold to medical colleges all continue to frame Black Americans' relationship to institutionalized medicine. In this vast, complex historical context, it is no wonder that mistrust is high for reasons that span well beyond "the Tuskegee Experiment." In our next section, we outline how the deficit-straw man fallacy worked in reporting, both in the early days of the pandemic and through the anxiety about vaccine acceptance, to funnel these complex concerns into a singular, solvable rationale for possible refusal.

The Deficit-Straw Man Fallacy at Work: Media and "the Tuskegee Experiment"

To examine this phenomenon, we read a wide range of news reports about Covid vaccine and "the Tuskegee Experiment" published between July 2020 and July 2021. Using a Nexis Uni search including those terms, we aimed to assess a wide range of media outlets to better understand how they were using this term alongside Covid vaccine acceptability among Black Americans. We use these articles as evidence of the breadth of this phenomenon across news outlets.

The oversimplification of Black Americans' relationship with the US medical system in popular media occurred early and often in response to Covid. A *Google News* search conducted on July 18, 2021, yielded 6,470 results for "the Tuskegee Experiment" from the previous year. Early reports about the pandemic immediately relied on "the Tuskegee Experiment" as an explanation for why Covid had a disproportionate impact on Black Americans. We discuss just the first few results as examples, but media coverage ranged from written articles to short segments in local broadcast news productions. In the *Financial Times*, reporters blamed the "Tuskegee Experiment" for fueling long-standing mistrust that led Black Americans to believe internet rumors that Black people could not get Covid.[31] Similarly, the *New York Times* linked Tuskegee to Black Americans' likelihood to believe a wide range of misinformation and conspiracy theories about not just Covid but AIDS as well, fueled by distrust in medicine caused by Tuskegee: "The effects of the Tuskegee syphilis study still reverberate in the form of distrust and sometimes avoidance of the health care system among Black Americans. In our current moment, this medical distrust has shown up in the form of those conspiracy theories and low-information rumors about Covid-19—akin to the false theories and rumors that were also prevalent during the AIDS era."[32] *USA Today* quoted a CDC official as blaming Tuskegee for historically low rates of participation in medical studies among Black Americans. The *Philadelphia Inquirer* located Tuskegee as chief among the reasons that public health enjoys very little trust, which was ultimately to blame for mistrust about CDC recommendations for masking and distancing early in the pandemic.[33]

It is no surprise, therefore, that early pandemic reporting that cast Tuskegee as responsible for making Black Americans more likely to believe conspiracy theories and mistrust medicine would eventually evolve into a concern about Black Americans resisting the Covid vaccine specifically. The Ad Council, an organization that produces public service announcement advertisements in response to current events and issues, created a PSA wherein descendants of Tuskegee patients encourage other Black people to take the Covid vaccine.[34] The reasoning behind this campaign was explained as Black people's distrust of the medical system and the US government. Even news articles that had nothing to do with Covid casually mention the Tuskegee experiment as the root of African American distrust of vaccines.[35] Another piece in *USA Today* examined the relationship between Tuskegee and low rates of vaccination among Black Americans generally (including low rates of flu vaccination) through the perspective of "David Graham . . . a 41-year-old black man who learned in high school how doctors failed to treat hundreds of black men in a federal study for their syphilis, so he isn't inclined to trust the government to get a vaccine for the pandemic right."[36] Within the context of this frame of Tuskegee, a range of health officials and practitioners chimed in to offer reasons that people like Graham should not be worried about vaccines, concluding that vaccines "prevent millions of illnesses and flu-related doctors' visits," and are overall "safe and effective."

This frame that "Tuskegee" is primarily responsible for Black Americans' potential low uptake of the Covid vaccine appears throughout thought pieces in popular media outlets. The writers at media outlets like the *Washington Post*, *Wall Street Journal*, and National Public Radio omitted the larger historical context for Black Americans' mistrust of medicine in favor of deep dives into the Tuskegee Experiment's effect on vaccine hesitancy. A *Washington Post* "Lifestyle" piece led with a story about how descendants of men from "the Tuskegee experiment" are trying to quell misgivings about the Covid vaccine.[37] The article profiled three Black people who are also members of an organization of descendants. Beginning with three descriptions of how excited they were to get vaccinated, the article pushed the message that while many Black people are "using the Tuskegee experiment" as an excuse not to get vaccinated, these descendants are doing the right thing and getting vaccinated. By this logic, the hope seems that those Black people who are skeptical will see the willingness of these individuals to get the vaccine as proof that it is safe. Even the news outlets that acknowledge deeper structural inequity start by explaining "Tuskegee" as the grounding event driving distrust.

Like the *Washington Post*, articles in the *Wall Street Journal* present "Tuskegee" as almost the sole reason for most Black Americans' hesitancy. The article "In Tuskegee, History Drives Distrust of Covid-19 Vaccines," focused on the residents of Tuskegee, Alabama, specifically. By centering those who live in the area where the experiments were carried out, reporter Julie Wernau presented the feelings of a few Black people who are especially close to the event and ties them to a national distrust of the vaccine. While much of the article discussed the perspective of Black residents of Tuskegee, Alabama, the introduction that details the significance of this information explained that a physician who has been working on national vaccine outreach says, "the legacy of the Tuskegee study has made many Black people wary of the shots."[38] The initial appeal to a national issue as an exigence for a piece about a specific local area shows that Black people in Tuskegee, Alabama, are being used as a stand-in for all Black Americans.

Wherever distrust of medicine and Black people are mentioned in the same context, it seems "Tuskegee" is also part of the conversation. Quinn et al., who explore flu vaccine uptake and beliefs among African Americans, find the same complexity that we know exists with vaccine hesitancy among other populations, ranging from access, cost, and socioeconomic status; living in "health deserts" where there is no history of medical care; health status; and age.[39] In addition, they found that "knowledge of Tuskegee" is associated with reduced uptake of flu vaccine among African Americans. However, it is worth noting that "Tuskegee" was the only historical incident specifically asked about in the study. Their research instrument (a questionnaire) did not ask about other historical incidents, personal family history, or historical context more generally, so even this finding lacks the nuance necessary to really make sense of the true weight of "Tuskegee."

The long history of medicine's mistreatment of Black people is so readily available, yet "Tuskegee" remains such a relied-upon explanation for the source of the mistrust that many Black Americans have of medicine. As we argue in this chapter, the deficit-based responses that the Tuskegee-Covid straw man allows in this case easily dismisses past abuses, yet we maintain that the abuses are both past and present, a more difficult argument to dispel.

The Path Forward: Modifying the Material Exigencies of Vaccine Hesitancy

If the purpose of most media coverage of vaccine hesitancy among Black Americans is to rebut it, the USPHS Syphilis Study provides not only a point of concession, but also dismissal. As stated, through the synecdochal reduction, the media deploys the straw man fallacy by only recognizing the one historical incident of abuse. Deficit-based rebuttals then can easily assert that "yes, 'Tuskegee' happened, and it was awful. But, that was in the past, and look at all that has changed and is now corrected." If all distrust can be attributed to one event, authorities weaken the bases of Black people's hesitancy by situating it as an outdated example and an already solved problem. Yet it is not.

As Washington proves in *Medical Apartheid*, even after the Belmont Report, informed consent for vulnerable groups is still a fraught enterprise to say the least. Ending in the 1970s, "Tuskegee" occurred in the recent past, not so long ago as to be out of the (white) social memory and without the graphic images of gynecological surgeries without anesthesia like those performed by J. Marion Simms. Its wrongs are stark and contribute to a myth that this kind of behavior is a thing that we no longer do. Finally, tragic as it was, it offers an easy deficit to resolve. Hearings have been held, court cases settled, and reparations made. As an event in human history, "Tuskegee," or the USPHS Syphilis Study is a closed case. In 1997, Bill Clinton issued a formal apology for the federal government's funding of the Study. Popular discourse and media representations can assert: "Tuskegee" was awful, but it's over, so Black Americans should move past it, at which point the rhetorical goal is to help move them out of that deficit by reminding them that "Tuskegee" is over.

As we discussed, the USPHS Syphilis Study *is* among the reasons cited for mistrust of medicine by Black Americans. But we argue that when the media reduces an ongoing history of mistreatment to a single event, the discursive damage is vast. First, it does harm to the ethos of doctors and academics as intellectual authorities by refusing to recognize factual evidence provided to support differing perspectives. Second, it forecloses opportunities for generative discussion on how to actually address historic inequities because the conversation is derailed by straw man arguments. Third, it creates further division between deliberative parties by painting one party as irrational. Fourth, it provides cover for those medical systems that have historically underperformed for Black Americans to continue their substandard treatment by taking attention away from the history of mistreatment presently unfolding. It allows the media to elide the multiple complexities of racism in medicine that create a straight through line from J. Marion Simms, to the USPHS Syphilis Study, to Black mothers being more up to five times more than white mothers during childbirth.[40]

Raquel M. Robvais aptly observes in this volume: "Covid discourse represents a continuation of history, a reiteration of white supremacy in disguised characterizations." For Black Americans, the abuses of today—within Covid and beyond—simply compound the effect of history and generational traumas, making *history* a key material exigence to be modified in vaccine skepticisms. Material exigencies in vaccine discourse constitute the real, material conditions that shape rhetorical situations, motivating discourse and demanding responses that, if unacknowledged, will drive ongoing discord and disrupt resolution.[41] The experience of being consistently dismissed, chastised, lectured, or ignored by medical professionals is an *ongoing* phenomenon, informed by history and activated in the present, constitutes a material exigence that will only serve to fuel skepticism as it remains unacknowledged, or only addressed through feigned acknowledgments through deficit-straw man arguments. The effort to acknowledge the endemic racism in medicine and make the changes necessary to make medicine and health care more equitable is set back by bad-faith reductionist depictions of the issue.

Most consequential for vaccination—casting the problem in such a manner blinds us to the real, material resolutions that might come to pass that could expand vaccine trust and levels of acceptance for those mistrustful of vaccination. This requires a re-imagining of response to vaccine concerns among hesitant communities, that sadly we did not see happening in the months following the vaccine roll-out. Data available following widespread availability of vaccines against Covid show that long-standing material barriers to vaccination, including access to vaccines and a trusted healthcare provider, continue to shape vaccine uptake in significant ways.[42] It is an established truism in vaccination that people *want* advice from trusted healthcare providers when it comes to vaccination. But if you do not trust your healthcare provider, or have access to one at all, then that is an immediate barrier to ground-up changes leading to trust in medicine, science, and health care. Modifying material exigencies requires addressing the exigencies driving distrust through a combination of acknowledging past and present abuses while changing the material outcomes of those abuses that perpetuate inequality today.

All good answers come from understanding. Let us not mistake distrust for paranoia or assume skepticism is misguided or wrong. More study is needed to fully understand the nature and scope of vaccine hesitancies for Black Americans; such research has been scarce and focused on structural or educational barriers that suppress vaccine acceptance. In many instances, those outliers who have argued for distrust have been proven correct. As we have already discussed, medical abuse of Black bodies is intertwined with the history of American medicine in the same ways that slavery is intertwined with the history of America. And moreover, simple acknowledgment of this fact does not go far enough to address such an acute issue as vaccine hesitancy because medicine's problem with Black people is profoundly chronic.

Structural changes are needed to see widespread change in mistrust of the medical system. Tomorrow's medical history is being written today, and the monumental shift that must occur to help heal the relationship between medicine and Black people has not yet happened. Sociologist Tressie McMillan Cottom describes the medical bureaucracy as one that must view a patient or stakeholder as competent in order to provide the promise of competent health care.[43] Black women, however, are rarely coded as competent, regardless of their level of educational or financial means. Famously well-connected and well-educated Black women have testimonies of dismissive doctors and nurses, sometimes with deadly consequences. On popular social media outlets, like Twitter, Facebook, and TikTok, Black women give advice for navigating the medical system in ways that may mitigate the effects of implicit bias against them. There is a popular sound on TikTok that says, "Doctors are to Black women what police officers are to Black men."[44] The original creator of the sound, @talkofshame, posted this at a time when national attention seemed to be turning toward the problem of health disparities, particularly among BIPOC viewers. She goes on to advise Black women to use this phrase when dealing with their doctors, "I will need you to document on record that you are refusing the treatment (or medicine) I've requested and the reason you are doing so." This trend on TikTok is just one example of the myriad tactics Black Americans have had to devise to protect themselves, proof that the need to mitigate structural inequity is not a phenomenon of the past.

As much as is lost by reductive explanations of the issue of health disparities in general and vaccine hesitancy specifically, there is still much to learn and apply in attempts to make things better. Through inquiry into this phenomenon, we have learned some lessons. Not least of these discoveries is that despite all of the misgivings expressed, as of April 2022, the percentage of vaccinated people who are Black/African American is about equal to their share of the US population.[45] While this information could be interpreted to mean that African Americans are beginning to trust medical authorities more, it is more likely a pragmatic reaction to regulations requiring vaccination for work and school. It also likely does not mean more trust in the system, but instead a resignation with the way things are and signs in popular media and legislation that failure to get vaccinated may close doors of access that African Americans cannot afford to close. In that case, the lesson to be learned is that while coercion works, it does not solve the problems that lead to resistance and distrust. We should not miss the opportunity to train a spotlight on the systemic issues that continue to leave Black Americans with less access to quality care as a whole.

The enslavement, dehumanization, exploitation, and oppression of Black Americans is materially manifest every day in large and small ways, from the connection between slavery, sharecropping, redlining, and the racial wealth gap, to the prevalence of certain socially determined health risk factors. These material realities force discursive responses that counter popular paradigms of physical, psychological, and social health. For affluent Americans who do not personally encounter racism and marginalization in their healthcare, the medical system may seem to work logically because popular understandings of health are Eurocentric in design and privileged in their application. However, for Black Americans, the material reality of history and the present creates a need to look skeptically at information that comes from historically untrustworthy sources. Instead of unquestioningly following the dictates of the medical system, many Black Americans look for the hidden agenda. When it comes to vaccination, the metric for success cannot be "shots in arms," but rather engaged communities of equal stakeholders.

NOTES

1. Susan Reverby, *Examining Tuskegee: The Infamous Syphilis Study and Its Legacy* (Chapel Hill: University of North Carolina Press, 2009).
2. Melissa L. Carrion, "'You Need to Do Your Research': Vaccines, Contestable Science, and Maternal Epistemology," *Public Understanding of Science* 27, no. 3 (2018): 310–24; Elena Conis, *Vaccine Nation: America's Changing Relationship with Immunization* (Chicago: University of Chicago Press, 2016); Bernice L. Hausman, *Anti/Vax: Reframing the Vaccination Controversy* (Ithaca, NY: Cornell University Press, 2019); Bernice L. Hausman, "Immunity, Modernity, and the Biopolitics of Vaccination Resistance," *Configurations* 25, no. 3 (2017): 279–300; Heidi Y. Lawrence, *Vaccine Rhetorics* (Columbus: Ohio State University Press, 2020); Jennifer Malkowski, "Confessions of a Pharmaceutical Company: Voice, Narrative, and Gendered Dialectics in the Case of Gardasil," *Health Communication* 29, no. 1 (2014): 81–92; Xiaoli Nan, Kelly Daily, Adam Richards, and Cheryl Holt, "Parental Support for HPV Vaccination Mandates among African Americans: The Impact of Message Framing and Consideration of Future Consequences," *Health Communication*

34, no. 12 (2019): 1404–12; Karen L. Walloch, *The Antivaccine Heresy: Jacobson v. Massachusetts and the Troubled History of Compulsory Vaccination in the United State*s (Rochester, NY: Boydell & Brewer, 2015).
3. Natalie Pierre Joseph, Jack A. Clark, Glory Mercilus, MaryAnn Wilbur, Jean Figaro, and Rebecca Perkins, "Racial and Ethnic Differences in HPV Knowledge, Attitudes, and Vaccination Rates among Low-Income African-American, Haitian, Latina, and Caucasian Young Adult Women," *Journal of Pediatric and Adolescent Gynecology* 27, no. 2 (2014): 83–92.
4. Heidi Y. Lawrence, Bernice L. Hausman, and Clare J. Dannenberg, "Reframing Medicine's Publics: The Local as a Public of Vaccine Refusal," *Journal of Medical Humanities* 35, no. 2 (2014): 111–29.
5. Alan Gross, "The Roles of Rhetoric in the Public Understanding of Science," *Public Understanding of Science* 3, no. 1 (1994): 3–23.
6. Celeste Condit, John Lynch, and Emily Winderman, "Recent Rhetorical Studies in Public Understanding of Science: Multiple Purposes and Strengths," *Public Understanding of Science* 21, no. 4 (2012): 386–400.
7. Irwin M. Rosenstock, "Why People Use Health Services," *Milbank Quarterly* 44, no. 3 (1966): 94, https://doi.org/10.2307/3348967.
8. Lawrence, *Vaccine Rhetorics*.
9. Mark A. Largent, *Vaccine: The Debate in Modern America* (Baltimore, MD: Johns Hopkins University Press, 2012).
10. Lawrence, Hausman, and Dannenberg, "Reframing Medicine's Publics."
11. Brendan Nyhan et al., "Effective Messages in Vaccine Promotion: A Randomized Trial," *Pediatrics* 133, no. 4 (2014): e835–42.
12. Jennifer Schumann, Sandrine Zufferey, and Steve Oswald, "The Linguistic Formulation of Fallacies Matters: The Case of Causal Connectives," *Argumentation* 35, no. 3 (2021): 361–88.
13. Bernice L. Hausman et al., "H1N1 Vaccination and Health Beliefs in a Rural Community in the Southeastern United States: Lessons Learned," *Critical Public Health* 30, no. 2 (2018): 1–7.
14. Patricia Roberts-Miller, "Dissent as 'Aid and Comfort to the Enemy': The Rhetorical Power of Naïve Realism and Ingroup Identity," *Rhetoric Society Quarterly* 39, no. 2 (2009): 170–88.
15. Elizabeth B. Arias, Betzaida Tejada-Vera, and Farida Ahmad, "Provisional Life Expectancy Estimates for January through June, 2020," data brief, *Vital Statistics Rapid Release* 15

(2021), https://www.cdc.gov/nchs/data/vsrr/vsrr015-508.pdf; Andreea A. Creanga et al., "Pregnancy-Related Mortality in the United States, 2011–2013," *Obstetrics and Gynecology* 130, no. 2 (2017): 366–E73; Donna Hoyert, "Maternal Mortality Rates in the United States, 2020," *NCHS Health E-Stats* (2022), DOI: https://dx.doi.org/10.15620/cdc:113967.

16. "The Syphilis Study at Tuskegee Timeline," CDC, https://www.cdc.gov/tuskegee/timeline.htm.
17. Susan M. Reverby, *Examining Tuskegee: The Infamous Syphilis Study and Its Legacy* (Chapel Hill: University of North Carolina Press, 2009).
18. Reverby abbreviates this to "the Study," which we use alongside the "USPHS Syphilis Study" when officially referring to the study in our chapter here. Our media research, however, examines articulations of "Tuskegee" or the "Tuskegee Experiment," as reflective of more popular nomenclature, also noted by Reverby. When referring to these reductionist naming practices—shortening "USPHS Syphilis Study at Tuskegee" to "Tuskegee Experiment"—we use the latter term in quotations when possible.
19. Reverby, *Examining Tuskegee*, 9.
20. Allan M. Brandt, "Racism and Research: The Case of the Tuskegee Syphilis Study," in *Sickness & Health in America: Readings in the History of Medicine and Public Health*, ed. Judith Walzer Leavitt and Ronald Numbers (Madison: University of Wisconsin Press, 1997), 395.
21. Reverby, *Examining Tuskegee*, 8.
22. Brandt, "Racism and Research," 399.
23. Harriet A. Washington, *Medical Apartheid: The Dark History of Medical Experimentation on Black Americans from Colonial Times to the Present* (New York: Anchor, 2008).
24. "The Legacy of Henrietta Lacks: Upholding the Highest Bioethical Standards," Johns Hopkins Medicine, https://www.hopkinsmedicine.org/henriettalacks/upholding-the-highest-bioethical-standards.html.
25. Washington, *Medical Apartheid*.
26. Eileen Welsome, *The Plutonium Files: America's Secret Medical Experiments in the Cold War* (New York: Delta, 2000).
27. Michel Foucault, "The Politics of Health in the Eighteenth Century," in *Power/Knowledge: Selected Interviews and Other Writings, 1972–1977*, ed. Colin Gordon (New York: Vintage, 1980).
28. Rana Hogarth, *Medicalizing Blackness: Making Racial Difference in the Atlantic World, 1780–1840* (Chapel Hill: University of North Carolina Press, 2017).

29. Nicole Charles, *Suspicion: Vaccines, Hesitancy, and the Affective Politics of Protection in Barbados* (Durham, NC: Duke University Press, 2022).
30. US Department of Health and Human Services, "Racial and Ethnic Disparities Continue in Pregnancy-Related Deaths: Black, American Indian/Alaska Native Women Most Affected," *CDC Newsroom*, January 1, 2016. Amy Norton, "Racial Disparity in Care Starts in NICU," *HealthDay News*, July 29, 2019. Monika K. Goyal et al., "Racial Disparities in Pain Management of Children With Appendicitis in Emergency Departments," *JAMA Pediatrics* 169, no. 11 (2015): 996–1002.
31. David Crow, "Coronavirus Fuels Black America's Sense of Injustice: African Americans Have Been Especially Vulnerable during the Pandemic, Laying Bare Disparities in Health, Housing and Employment," *Financial Times*, June 10, 2020, https://www.ft.com/content/7f679362-0084-47d0-a67f-661da639e78c.
32. "'A Terrible Price': The Deadly Racial Disparities of Covid-19 in America," *International Center for Multigenerational Legacies of Trauma*, May 12, 2020.
33. Ken Alltucker and Karen Weintraub, "NIH Director Urges Diverse Research for Virus Vaccines," *USA Today*, June 24, 2020, 4.
34. Ethan Jakob Craft, "Ad Council Taps Descendants of Tuskegee Syphilis Study Victims for Vaccine PSA," *Ad Age*, June 30, 2021.
35. Rafu Staff, "Baseball Great Hank Aaron Was a Legend Off the Field As Well," *Rafu Shimpo: Los Angeles Daily Japanese News*, January 26, 2021.
36. Jayne O'Donnell, "'Tuskegee Always Looms in our Minds': Some Fear Black Americans, Hardest Hit by Coronavirus, May Not Get Vaccine," *USA Today*, April 19, 2020, https://www.usatoday.com/story/news/health/2020/04/19/coronavirus-vaccine-black-americans-prevention/5146777002/.
37. David Montgomery, "Descendants of Men from Horrifying Tuskegee Study Want to Calm Virus Vaccine Fears," *Washington Post*, April 27, 2021.
38. Julie Wernau, "In Tuskegee, History Drives Distrust in Covid-19 Vaccines," *Wall Street Journal*, February 25, 2021.
39. Sandra Crouse Quinn et al., "Breaking Down the Monolith: Understanding Flu Vaccine Uptake Among African Americans," *SSM—Population Health* 4 (2018): 25–36.
40. Julie Wernau, "History Drives Distrust in Covid-19 Vaccines for Black Americans in Tuskegee," *Wall Street Journal*, February 25, 2021.
41. Lawrence, *Vaccine Rhetorics*.
42. Joyce Frieden, "'Pandemic of the Unvaccinated?' Not Really, Advocate Says," *MedPage Today*, August 25, 2021.

43. Tressie McMillan Cottom, "Dying to Be Competent," in *Thick: And Other Essays* (New York: New Press, 2019).
44. Kiki Monique, post to "@TalkofShame—Doctors Are to Black Women What Police Officers Are to Black Men," TikTok, July 25, 2020, https://www.tiktok.com/@thetalkofshame/video/6853409941986741509?lang=en&is_copy_url=0&is_from_webapp=v1&sender_device=pc&sender_web_id=6949006183970981382.
45. Nambi Ndugga et al., "Latest Data on COVID-19 Vaccinations by Race/Ethnicity," *Kaiser Family Foundation*, July 14, 2022.

PART 2

Essential and Disposable

Covid and Essential Workers

Medical Crises and the Rhetorical Strategies of Disposability

Marina Levina

ON MARCH 31, 2020, A COUPLE OF WEEKS INTO THE COVID SHUTDOWN, THE Brookings Institute, a prominent think tank, released a report with a set of recommendations on how to protect essential workers during the pandemic.[1] Based on the list released by the Department of Homeland Security, which designated "Essential Critical Infrastructure Workers" as those who "protect their communities, while ensuring continuity of functions critical to public health and safety, as well as economic and national security,"[2] the Brookings Institute estimated that essential workers represent at least 39 percent to 43 percent of the US workforce. The report acknowledged that "this is a staggering share of all workers, confirming the sheer scale necessary to keep us safe and economically resilient during a pandemic."[3] The report continued that "much like a wartime economy, this unique situation calls for the federal government to create a short-term social contract with the essential workforce."[4]

The report exemplifies the tension of constructing essentiality during the times of Covid. On one hand, essentiality functions to designate bodies as those with an irreplaceable value. After all, as the report shows, they are responsible for the safety and security of communities, both local and national. They are so essential to the very functioning of the nation-state during the time of an extreme crisis that the government bears a special, moral responsibility for their protection and compensation, akin to those owed to soldiers in the time of war.[5] On the other hand, what makes these bodies essential is that they are most likely to be sacrificed for the sake of the perceived economic security of the nation-state.[6] The bodies are essential precisely because they are disposable and must be sacrificed for the sake of economic prosperity and expansion.

In this chapter, I examine the rhetorics of essentiality, which emerged during the Covid pandemic. I argue that a designation of certain types of work as "essential" during the pandemic not only illuminates structural labor inequalities as they intersect with race and gender, but also the role that rhetoric plays in designating certain bodies as essential and therefore, ironically enough, without value. In other words, essentiality is rhetorically constructed to grant certain bodies and labor an essential value, which also marks them as disposable. Here, essentiality serves as a rhetorical strategy of disposability. The rhetorics of essentiality therefore render bodies valuable for disposability and marking them as essential makes disposability palatable. What is particularly interesting about this rhetorical juxtaposition between essentiality and disposability is that they are antonyms of each other.[7] To reconcile this relationship between these nearly opposing terms, we need to consider what Nathan Stormer calls the violence of consensus,[8] or how supposedly opposed rhetorical strategies are reconciled to render sacrifice of some for the benefit of others not only palatable, but presumably unavoidable. The archive that I collected here is obviously not exhaustive and does not represent the entirety of the complicated rhetorical and discursive response to the pandemic. Moreover, as I suggest in the conclusion, there has been pushback against essentiality/disposability both in popular and academic writing. However, the archive presented in the chapter—chosen specifically for its detailed engagement with the concept of essential workers—represents a rhetorical and cultural consensus that frames essentiality and disposability in a way that enacts sacrificial violence on the most vulnerable populations. Through the essay, I use critical textual analysis to elucidate the meaning behind this archive.

In an article on essential workers and the in/visibility of racial capitalism, Hareem Khan argues that categorization of workers as essential is "a racial tactic to demand their labor while evading accountability for workers' survival."[9] He argues that since most essential labor is performed by Black and Brown people, the codification of labor as essential marks Black and Brown bodies as "existentially essential." While "lauded as heroes of a capitalist state in the national public discourse, their disposability becomes glaringly real as threats from employers force workers to continue their shifts despite the risk of literal death."[10] The connection between disposability and race is further explicated by Lisa Flores, who argues that disposability functions as a rhetorical mechanism of racialization. In her analysis of rhetorical constructions of Mexican bodies in the United States, she argues that "disposability is one technique through which whitened violence is perpetuated."[11] Both Khan and Flores draw connections among essentiality, disposability, and the functioning of white supremacy and the capitalist regime that renders Black and Brown bodies consumable and disposable. I extend these arguments to examine how disposability is made not only tolerable, but, indeed, essential in the time of crisis. Specifically, I examine how essential bodies and labor were defined during the pandemic; how disposability was made essential through rhetoric of sacrifice, heroism as well as affects of care; and how disposability functions by marking certain bodies as essential enough to be sacrificed.

Defining Essential Bodies

In her book on HIV/AIDS pandemic, Paula Treichler argues that a pandemic is first and foremost an epidemic of signification. She insists that we need to consider a pandemic not only in terms of (re)production of virus through the body of the nation-states, but also in terms of re(production) of meaning about sexuality, desire, marginalization, gender, and race. She writes, "an epidemic intensifies existing social divisions and codifies cultural stereotypes because there seems to be no time to do otherwise. Ideas, metaphors, and images circulate efficiently. The long-standing use of the human body as a symbol of society ... takes on special force in an epidemic."[12] In other words, a pandemic as a crisis further clarifies what can be done to the body even before the crisis occurred. In the time of a pandemic, we fall back on existing conceptions of which bodies are essential and disposable, even as we claim that we are challenging pre-existing thinking. In the case of essentiality, discourses that defined and clarified what counts as essential work simply evoked existing narratives of sacrifice as essential to the functioning of the nation-state.

At the beginning of the pandemic, US Department of Homeland Security Cybersecurity and Infrastructure Security Agency list of "Essential Critical Infrastructure Workers" identified essential workers as those

> who conduct a range of operations and services that are essential to continued critical infrastructure viability, including staffing operations centers, maintaining and repairing critical infrastructure, operating call centers, working construction,

and performing management functions, among others. The industries they support represent, but are not necessarily limited to, medical and healthcare, telecommunications, information technology systems, defense, food and agriculture, transportation and logistics, energy, water and wastewater, law enforcement, and public works.[13]

The list suggests that the category of essential worker encompassed most of the workforce in the United States. Taken at its face value, this list implies that all labor is essential and therefore must be treated as such.

However, what it means to treat labor as essential is not necessarily clear. While our society might like to believe that designating labor as essential means valuing lives of those who perform this labor, the pandemic has illustrated that to designate labor as essential means to treat bodies who perform it as disposable and sacrificial. Because essentiality is deeply tied to the interworking of late-capitalist society with its artificial scarcity models, treating labor as essential means that certain bodies are essential precisely because they need to be disposed of in order to assure the continuous functioning of capitalist regimes. As Henry Giroux argues, "Under the logic of modernization, neoliberalism, and militarization, the category 'waste' includes no longer simply material goods but also human beings . . . Excluded from any long-term goals and a decent vision of the future, these are the populations who have been rendered redundant and disposable in the age of neoliberal global capitalism."[14] However, while Giroux suggests that certain bodies must simply be disregarded in order to assure the functioning of global capitalism—and that is certainly often the case—Covid illustrates that during the time of crisis, disposability becomes a much more complicated discursive and rhetorical practice, intimately tied to making bodies essential before they can be disposed. Within Covid narratives, essentiality has become intimately tied to the metaphors of war and sacrifice on the part of essential workers. The discursive practices parcel the broad category of "essential" labor to construct a subset of essential workers as frontline workers. For example, the Brookings Institute further delineates the distinction between frontline and essential workers. It argues that "protecting all essential workers is important, but defining the subset of essential workers who must physically report to their jobs and are most vulnerable to health risks—what we call 'frontline' workers—demands greater attention . . . We define 'frontline workers' as *employees within essential industries who must physically show up to their jobs*."[15]

The category of "frontline worker" is rhetorically significant for a few reasons. First, the metaphor of the "front" connects workers with the idea of war, where they become configured as soldiers in the pandemic war. This connection enables a rhetorical move toward choice and sacrifice, where a certain category of workers are represented as noble sacrifices, which then makes disposability palatable. Workers' bodies are then rendered essential for sacrifice to make sense. Much like soldiers in the war, their bodies become stand-ins for the nation-state—therefore making disposability and death an essential part of life. As Carolyn Marvin and David Ingle argue, the nation-state demands blood sacrifice, and much like in other religious rituals, the sacrifice is only meaningful if it is done willingly.[16] They maintain that soldier bodies are constructed as an extension of the body of the nation-state so that their death serves as a stand-in for the sacrifice by the totality of the nation-state. The analogous construction of the frontline worker connects labor and war in the pandemic. For their sacrifice to be meaningful, the workers must choose to show up to work much like soldiers must choose to show up to the battlefield. Of course, this obfuscates the structural inequalities that make these choices ineligible. Moreover, the sacrifice of essential workers is embedded in what Achille Mbembe defined as necropolitics, or the right and capacity of sovereignty to dictate who must die. He argues that "to exercise sovereignty is to exercise control over mortality and to define life as the deployment and manifestation of power."[17] Necropolitics and necropower account for "the creation of death-worlds, new and unique forms of social existence in which vast populations are subjected to conditions of life conferring upon them the status of living dead."[18] Here, death-worlds are essential to the functioning of sovereignty and the biopolitics of death. In other words, sacrifice becomes essential to the functioning of power. Necropolitics defines sovereignty as control over death. Mbembe's definition extends Giorgio Agamben's argument that power works through the creation of a permanent state of exception, or spaces in which, as Cindy Patton argues, "laws cannot be broken because the rule of law has already been suspended."[19] The state of exception creates a zone of indistinction where it is "not so much a spatiotemporal suspension as a complex topological figure in which not only the exception and rule but also the state of nature and law, outside and inside, pass through one another."[20] The zone of indistinction manages the sacrifice of bodies that are essential to the functioning of the death-worlds.

In the pandemic's zone of indistinction, the topology of sacrifice and death is rendered meaningful through rhetorical articulations of choice on behalf of essential workers. This has been discursively accomplished through an intertwining of sacrifice with an affect of care. In much of the pandemic's media coverage, essential workers are positioned as not only those who sacrifice for the better of the country, but also those who do so because of some higher calling or care. For example, an story on *Vox*, which features an interview with nursing home staff, states that "essential workers are really *care* workers, in every sense of the word."[21] When asked "if she's considered quitting, given the stress of the situation," one of the nurses replies "my heart won't let me, because then who's going to look after these residents?"[22] It is important to note here that *Vox*'s article advocates for hazard pay for essential workers, and it is common that sacrifice, morality, and care are interconnected in rhetorics of those advocating for the essential workers. For example, in a *Washington Post* op-ed, William J. Barber II (a co-chair of the Poor People's Campaign) and Joe Kennedy III (D-Mass 4th District), both longtime advocates for the working class, argued that for essential workers, "sacrifice and ... service are a moral calling for all of us."[23] Another op-ed in *New York Times* authored by Yasin Kakande—a journalist and author from Uganda currently working as a home health aide—addresses the fact that a lot of essential workers are immigrants, often without legal protection, but insists that "migrants like me and my brother are here because we want to work and provide for our families, just like you. We are proud to be a part of the essential work force."[24] And a *New York Times* article, examining the fact that most of "essential" personnel are women, states "from the cashier to the emergency room nurse to the drugstore pharmacist to the home health aide taking the bus to check on her older client, the soldier on the front lines of the current national emergency is most likely a woman." The article then proceeds to interview another home health aide, stating that, for her, "there is a fundamental question before her, one faced by countless other women keeping the country alive: If she does not do this, who will?"[25]

In these narratives, essential workers are constructed not as stuck working in dangerous working conditions due to the structural inequities, but rather as self-aware warriors who are choosing to help others despite the dangers to themselves and their families. For example, when the New York region was at the epicenter of the pandemic, the owner of a medical marijuana facility remarked that few of his employees balked at working during the pandemic: "Our employees understand the medicine that they're producing and the importance of it in the community."[26] He continued: "They've been so helpful and understanding about being on the front lines. Coming in contact with hundreds of patients every day, they've been doing it like champions."[27] Another article about essential work during the NYC outbreak—one of the worst outbreaks of Covid-19 in the United States—writes, "as shoppers swarm stores, snapping up everything from milk to toilet paper, cashiers are there to ring them out. Stockroom employees replenish shelves as soon as shipments arrive. Their presence is a source of calm, signifying that, even as demand has surged, supply chains remain intact and the essentials that people need remain available."[28] It then quotes a supermarket manager, who states, "On a personal level I'm worried about my health, too, but at the end of the day, what we're doing is important to a lot of people, so it's a sacrifice we have to make." The manager remarks that nearly all his employees have shown up for work every day. The same article quotes a local food and commercial worker union representative, who states that "workers in food stores are the ones keeping this nation from going into civil unrest."[29]

In these stories, sacrifice and care come together to form a narrative of heroism. For example, a Brookings Institute report states that grocery workers are among the true heroes of the pandemic, providing basic necessities to keep Americans alive and human comfort for their customers during an anxious time. It then quotes a cashier who says, "I choose to be happy and positive . . . If you can talk and make someone laugh, that might be the only positive thing in their life that day. That is what I choose to do."[30] Here, heroism is a result of not only showing up to work, but rather doing so willingly, driven by a higher purpose of care as opposed to the economic structures based on unsafe working conditions. In fact, heroism has become a common trope in describing essential workers. Another Brookings Report states that, despite the hardships and health risks, millions of essential frontline workers continue to do their jobs during the Covid-19 pandemic. The report praises "these hardworking heroes [who] are keeping Americans fed, picking up their trash, providing them life-saving medicine, delivering their groceries and packages, preparing their food, cleaning their hospitals, caring for those who are most vulnerable, and keeping us safe—often while earning low wages and few benefits.[31]

Rhetorics of heroism have also shaped the response for support of essential work. For example, a motion introducing "hero pay" in LA county, stated "grocery and drug retail workers are among the heroes of this pandemic, putting their lives on the line—often for low wages and minimal benefits—in order to sustain our food system and maintain healthy communities."[32] The solution of "hero pay" would require employees to offer raises to workers during the pandemic. In New York City, there are plans on the way for construction of the Circle of Heroes Essential Worker Monument. At the announcement of the monument, New York governor Andrew Cuomo stated,

> In the beginning of the pandemic when people were told to stay home, essential workers went into work day after day, making sure their fellow New Yorkers were safe,

fed and cared for. While we will never be able to fully repay our essential workers, we can honor and celebrate them with this monument that will stand forever as a tribute to all that they have done for New York in our greatest moment of need and beyond. These heroes continue to inspire us every day and we are forever grateful for their service and sacrifice.[33]

The rhetorics of heroism are important because they symbolize a temporal and situational exception. Heroism exists as an affective, spatial, and temporal apparatus that defines not only what can and cannot be done to bodies under extraordinary circumstances, but also how those bodies are marked as exceptional and therefore sacrificial. For example, the daily 7:00 P.M. citywide clapping for medical and other essential workers in New York City, and other major cities around the world, marked one of those celebratory spaces—a "daily clap for those who are risking it all."[34] This spontaneous expression of gratitude has been rhetorically constructed as a "way to connect with each other," and "a fashionable way" of showing support for essential personnel.[35] The clapping is a performative ritual to mark certain bodies as heroic. Here, and in other instances, the workers are portrayed as heroic because they are seen as choosing bravery and service under exceptional circumstances. This is, of course, a misnomer. The work was performed because it was essential to the workers in order to pay their bills.[36] In other words, their own survival was dependent on their own death—echoing back to death-worlds, which require those living in it to become a living-dead—always dead and always alive at the same time. Those who were constructed as essential or heroic were always already existing in a state of exception, or perpetual precarity, where what can and cannot be done to their bodies in the time of a crisis was predetermined by the permanent state of exception of late-capitalism.[37]

Instead of acknowledging that society has always marked certain bodies as disposable in the time of crisis, the rhetorics of heroism have combined the positionality of sacrifice and affects of care in order to mark the always already disposable bodies as essential. Here rhetorics of essentiality of sacrifice and heroism coupled with constructed affect of care became the strategy of disposability. In the day-to-day state of exception, society assumes that certain bodies can be disposed in order to sustain the daily functioning of capitalist regime. However, in times of crisis, such as the pandemic, the rhetorical strategy of disposability marks death as meaningful and therefore unavoidable. Even those who acknowledged problematics with the rhetorics of heroism did not go far enough to question the very structure of a regime where the bodies of essential workers were marked for disposability prior to Covid.

For example, in a *Washington Post* op-ed on pandemic adaptations we should keep, Benjamin Lorr was hopeful that we will keep appreciation for essential work while acknowledging that

> It didn't take long to move from "essential worker" to "hero." And while it seems kind of definitional that heroes opt into their heroics—as opposed to being conscripted by economic necessity—we can leave learning the distinction between heroism and extortion for a 2021 goal. Right now, I'm just glad for awareness. May we keep an understanding of how much we depend on these workers, and someday soon, may that awareness grow into . . . bringing them higher wages, basic benefits and a status equal to all they deliver.[38]

I would argue that there is no difference between heroism and extortion in the capitalism regime, which asks for heroism as a necessary condition of work. Capitalism consumes that which it purports to create. Consumption of bodies is an essential characteristic of consumer capitalism as it exists in the current form. As Jasbir Puar argues, "capacity and debility are seeming opposites generated by increasingly demanding neoliberal formulations of health, agency, and choice . . . Which bodies are made to pay for 'progress'? . . . The body is always debilitated in relation to its ever-expanding potentiality. Debility is profitable to capitalism, but so is the demand to 'recover' from or overcome it."[39] The narrative of heroism demands a swift recovery from the debilitating effects of a pandemic in order to make bodies reinvigorated and consumable for the functioning of late-capitalism. Therefore, while higher wages and benefits are important, they do not solve the problem clarified and crystalized by Covid—that capitalism is a death-world that constructs heroism, sacrifice, essentiality, and care to make consumption of bodies more meaningful and therefore more filling. Disposability is a condition of life in capitalist society. In the next section, I examine how essentiality has become a strategy of disposability and how rhetorics of sacrifice, heroism, and care have become encircled in the logic of disposability.

From Essentiality to Disposability

In June 2020, the Center for Employment Equity at the University of Massachusetts at Amherst published a report about essential workers, which stated, "only a few months ago low wage workers in the United States were largely treated as disposable, the victims of their own choices and societal neglect. In the wake of the Covid-19 pandemic it is now apparent that these disposable workers are essential."[40] This connection between essentiality and disposability is drawn throughout the media coverage of essential work, especially when it comes to immigrant labor. For example, an article in *The Atlantic* on farm workers, who most of the time are migrant workforce, states that migrant workers "know they are essential workers. But with little protection from the federal government and employers, many of them feel that they're treated as expendable."[41] And in the *New York Times* op-ed, Alfredo Corchado, Mexico border correspondent for *The Dallas Morning News*, passionately writes, "The vulnerable—Dreamers working in health care; hotel maids; dairy and poultry plant workers; waiters, cooks and busboys in the $900 billion restaurant industry—still work to feed their families while feeling disposable, deportable by an ungrateful nation. . . . I worked alongside them, my brothers and cousins, too, essential links in a supply chain that kept America fed, but always a step away from derision, detention and deportation."[42]

While these pieces make important points about how blue-collar labor is devalued in this country, especially when that labor is performed by Black and Brown bodies, they fail to consider how the very category of essentiality works not to make bodies *less* disposable, but rather serves as a rhetorical strategy of disposability. Hence, marking labor as essential always already constructs certain bodies as being disposable. Moreover, as Lisa Flores argues, migrant labor emphasizes "two different kinds of immigrants, those invited to become American and those desired as disposable labor."[43]

In the same op-ed, Alfredo Corchado interviews Joe L. Del Bosque of Del Bosque Farms, one of the largest organic melon growers in the country who employs about three hundred people on hundreds of acres:

> Sadly, it's taken a pandemic for Americans to realize that the food in their grocery stores, on their tables, is courtesy of mostly Mexican workers, the majority of them without documents," Mr. Del Bosque told me. "They're the most vulnerable of workers. They're not hiding behind the pandemic waiting for a stimulus check." Even with unemployment projected to be 15 percent or higher, Mr. Del Bosque told me he doubts he'll ever see a line of job-seeking Americans flocking to his fields.[44]

Taken as a part of the op-ed that argues for indisposablity and dignity of migrant work, the rhetorical construction of labor here is troubling. Mexican workers are portrayed as worthy of respect, and potentially of documented status, only because they are hardworking. Throughout these pandemic narratives, the essentiality of bodies is deeply connected to their usefulness. As Sarah Ahmed argues, "Use becomes a technique that is exhaustive of the fullness of a subject's potential; correct use is when nothing is left idle. Use becomes a command as well as a threat: if to be idle or useless is not to support what is being accomplished, the to be idle or useless is not to be supported."[45] The usefulness, or essentiality, of the undocumented Brown bodies based upon their ability to perform labor deemed to be too much by those who are documented is what marks them as supposedly indispensable.[46]

And, at the same time, the labor is not sustainable, and the body that performs it will become disposable as soon as the labor is completed. Therefore, the ability to perform labor, or essentiality of the body, is what makes the body always already disposable. Within the twin logics of capitalism and necropolitics, where bodies' usefulness is tied to their ability to perform labor, aging migrant bodies are marked for both symbolic and physical death.[47] As essentiality is deeply tied to the body's ability to perform labor and the ability to perform labor is always temporary, the body is always already dispensable even as it is still working. Therefore, being able to work—or being able to perform labor—is essential to being disposable. A healthy body—as defined through its ability to perform labor—is rendered disposable not because it is inessential, but precisely because it is essential to the workings of capitalism. I contend that Covid illustrates how the late-stage capitalism relies upon rendering bodies essential by insisting on their ability to perform necessary labor. Once the body is marked as essential it can be sacrificed for the supposed good of the economy. Therefore, disposability relies on an ableist construction of labor.

For example, during debates over vaccine priority, it was widely agreed that health care providers should be the first to receive vaccinations. After that, things got murky on state and nation-state levels. Experts disagreed on whether the next group to get vaccines should be those over sixty-five years old (because they are most likely to die from Covid) or essential/frontline workers. While the World Health Organization and many countries developed frameworks that prioritized older populations,[48] this was not a clear-cut case. As some public health experts pointed out, prioritizing older population meant prioritizing white people, as the life expectancy of the white population is longer than that of the Black or Brown population. As quoted in a *New York Times* article on vaccine distribution, Harald Schmidt, an expert in ethics and health policy at the University of Pennsylvania, argued that, "it is reasonable to put essential workers ahead of older adults, given their risks, and that they are disproportionately minorities. Older populations are whiter." He continued, "Society is structured in a way that enables them to live longer. Instead of giving additional health benefits to those who already had more of them, we can start to level the playing field a bit."[49] And at the same time, a disproportionate amount of essential workers are workers of color. Camara Phyllis Jones, past president of the American Public Health Association, pointed out in the *Washington Post* that "People are thinking about risk at an individual level as opposed to at a structural level. People are not understanding that where you work and where you live can actually bring more risks than your age."[50] Another consideration is whether the goal of the vaccines should be to prevent death or stop the spread of the disease. Curbing the spread of the disease means prioritizing essential workers, while preventing death might mean gearing the vaccine toward older population.[51]

In other words, ethical and epidemiological determinations behind vaccine distribution are complex and must consider many factors. However, as we already know, in the United States, and most of the world, the vaccine distribution prioritized the older population over frontline workers to whose sacrifice we were supposed to owe so much. For example, Florida Governor Ron DeSantis vowed that "we are not going to put young, healthy workers ahead of our elderly, vulnerable population."[52] These determinations are a part of what Allison L. Rowland calls *zoerhetorics*, or "discursive and material practices that transvalue lives across a particular public."[53] She argues that zoerhetorics "discursively include and exclude certain living beings from what we might call the good life . . . they matter because they affect the livability of life."[54] Rowland directs our attention not only toward dehumanizing speech aimed at diminishing lived experience, but also at humanizing speech aimed to, in Jasbir Puar terms, *capacitate* life, thus rendering it possibly more invested in and by the biopolitical and necropolitical regime. Puar argues that capacity is intimately tied to the biopolitics of debilitation, where "debilitation is not just an unfortunate by product of the exploitative workings of capitalism; it is required for and constitutive of the expansion of profit. Certain bodies are employed in the production process precisely because they are deemed available of injury-they are, in other words, objects of disposability, bodies whose debilitation is required in order to sustain capitalist narratives of progress."[55] I would argue that offering vaccines first to older populations, while labeling the essential workers heroic, highlights how Black and Brown bodies specifically are capacitated and humanized for disposability and sacrifice. Additionally, the zoerhetoric of heroism is so deeply tied to disposability that we need to shy away from declarations of heroism and essentiality all together.

Instead, we need to take an unflinching look at how and why our economic system demanded expendability and disposability long before the pandemic.

Conclusion: Complicating Heroism

In this essay, I have examined how essentiality and disposability intersected during the pandemic to mark certain bodies as essential and therefore disposable as well as heroic and therefore sacrificial. However, it is important to acknowledge the rhetorical pushback against the narrative of heroism. *Statnews*, for example, argued that we should not be labeling essential workers heroic because that forecloses the workers' own stories and experiences. It states, "labeling frontline workers as heroes without first listening to them forecloses their narrative possibilities—and our historical lessons. We say heroes for us, not for them. So please, change your language: Actions are heroic, but people are people."[56] This critique still centers the rhetorics of heroism as unproblematic while acknowledging that such narratives do limit the stories we tell about essential work. This critique forecloses the opportunity for critical discussion about heroism, essentiality, and disposability. More powerful is the pushback among workers themselves against the rhetorics of heroism and essentiality. In a powerful editorial in the *New York Times*, Sujatha Gidla, NYC metro conductor writes, "the conditions created by the pandemic drive home the fact that we essential workers—workers in general—are the ones who keep the social order from sinking into chaos. Yet we are treated with the utmost disrespect, as though we're expendable. Since March 27, at least 98 New York transit workers have died of Covid-19. My coworkers say bitterly: 'We are not essential. We are sacrificial.' We are stumbling upon dead bodies."[57] The visceral description of death that haunts those who work is disturbing and powerful because it forces us to consider that heroism plain and simple signifies encounters with death as a condition of life in the late-capitalism. Gidla also makes an important rhetorical pivot away from essential workers to workers in general, marking the importance of considering death as a condition of work in general. It is through the rhetorics of heroism and essentiality that we mark disposability and death as palatable and necessary to life and labor in current economies. And, at the same time, I would like to argue that while Covid crystalized what we are willing to do to bodies during a time of crisis, the sacrifice of bodies that renders them as both essential and disposable is not a new development. It is perhaps a natural extension of survival in the systems of inequalities built into socioeconomic global assemblages.

I would like to suggest that as scholars we need to pay particular attention to the discursive formations that construct these enmeshments of supposedly unproblematic terms. We also need to question our own response to a crisis and its contribution to the very systems of power we critique.

NOTES

1. Adie Tomer and Joseph W. Kane, "How to Protect Essential Workers during COVID-19," *Brookings*, March 31, 2020.
2. Christopher Krebs, "Memorandum on Identification of Essential Critical Infrastructure Workers during COVID-19 Response," *U.S. Department of Homeland Security (DHS)*, March 19, 2020.
3. Tomer and Kane "How to Protect."
4. Tomer and Kane, "How to Protect."
5. Tomer and Kane, "How to Protect."
6. At the beginning of the pandemic, Texas lieutenant governor Dan Patrick attracted national publicity when he stated that he would rather die than sacrifice the nation's economy due to Covid lockdowns.
7. I would like to thank the editors for this astute observation.
8. Nathan Stormer, "On the Origins of Violence and Language," *Quarterly Journal of Speech* 99, no. 2 (2013): 184.
9. Hareem Khan, "Existentially Essential: In/Visibility Under Racial Capitalism," *Journal of Asian American Studies* 23, no. 3 (2020): 477.
10. Khan, "Existentially Essential," 480.
11. Lisa A. Flores, *Deportable and Disposable: Public Rhetoric and the Making of the "Illegal" Immigrant* (University Park: Penn State University Press, 2021), 79.
12. Paula A. Treichler, *How to Have Theory in an Epidemic: Cultural Chronicles of AIDS* (Durham, NC: Duke University Press, 1999), 45.
13. Brandon Wales, "Advisory Memorandum on Ensuring Essential Critical Infrastructure Workers' Ability to Work during the COVID-19 Response," *DHS*, December 16, 2020.
14. Henry A. Giroux, "Violence, Katrina, and the Biopolitics of Disposability," *Theory, Culture & Society* 24, nos. 7–8 (2007): 308.
15. Tomer and Kane, "How to Protect."
16. Carolyn Marvin and David W. Ingle, *Blood Sacrifice and the Nation: Totem Rituals and the American Flag* (Cambridge: Cambridge University Press, 1999).

17. Achille Mbembe, "Necropolitics," *Public Culture* 15, no. 1 (2003): 11–40, 12.
18. Mbembe, "Necropolitics," 40.
19. Cindy Patton, "Pandemic, Empire and the Permanent State of Exception," *Economic and Political Weekly* 46 no. 13 (2011): 104.
20. Giorgio Agamben, *Homo Sacer: Sovereign Power and Bare Life* (Stanford, CA: Stanford University Press, 1998), 37.
21. Emily Stewart, "Essential Workers Are Taking Care of America. Are We Taking Care of Them?," *Vox*, April 23, 2020.
22. Stewart, "Essential Workers."
23. William J. Barber II and Joe Kennedy III, "Opinion: The Pandemic Changed Our Definition of 'Essential.' Will We Act on What We Learned?," *Washington Post*, April 27, 2020.
24. Yasin Kakande, "Opinion: We Are Not Enemies. We Are Essential Workers," *New York Times*, May 18, 2020.
25. Campbell Robertson and Robert Gebeloff, "How Millions of Women Became the Most Essential Workers in America," *New York Times*, April 18, 2020.
26. Patrick McGeehan and Matthew Haag, "These Stores Are 'Essential' in the Pandemic. Not Everyone Agrees.," *The New York Times*, March 27, 2020.
27. McGeehan and Haag, "These Stories."
28. Michael Corkery, David Yaffe-Bellany, and Rachel Wharton, "When Stocking Grocery Shelves Turns Dangerous," *New York Times*, March 20, 2020.
29. Corkery, Yaffe-Bellany, and Wharton, "When Stocking."
30. Molly Kinder, "Grocery Workers Are Keeping Americans Alive during the COVID-19 Pandemic. Here's What They Need," *Brookings*, March 25, 2020.
31. Molly Kinder, "Meet the COVID-19 Frontline Heroes," *Brookings*, April 10, 2020.
32. Hila L. Solis and Holly J. Mitchell, "'Hero Pay' for Frontline-Grocery and Drug Retail Employees in Los Angeles County," County of Los Angeles, February 23, 2021, 3, file.lacounty.gov/SDSInter/bos/supdocs/153987.pdf.
33. "NY Plans Circle of Heroes Monument for Essential Workers in Battery Park City," *NBC New York*, June 23, 2021.
34. Andy Newman, "What N.Y.C. Sounds Like Every Night at 7," *New York Times*, April 10, 2020.
35. Newman, "What N.Y.C Sounds Like."
36. Of course, while many essential workers cannot afford to not work, we must not discount the class differences among different groups of essential workers. Specifically, within the healthcare industry, surgeons, and other high-level physicians could conceivably choose

not to work through the pandemic and yet have chosen otherwise. Further research is needed to explore the issue of class in the theorization of heroism.

37. Agamben, *State of Exception*.
38. Lara Bazelon et al., "Outlook: What We'll Keep," *Washington Post*, April 27, 2021.
39. Jasbir K. Puar, *The Right to Maim: Debility, Capacity, Disability* (Durham, NC: Duke University Press, 2017), 13.
40. Clare Hammons, Jasmine Kerrissey, and Donald Tomaskovic-Devey, "Stressed, Unsafe, and Insecure: Essential Workers Need a New, New Deal," Center for Employment Equity, University of Massachusetts, Amherst (2020).
41. Madeline Leung Coleman, "Essential Workers Are Being Treated as Expendable," *Atlantic*, April 23, 2020.
42. Alfredo Corchado, "Opinion: A Former Farmworker on American Hypocrisy," *New York Times*, May 6, 2020.
43. Flores, *Deportable and Disposable*, 5. Flores's text provides an in-depth analysis of rhetoric of migrant labor.
44. Corchado, "A Former Farmworker."
45. Sara Ahmed, *What's the Use?* (Durham: Duke University Press, 2019), 104.
46. Ahmed, *What's the Use?*, 3.
47. Ahmed, *What's the Use?*, 4. Lisa Flores argues, "the larger rhetorical climate around Mexicans installed the critical pieces that situated Mexicans as transient, cheap labor—recruitable and returnable. This framing of Mexicans as needed temporary labor informed early policy and practice, and continues, in a somewhat different variant, to underwrite efforts to perpetuate Mexican migration even as dominant discourses promised a seemingly tenacious invasion" (*Deportable and Disposable*, 4).
48. Peter Beaumont, "Covid-19 Vaccine: Who Are Countries Prioritizing for First Doses?," *Guardian*, November 18, 2020); and "WHO SAGE Values Framework for the Allocation and Prioritization of COVID-19 Vaccination," *World Health Organization*, September 14, 2020.
49. Abby Goodnough and Jan Hoffman, "The Elderly vs. Essential Workers: Who Should Get the Coronavirus Vaccine First?," *New York Times*, December 5, 2020.
50. Lena H. Sun, Isaac Stanley-Becker, and Akilah Johnson, "Essential Workers Get Lost in the Vaccine Scrum as States Prioritize the Elderly," *Washington Post*, January 31, 2021.
51. Sun, Stanley-Becker, and Johnson, "Essential Workers."
52. Isaac Stanley-Becker, "Some States Buck Federal Vaccine Recommendations and Prioritize the Elderly over Essential Workers," *Washington Post*, December 29, 2020.
53. Allison L. Rowland, *Zoetropes and the Politics of Humanhood* (Columbus: Ohio State

University Press, 2019), 2.
54. Rowland, *Zoetropes*, 2.
55. Puar, *Right to Maim*, 81.
56. Matthew Lewis, Zac M. Willette, and Brian Park, "Calling Health Care Workers 'Heroes' Harms All of Us," *STAT*, May 21, 2020.
57. Sujatha Gidla, "Opinion: 'We Are Not Essential. We Are Sacrificial,'" *New York Times*, May 5, 2020.

Covid and Being a Doctor

Physicians' Published Narratives as Crisis Archive

Molly Margaret Kessler, Michael Aylward, and Bernard Trappey

IN RECENT HISTORY, NOTHING HAS STRAINED HEALTHCARE PROVIDERS' (HCPs) ability to deliver healthcare as much as the Covid pandemic. As one physician wrote of his experiences early in the pandemic: "Recent weeks have brought a massive and hurried adaptation that risks changing the ancient and sacrosanct practice of medicine."[1] Covid's scale, urgency, and uncertainty have amplified systemic challenges facing physicians in ways we are only beginning to understand. Further, events and activism in recent years have pushed some in the medical community to reckon with embedded structural racism central to medicine's past and present. These immense pressures often leave physicians struggling to process the emotional, physical, and mental impacts of practicing medicine. Consequently, physicians are increasingly turning to narrative writing to explore the embodied, structural, and practical experiences of their professional roles.[2]

Reflective narratives allow authors to exert a sense of control over situations in which they might otherwise feel powerless, manage the chaos of difficult or traumatic events, and better understand themselves and their actions as HCPs.[3] Publishing these narratives also presents an opportunity for HCPs to reflect and dialogue *communally* about the experiences of practicing medicine. Commonly written *by* physicians and *for* other physicians, HCPs, and biomedical researchers, HCP-authored narratives often present a different discourse than we encounter in mass media or clinical encounters with providers. While these narratives can be accessed by readers beyond the medical community, for example, rhetoricians, scholars in the medical humanities, patients, and other invested readers can access these stories behind journal paywalls) the typical primary audience is other HCPs such as medical students, physicians, nurses, and therapists.

Published physicians' narratives therefore occasion a unique opportunity to hear what physicians have to say about their experiences and what they prioritize as significant. These narratives remain a largely untapped opportunity for rhetorical inquiry that would facilitate understanding of physicians' realities, perspectives, concerns, experiences, and overall rhetorical practices. Researchers have argued that physicians' stories "have potential to uncover new insights into what physicians perceive as flawed about the health systems they practice within and, moreover, what they think they can do about it."[4] These narratives provide a particularly rich site for examining the rhetorical complexities of providing healthcare in the time of Covid.

This chapter, collaboratively written by a rhetorician (Molly Margaret Kessler [MK]) and two practicing physicians (Bernard Trappey [BT] and Michael Aylward [MA]), reports on analysis of seventy narratives published in four key medical journals between April 2020 and April 2021. We examined physicians' narrative writing during the first year of the pandemic to interrogate how—according to physician-writers—structural, cultural, political, and biomedical systems have changed throughout the Covid pandemic and what it has meant to deliver healthcare in and after crisis. We asked: What stories have physicians told about their pandemic experiences? What elements of medical practice were transformed by the pandemic, specifically—what was defined as essential and/or disposable by the pandemic? And what can these narratives tell us about what it means to be a HCP navigating the myriad issues surfaced or silenced by Covid? In addressing these questions, we examine the issues, meaning-making practices, and experiences addressed by physician narrative writing to understand how medicine has been transformed by Covid and other ongoing crises (i.e. political, racial). Our research is intended to be both descriptive and generative in hopes of catalyzing future research and intervention within the biomedical systems and experiences that physicians narratively navigate.

Before moving forward, we want to acknowledge the positions and perspectives from which we individually and collaboratively conducted this project. As BT explained:

I practice both adult and pediatric hospital medicine and, at the beginning of the pandemic, volunteered to change my practice location to a Covid-only cohort hospital, caring exclusively for Covid patients. I chose to do this because it allowed me to concentrate my clinical shifts into longer blocks and to live in a hotel in order to protect my wife, who was pregnant with our first child at the time. Since my son was born in late August of 2020, I have returned to my usual hospital medicine practice, where I continue to care for both adults and children with Covid.

For her part, MK described her positionality in the following terms: "As a rhetorician of health and medicine, I am interested in the rhetorical work that is happening within and through physicians' published narratives, however, I approached this project from the dual perspectives of researcher and immunocompromised patient." And, finally, MA explained: "I practice primary care internal medicine and pediatrics in a Federally Qualified Healthcare Center which serves a diverse population of underserved patients. I am also a residency program director responsible for the training of approximately forty residents per year." In addition to exploring our identities here, we reflectively engage these identities throughout this chapter.

In what follows, we provide context for and description of published physicians' narratives, explain how we collected and rhetorically analyzed those stories, and present key findings to inspire thinking about Covid and physicians' complex lived realities at the nexus of medical, ethical, social, and political uncertainty. Finally, we reflect on our individual and collaborative experiences working on this project as an interdisciplinary team during Covid.

Rhetoric, Narrative, and Medicine

Stories in health and medicine are important for a variety of stakeholders ranging from patients and providers to caregivers and the general public. Researchers across rhetoric of health and medicine (RHM), narrative medicine (NM), and medicine have studied stories to understand meaning-making and lived experiences within health and medicine.[5] Judy Segal demonstrated the power of engaging stories as public rhetoric, specifically to illuminate how dominant stories are deeply entangled and, at times, in conflict with individuals' lived experiences with illness.[6] Similarly, NM scholars not only acknowledge that lived experiences and narratives offer important insight when calibrated with scientific and empirical knowledge, but further argue NM "will lead to more humane, more ethical, and perhaps more effective care."[7] NM, thus, has been catalyzed in response to the growing awareness that patients' stories about their lived experiences are critical to successful healthcare.

Together, NM and RHM, while distinct in many ways, are aligned in their interest in the meaning-making of stories. Researchers in both fields have most extensively engaged *patients'* stories, which has been important in advocating for patients, resisting paternalism within medicine, and rehumanizing patients who have been dehumanized by biomedical institutions.[8] Other types of stories, particularly HCP narratives, have been studied less, despite their rhetorical importance. We extend previous work in RHM and NM by centering physicians' published narratives to gather insight into Covid and healthcare delivery and the rhetoricity of HCPs' Covid experiences and stories. Specifically, we approach physicians' narratives as rhetorical objects with much to teach us about the inner workings of healthcare and how HCP experiences have been upended, exacerbated, halted, or otherwise impacted by the pandemic. We examine stories or narratives—terms we use interchangeably—for the rhetorical work they do and what they can reveal about the inner workings of healthcare.[9] Focusing less on the particular rhetorical moves or features within text, we center the broader meaning-making work depicted and enacted by HCP narratives as a living archive.

Research Approach

Following Moniz et al.,[10] we analyzed narratives published in four of the highest impact North American medical journals: *Journal of the American Medical Association* (*JAMA*), *New England Journal of Medicine* (*NEJM*), *Canadian Medical Association Journal* (*CMAJ*), and the *Annals of Internal Medicine* (*Annals*). Each of these journals includes a specific section for physicians' narratives: *JAMA*, "A Piece of My Mind"; *NEJM*, "Perspective"; *CMAJ*, "Encounters"; and *Annals*, "On Being a Doctor."[11] Typically, these narratives are one to two pages in length, written in first-person, composed by individuals or small collaborative teams, and explore pressing or emergent issues that impact providers. Our dataset includes seventy such narratives published between April 2020 and April 2021 that significantly discuss Covid, which allowed us to capture a year-long snapshot of Covid-related experiences.[12]

Final Coding Schema

CODING CATEGORY	MEANING-MAKING THEMES What shaped the meaning/experience in this story?	ELEMENTS What elements participated in the primary meaning-making forces/themes?	EMOTIONS
Codes	• Uncertainty • Isolation • Transformation of practices/role • Obligation/sense of duty • Intersecting public crises/context	• PPE (personal protective equipment) • Resource scarcity • Visitor restrictions • Decontamination • Trainee experience • Policies/politics • Discrimination/social oppression • Misinformation • Patient experience	Coded in situ

Our coding schema (see the table) was generated iteratively and features three mains categories: meaning-making themes, elements, and emotions. For themes and elements, we developed guiding questions to support the consistent application of the codes. We treated meaning-making themes as the larger umbrella category in which elements fit. For example, if we coded "uncertainty" as a theme, we then turned to the elements category to capture the elements that participated in the experience of uncertainty. The unit of analysis for each code was the whole narrative because codes frequently unfolded over an entire piece. For each narrative, we coded no more than three meaning-making themes and no more than three elements; the three most significant codes in each category were applied.

We also analyzed each narrative for the emotions/affective experience it generated. We intuitively open-coded the emotions we felt were communicated rather than use a priori categories.[13] Many narratives were highly evocative for us given our various first-hand experiences throughout the pandemic.

Findings

Our findings highlight salient themes that illustrate one view of transformative experiences precipitated by the pandemic. These narratives enabled physicians to ask:

Who are we as healthcare professionals? What does it mean to practice medicine? And, what can/should medicine look like moving forward? Our analysis attempted to capture physicians' own answers to these questions, however limited and incomplete, as they were forged through the Covid pandemic.

Emotions

Unlike our content codes, we did not attempt to norm or combine our individual codes for the emotions/affective responses we coded in situ. As our goal in this analysis is descriptive and reflective, we report on our collective emotions coding. To help characterize the emotion codes that we identified in these narratives, we created a word cloud that illustrates the presence of and relationships among the emotions we identified (see figure).

As the word cloud shows, fear, anxiety, frustration, and grief were most commonly coded across the three of us. These emotions depict the negative experiences that were both showcased by writers through their narratives and felt by us as readers. Interestingly, hope and gratitude were among emotions commonly coded, though often those emotions were simultaneously coded with other, conflicting emotions like fear or anxiety. For example, some narratives described fear of contracting the virus due to lack of proper PPE but concluded with comments that depicted a sense of gratitude for fellow frontline healthcare workers; in such instances, both fear and gratitude may have been coded. Fear was the most present (in approximately 45 percent) emotional experience in these narratives—fear about the uncertainty of Covid, for patients' lives and physicians' own lives, of accidentally bringing Covid home and infecting loved ones, about the future of medicine.

The emotions presented and experienced throughout these narratives have important rhetorical, public, pedagogical, and community-building functions. As Emily Winderman and Jamie Landau argue, writing within science and medicine has the power to "strategically modulate public emotion."[14] We found that the emotions throughout these narratives encourage empathy, community, and learning in readers including but not limited to physicians. Specifically, emotions like fear and despair (re-)humanize the physician writers at a time when they were (and still often are) publicly dehumanized through rhetorics of heroism and disposability through essentiality. For readers, especially those who are not HCPs, the emotional experiences shared throughout these stories may serve as reminders of the often harsh,

Word cloud depicting the emotions we coded. Created by Molly Margaret Kessler, Michael Aylward, and Bernard Trappey.

traumatizing realities that physicians, nurses, and other HCPs have faced throughout the pandemic. Although HCPs have been celebrated as heroic essential workers, their essentiality has been harrowing for many.

As we have noted, it is hard to read these narratives and not be moved by them. MK recalled:

> My own lived experiences differed dramatically from what physicians described in their narratives, yet the feelings enacted in these narratives deeply resonated with me. The fear, uncertainty, and anxiety felt by physicians—especially in the early months of the pandemic—mirrored my own story and memories. While reading, I often had to pause to give myself an emotional break. The handful of narratives written by physicians local to me in Minnesota and those written with explicit discussions of George Floyd's murder felt especially powerful and required additional emotional checking for me as I read and attempted to analyze them.

Likewise, MA noted:

> Reading these pieces, in order, was a harrowing reliving of 2020. The bewildering, daily changes of policy and protocol. The infuriating frustration of no testing, then

not enough testing, for far too long. The many decisions I made, both clinically and on behalf of the residents I oversaw, that were ill-informed and poorly communicated and that were overturned the following day. And throughout, the fear that my family would get sick, the massive upheaval of the education system, and the distance from parents and grandparents. Throughout, the powerful feeling of helplessness and doing the best we could with what we had: I think we, collectively, got a lot of things wrong during the pandemic, but I feel that the corpus of pieces we analyzed "felt right" in terms of capturing the thoughts, feelings, and themes that arose during these times.

Themes: What Shaped the Meaning-Making/Experience in This Story?

With the affective dimensions of these stories in mind, we present findings from select content codes identified as most significant in terms of presence in our dataset and how transformative these themes/experiences seemed for the authors. For each, we provide a brief description followed by excerpts from the narratives that exemplify the code. We also include percentages that represent the frequency codes were applied to the seventy narratives we analyzed. Finally, we offer reflections as our individual identities as patients, providers, and researchers intersect with narratives' various rhetorical themes and elements.

Obligation/Sense of Duty

Approximately 20 percent of the narratives grappled with "obligation/sense of duty," which included discussions of the conflicts or challenges that emerged around professional commitments. Often, these stories detailed conflicts between physicians' desire to care for patients and their own health conditions that put them at increased risk of severe Covid.[15] Guilt, shame, and confusion arose in many stories for physicians who could not join the "frontlines." One physician grappled:

> Making yourself the hero of the story is a narrative cliché, yet many of us tell an "I want to help people" tale when seeking entry into the profession. For some clinicians, the pandemic offers an opportunity to take on that role as never before. But for

those who can't, the stories of heroism may be as silencing as they are intoxicating. Clinicians on the sidelines must confront not only shame and guilt, but also the loss of their primordial story. Who are you, if you can't be the hero you imagined yourself to be?[16]

BT often related to stories that described the complexity of a sense of duty:

> Mirrored in some of these stories was my own struggle with the decision to volunteer to put myself on "the frontlines."[17] In reading these stories, I relived the very real conflict between the desire to live up to the hero label that society was placing on healthcare and other essential workers and the sneaking suspicion that, in contrast to fiction, real life heroes are those society builds up and celebrates in order to assuage the guilt of the necessary casualties of moments like these. As calls to "flatten the curve" were replaced first by calls to reopen the economy and arguments about the sanctity of haircuts and later by protests against mask mandates and disinformation campaigns against vaccines, I found myself wondering again and again, "What are essential workers but those whom we are willing to sacrifice at the altars of convenience, capitalism, and self-determination?" We are fortunate that medical journals have provided space to capture the voices of physicians in these reflections when there are so many other "essential" voices that will never be heard.

Early in the pandemic especially, physicians seemed to use these narratives to weigh conflict between a perceived obligation to care for patients and the risk of exposing themselves and loved ones to the virus. Many physicians narrated the emotional distress their professional sense of duty caused particularly in the context of Covid's immense uncertainty. The following excerpt comes from a piece BT wrote and published in *JAMA*:

> The day before I worked the opening shift, my wife and I used an online service to complete our first wills. Our neighbors witnessed as we signed them on the front porch. Later, I carried my bags out to the car, all of the things that I would need to live in a hotel for the next month. A cold, spring rain fell as my wife and I stood on our front porch and hugged. I could feel the slight bump that was just starting to signal that she was carrying our first child. We cried and hoped that it would not be the last time we ever touched. But despite the fear and the lack of knowledge

of what the weeks ahead would hold, there was also a sense of clarity and purpose. When the first patient with Covid-19 arrived, I had no doubt that I was where I was supposed to be.[18]

Uncertainty

We coded nearly half (46 percent) of the narratives for uncertainty or discussions of the lack of knowledge or data regarding Covid. Uncertainty was often animated as writers struggled to treat Covid, predict and prepare for the many lives Covid might take, and develop plans to navigate the pandemic. One narrative questioned "the unsettling uncertainty about the duration and extent of the pandemic are familiar to any patient with cancer: How long will this last? Will it get worse? Is there an effective treatment? Will life ever go back to normal?"[19] Another described the pandemic's uncertain doom: "It's like we are standing on a wide flat beach, with a 10-story high tsunami that curves out, not in, looming over us."[20] Additionally, physicians grappled with the uncertainty about their own lives and the potential of contracting and spreading Covid. As one physician wrote, "I'm as likely to be a vector as a victim."[21]

BT remarked on the perspective afforded by time.

> It is surprising how quickly the memory of the details of the early days of pandemic fades. (Re)-reading these pieces was an intensely meaningful reflective exercise, as I was prompted to remember and, in many ways, relive the unprecedented uncertainty of caring for patients infected by the virus during those early days. I found myself awash in both the anxiety and helplessness of those early days of the pandemic as well as the regret and frustration over mistakes and misunderstandings that I now recognize from my vantage point in 2021.

Isolation

Narratives in which isolation was a major theme (approximately 36 percent) described how the changes prompted by the pandemic led to unprecedented isolation, particularly as physicians managed PPE and extraordinary precautions to protect loved ones. Several narratives recounted the challenges—emotionally, ethically, and practically—of witnessing isolation in patients, such as those suffering alone due to visitor restrictions and quarantine protocols. Consider the following scene depicted in one narrative:

> No visitors were permitted, of course, so the only faces she saw in person were masked and goggled; her care team had the disconcerting look of alien invaders. I can only imagine how frightening it must be as a patient to be sick and dependent on a care team of faceless people—a legion of attendants with eyes, nose, and mouth obscured by masks and eye shields.[22]

Many narratives also described personal isolation as the humanity of practicing medicine was disrupted by the move to telemedicine. One physician explained,

> The [Covid] pandemic has separated primary care physicians like me from most of our exam-table encounters. We now connect with our own patients through the phone speaker or the computer screen... we take turns seeing each other's patients. We're all happy to help, but we're also all homesick. For most physicians, seeing patients in person is the lifeblood that keeps us going through all the frustrations of paperwork and documentation.[23]

This experience resonated with MA, who remarked on the rapid integration of technology into everyday practice:

> During Covid's early phase, we had, like many other clinics, a rapid implementation of telemedicine in our clinic. It was exciting to be able to reach and interact with patients in new ways, meet them where they were, and provide them with a level of access to healthcare despite the pandemic. We also had to develop policies and protocols and figure things out as we went, so there was a real collaborative approach—we often would reach out to other clinics to see what they were doing. Over time, however, the luster wore off. My patient population had difficulty navigating the requirements and technology of video calls, so we largely did phone visits. Many of those phone visits were around Covid triage and, later, testing, which were both rote and formulaic as well as infused with a feeling of helplessness—I had nothing to offer. This transitioned to phone clinic sessions at home, trying to provide adequate care, but constantly feeling like I fell short. The lack of sharing a physical space wore on me, as did the lack of being able to engage and interact with my colleagues. I realized how much of

medicine is done "in the hallways" when we talk to nurses and medical assistants, or bounce an idea off of a colleague. A chat app was a poor and unfulfilling substitute.

Intersecting Public Crises/Context

Twenty-one percent of narratives included discussion about intersecting public, social, and political issues that influenced the practice of medicine throughout the pandemic, particularly the extreme racial injustices that were increasingly being acknowledged within medicine and dominant public discourse throughout 2020. One narrative repeatedly and evocatively used the phrase "Please—I can't breathe" to illuminate the stark, but often invisible, connections between racial injustice and Covid:

> One of every 1850 black Americans have lost their lives in this global fight against a novel virus that could have harmed anyone. And yet—because of racism and the ways humans use it to hoard resources and power for some, while depriving others—it has killed an enormous number of black people.
>
> "Please—I can't *breathe*."
>
> And black people are three times as likely to be killed by police as white people. Both these realities are acutely threatening black lives right now. But prevailing gaps in maternal and infant mortality have long threatened our survival beginning before we are even born.
>
> "Please—I can't *breathe*."[24]

Narratives discussing intersecting public/social crises, though fewer in number than we expected, stood out as perhaps the most significant narratives in our dataset emotionally and rhetorically, as the excerpt exemplifies. This code also included narratives that called out the complex, harmful relationship between essentiality and disposability that Covid exposed. One narrative articulated this complexity:

> "Stronger together," say the screen savers on every screen in the hospital, the banners on the sides of the shuttle bus. What I'll see in the coming weeks is just how much this isn't true, how so many of our sickest patients are Black or Brown ... "essential" and yet unprotected. I will see a 46-year-old Black man, infected with SARS-CoV-2 die instead from having a police officer kneel on his neck. I

will see those who protest police brutality, though masked and mostly peaceful, tear-gassed and shot with rubber bullets. I will see unregulated corporate bailouts, record unemployment, record housing insecurity. I will see political polarization recast common-sense public health policy as liberal propaganda. I will see your death multiplied by 10,000, by 100,000, all those bodies, mothers and fathers, daughters and sons. I wish I could tell you how sorry I am, for my fear, for our nation, for what happens next.[25]

These narratives demand that readers consider ethically, medically, and socially fraught questions: Which bodies matter and which are disposable? Who is allowed to breathe, allowed access to air? With whom should air be shared and whose access to air is/should be controlled, supported, mitigated, or prevented whether through masks, police brutality, or intubation?[26] We must attend to the deeply problematic entanglement of race, history, and medicine that has/does enable particular bodies (white) to be valued and prioritized over others (Black and other minoritized bodies) as Raquel M. Robvais argues in this volume. Thus, we might see these narratives further encouraging us to ask: How do we assign value, compare, and hierarchize bodies as we acutely and chronically navigate Covid and social injustice? And, in turn, how do we make decisions about whose lives deserve to be saved, and whose are allowed to be taken?

Finally, stories coded for this theme emphasized Covid's short- and long-term impact on healthcare access, particularly due to mandated pauses in routine visits, screenings, and procedures. "Primary care physicians," one physician wrote,

> have been steeped in a rising anxiety that fills the emptiness of once-bustling offices. At its worst, we feel a helpless dread. In easier moments, we still experience a premonitory exhaustion—knowing that the proverbial "marathon" ahead is insufficiently long and costly to describe what is coming to primary care clinics. Long after the last patient in the United States recovers from [Covid] many others will still be afflicted. They will have lost their jobs, and with them, their health insurance. They will have missed office visits and screening tests that might have prevented or delayed illness or even death. They will have suffered emotionally from the stress of isolation, and they will have become fearful of clinics and hospitals. They will have lost access to care in unexpected ways, like the undocumented couple who didn't come to their appointments last week. When the pair encountered the symptom screening station at the hospital entrance, they left assuming they would be turned away.[27]

Transformation of Practice

The most dominant theme we identified (coded in 67 percent of the narratives) was "Transformation of Practice." Especially early in the pandemic, authors wrote about rapid, unprecedented changes, including how and where they saw patients and how they prepared to see patients (donning/doffing PPE). One physician recounted: "A month ago, our first cases alarmed us; a week ago, our hospital was at surge level three: a series of tarps separated our Covid ward from the rest of the hospital. Now we are at level five: the whole hospital is essentially the Covid ward. At level six, we may expand to a school gymnasium."[28] In some cases, transformations of practice even included temporarily switching the area of medicine physicians practiced; that is, physicians described moving from primary care to emergency departments and Covid units or moving from roles as surgeons to providers at testing sites when nonemergency surgeries were paused during surges.

Many stories reflected on intense emotional and psychological transformations precipitated by Covid that spilled beyond the practice of medicine. One physician wrote, "This frightening pandemic has not only washed away our hospital routine, canceled our plans, and overturned our priorities; it has also torn apart our families, struck our friends and colleagues, and made unmistakably clear to our forgetful minds that we're all engaged in the same struggle."[29] Others expressed concern that their lives and selves—personally, professionally, physically—would be forever changed by their experiences of the pandemic:

> The weeks since Boston temporarily beat back Covid have been more difficult than I ever expected. When I fall asleep, I'm haunted by memories of patients I cared for but never met. I hear their families' wails, expressions of gratitude and, most often, stunned silence. I can't remember their names, but I also can't forget their stories ... Covid continues to live in my muscles. It permeates my marrow ... How can we speak about transforming our system when we haven't yet reckoned with how Covid has transformed those of us on the front lines?[30]

Remarking on these dramatic changes brought by the pandemic, BT explained:

> The above line haunts me. The pandemic changed (and continues to change) my practice dramatically, but even more, it has changed me. My current relationship with my work would be unrecognizable to the person I was in February 2020. Before then, I had never questioned my role in medicine or that it was a lifelong

commitment. Now I find myself looking at my work and my job with a more critical eye and daydreaming (not seriously, but consistently) of walking away. I know that I am not alone. It has not been widely reported, but attrition among healthcare workers, particularly among nurses, has increased dramatically since the start of the pandemic. Our hospital remains busier than it has ever been in my thirteen years working there. I fear that, in addition to the strain of the most recent surge of Covid, this is due to the fact that the for-profit health care system has incorporated the wrong lessons from the pandemic—among them that the goodwill and dedication of healthcare workers is an infinite resource and that we can continue to do less with more.

On this subject, MA offered:

The rapid and multiple practice transitions were jarring. My clinic first set up a series of military style outdoor isolation tents and barricades that were straight out of *Contagion*. Over days this evolved and changed, as did our triage protocols. We had no testing, and, frankly, had no idea what we were doing when it came to identifying patients who may have or been exposed to Covid. And then the pandemic hit full force, and we started doing telemedicine from home. The clinic became a shell of its former self, and weeks would go by without seeing a given colleague or interpreter or nurse. Meanwhile, I wondered where all the patients who needed to be seen had gone. How were chronic diseases going to be managed? How do we keep people out of the emergency rooms that were becoming overwhelmed with patients? Most of all, how do we keep our patients and each other safe? One thing is clear to me: we cannot go back to the way things were. We need to re-evaluate through the lens of what we now know, and we must collectively choose the practices—medically and socially—that move us forward.

Elements: What Elements/Actors Participated in the Meaning-Making?

In addition to identifying the major themes, we indexed specific elements and practices that participated within major rhetorical themes. For instance, when we coded transformation of practices, we then turned to our elements category to help capture *what* exactly was transformed and *how* those transformations were occurring. Below, we highlight the most salient elements we identified.

Visitor Restrictions

In nearly 22 percent of narratives, visitor restrictions was coded for any discussions of hospital policies that limited or inhibited visitors for both Covid patients and non-Covid patients. These discussions often emphasized the impact these policies had on patients, providers, and the families of those hospitalized, particularly during end-of-life care. For example:

> The repetitive, staccato tone of the code pager sounds, followed by a voice overhead announcing the patient's location. I spin down four flights of stairs and see people in yellow contact gowns forming a line for chest compressions. I feel nauseous. A resident calls out in my general direction that the family needs to be contacted. When no one volunteers, I step outside to the hallway to find a computer. I locate a phone number for the patient's emergency contact—his sister—but hesitate before calling. She is about to learn from a stranger that her brother has died and we are trying to bring him back.[31]

Physicians wrestled with the "ethical and health care dilemma" of visitor restrictions and consequent challenges, particularly regarding communication, that they faced: "Instead of our usual promise that 'We'll do everything we can to keep him alive until you get here,' we find ourselves telling families, 'Because of hospital policy, we cannot allow visitors at this time.' This conversation sometimes takes place at the doors to the ICU, over the phone, or in front of the hospital, as families beg to see their loved ones before they die."[32] This forced separation was also difficult for MK, who explained:

> As an immunocompromised person I had to quarantine for months at home due to increased Covid risk; for months, my only experience leaving my home was going to the hospital *alone* to undergo tests or treatment. Fortunately, none of my experiences were Covid-related; nevertheless, I distinctly remember the hospital feeling apocalyptic and desolate. Despite my years of experience as a chronic illness patient and my fluency in medical discourse, I struggled to manage all my visits by myself and found myself desperate thinking of fellow patients being left to navigate

their healthcare on their own or simply not at all. As one narrative put it, "the absence of loved ones . . . means that as our patients endure illness, there is no one beside them to ask questions, advocate for further testing, notice subtle changes in appetite or behavior, or insist that the problem that brought them to the hospital be solved before they're sent home. So these roles—noticing, advocating, accompanying—are my job now, too."[33] While it struck me that those roles seemed new to this physician, it both comforted and haunted me to hear the lengths providers were going to care—medically, emotionally, psychologically—for patients.

Patient Experience

Patient experience was the most commonly coded rhetorical element (43 percent) across coding categories. Physicians routinely noted with concern the changes that were rapidly and dramatically reshaping the provision of healthcare and how these changes affected vulnerable patients specifically. Writing about her time working in a Covid ICU and caring for a patient she had known for many years, one author wrote about the communal suffering between provider and patient: "Even with all I know about her, even with our shared history, I am also negotiating her absence. She is another Covid patient in another ICU bed in another ICU pod created to accommodate a seemingly endless surge. Sometimes the suffering itself feels endless. For all of us."[34]

This concern for patient experience was not limited to patients infected with Covid; authors struggled with how to best provide care to patients of all kinds when the healthcare system was overrun by patients with Covid, as in the case of an oncology fellow whose patient developed uncontrolled pain related to her terminal cancer: "Ms. M. was delirious, and I could hear her in the background, moaning in pain. The coronavirus pandemic had stretched all health care, including hospice, to its limits. The overwhelmed hospice agency was unable to evaluate her or transition her to inpatient hospice."[35] The intense difficulty of caring for people in pain resonated with BT, who recounted:

> Patient experience remains deeply affected by the pandemic. Though visitor restrictions have been loosened, they remain in place, and delays in care seem to have become commonplace as our healthcare system faces both fourth-wave Covid and (for reasons not well understood) a months-long non-Covid surge in the need for care.

Discrimination/Social Oppression

Twenty percent of narratives specifically described experiences with or concerns about discrimination/social oppression. While the "intersecting public crises" theme captured discussions *about* Covid's connection to other public crises, this element code was applied to stories in which discrimination/social oppression such as racism, xenophobia, or homophobia was present or influential in the experiences and practices of HCPs. Most often, racism was the rhetorical element experienced or discussed in stories that prompted us to apply this code.

Authors argued this pandemic is just the latest public health crisis facing American Black communities. Several authors explored how structural racism in both healthcare and broader society enabled the disproportionate toll Covid took on patients of color. As one narrative put it, the "pain" of Covid is "multiplied by ... social determinants of health—glaring among them being Black in America."[36] Another narrative, mirroring DiArron M.'s sentiment in this volume, reminded: "The truth is black people cannot breathe because we are currently battling at least two public health emergencies, and that is a conservative estimate."[37]

As other chapters in this collection reiterate, the impact and experience of Covid for marginalized communities have been exacerbated by the long-standing and deeply-entrenched legacy of medical racism against Black Americans. Narratives by Black physicians in our dataset articulate this compounding effect, as they wrote about the unique racist harm that manifested throughout the pandemic's most intense months. One medical student, a Black man in the middle of his clinical training, recounted his mixed emotions about returning to clinical medicine amid the social unrest catalyzed by George Floyd's murder after his program had been halted by the pandemic: "in the midst of the continued pain this pandemic has caused, I continue to be reminded that—despite my hard work and education—I am more likely to be killed by a police officer than by the virus, just like any other Black man in this society.[38]

Additionally, a few narratives mentioned experiences of discrimination against other minoritized communities. One physician, writing from a rural Indigenous community in Nevada, described the long-standing anti-Indigenous discrimination and the bias she saw in media coverage of Covid's impact on Indigenous communities:

> The national media reports on the severity of the Navajo Nation outbreak and hits the usual notes of poverty, isolation, and lack of running water. These reports are

factually accurate: the virus penetrated towns that utility companies have never managed to reach. But I yearn for stories that mention the diversity of talent and experience here, the resourcefulness. Outsiders seem surprised that the rural landscape hasn't protected us. I don't think the Navajo are surprised. From smallpox to H1N1 influenza, infections from the outside have always found their way here. It's just infrastructure that hasn't. It's not news.[39]

PPE

Several narratives (14 percent) contained vivid descriptions of the uncomfortable and unfamiliar embodied experience of wearing PPE for long periods. For example, "the hours go by, and your nose hurts more and more, the mask cuts through your skin and you can't wait to take it off and finally breathe. Breathe. It's what we all want these days, doctors and patients, nurses and care workers. All of us. We want air."[40] Other narratives shared the coping strategies emerging among HCPs as they endured the intense, long-term engagement with PPE:

> We share [Covid] hacks: We encase our cell phones in plastic wrap before going to work so that, on arrival home, we can peel it off (and maybe wipe the phone down again—can't hurt). The nurses show me how to use a skin protectant similar to moleskin on the bridge of my nose to reduce abrasion and breakouts caused by hours of pressure from my N95 mask. I can't wear my hospital ID on the exterior of our single-use yellow isolation gowns, so I use a black Sharpie to write "Dr. Doyle" in large block letters across the top of my reusable welder-style face shield. I have to periodically refresh the letters, because they continually fade under the effect of the meticulous antiviral wiping I perform on the shield multiple times a day.[41]

BT: The frequent discussion of PPE and the complicated donning and doffing and decontamination rituals were an effective reminder of the paranoia that came with uncertainty and unknowing. In the early days of the pandemic, PPE was our precious, if uncomfortable, armor. It was our only form of protection, and any misstep in removal or any misplaced hand gesture seemed to carry with it the threat of catastrophe. Now with the knowledge and experience that come with time and the added protection of the vaccine, the extra steps of putting on and removing protection feel automatic and mundane, a small annoyance amid the routine of the day.

Discussion

Collectively, these narratives offer a unique opportunity to examine the priorities, pressures, and issues that physicians faced throughout the primary months of the pandemic. They illuminate physicians' day-to-day realities and their reflections on the broader impact of the Covid pandemic on patients, families, and society. We have highlighted themes and elements we found to be most rhetorically significant within these narratives, knowing that we paint an incomplete yet important picture of how physicians' lives, roles, and experiences, alongside the systems and culture of Western medicine, were transformed by Covid.

The primacy of transformation of practice, particularly in tandem with discussions of telemedicine and visitor restrictions, suggests that HCPs are still wrestling with what is truly essential in the practice of medicine and what might be disposed of. The literal overnight implementation of telemedicine, as challenging and uncomfortable as it was for many, proved that the physician/patient relationship can transcend the confines of the exam room walls. Universal visitor restriction policies highlighted how, particularly for the sickest patients, the typical ethical relationship between the patient and provider was subverted in the interests of broader public health and workforce needs. These narratives demonstrated that the presumed disposability of these interactions brought a great deal of distress to providers, patients, and those closest to them. In fact, during data analysis, MA commented that visitor restrictions might be viewed in retrospect as a well-intentioned but tragic mistake with long-lasting consequences.

In addition to the significance of what *is* present in these narratives, what *is not* present provides valuable insights into the physicians' experiences throughout the pandemic. We were surprised to find that these narratives, overall, did not reflect the public discourse surrounding Covid, even as it evolved through time. We anticipated more meaningful discussions about the political landscape of 2020, policy decisions about mask mandates and shelter-in-place orders, and the intense surge of dis- and misinformation. When commentary on broader political context did appear, it was often passing and discrete. For instance, in a narrative otherwise about a specific experience with a dying patient, one physician wrote, "Thirty days before I met you, we didn't wear masks in the streets or in the halls of the hospital. The CDC said they were no use. Back then, the federal government had few plans for facing the pandemic other than sitting still and hoping for the best."[42] Though subtle references were sprinkled throughout narratives, explicit discussions of politically tenuous topics were absent.[43] We were also surprised to find no mentions of the vaccine, even in the later months of 2020 and early 2021, when physicians had access to the vaccine and as the vaccine was made more publicly available. It is possible that these omissions were due to editorial oversight or delayed publishing timelines or because we ended data collection in April 2021, when vaccines were not yet fully available to the US general public. Perhaps authors, consciously or unconsciously, avoided politically charged issues due to fear of retribution or of causing trouble within their workplaces. Perhaps physicians had less to say about the vaccine, as vaccine acceptance is high among physicians, and they were the earliest to receive it. In any case, the absence of mention feels noteworthy given the backdrop of omnipresent public debate and controversy.

We have emphasized that these narratives were written by physicians, which is mostly true; however, several (about 28 percent) of the narratives were written by physicians-in-training (medical students, residents, or fellows), one by a doctor of nursing, and one narrative collaboratively written by a nurse, doctor, and professional musician. We did not find significant differences in narratives written by different HCPs, with the exception that medical students, residents, and fellows commented on their experiences specifically as trainees, which included the stress of entering medicine during a pandemic and anxiety around feeling unprepared. That said, the perspectives and experiences represented in our dataset are limited by the writers' professional identities and individual experiences; therefore, we do not intend to suggest that these narratives speak for all HCPs or even all physicians. Undoubtedly, physicians in rural areas and/or underserved communities likely had less time or resources to write and publish narratives over the last year. Also, the experiences of nurses, certified nursing assistants, or medical assistants, would certainly add nuance to the findings presented. With these limitations in mind, our findings do archive some of Covid's unique challenges and how physicians' transformed and persisted in the early days of the pandemic.

Conclusion

Few professions have an outlet for recording the deeply personal thoughts, feelings, and experiences of their members during key moments in history. Even fewer have the opportunity or outlet to voice fears, concerns, and struggles in highly read and elite spaces like medical journals. Therefore, we feel fortunate that medicine provided space for stories like those analyzed in this dataset because they have much to tell us about the day-to-day life of physicians throughout the pandemic, and at the same time, they have much to tell us about systemic and structural issues that emerged or quelled under the unique circumstances of Covid. Physicians generously recorded their individual stories, describing in sometimes great detail the uncertainty, fear, and isolation of the past year, as they wrestled with the grief and sadness they were experiencing and witnessing, and as they attempted to make sense of what it meant to practice medicine among unprecedented societal change and human suffering. They also provided deep insight and an immutable record of the first year of the pandemic. Nonetheless, a troubling divide within the category of "essential workers" gets underscored in this collection as authors describe the economic and social privilege required to make major life changes to protect themselves and their families. The themes, elements, and emotions within these narratives illustrate the messy and, at times, painful process of transformation that medicine has undergone and will need to continue to undergo as it grapples with and recovers from the stresses and traumas of the pandemic.

When we embarked on the process of rhetorically engaging these narratives and writing this chapter in the spring of 2021, it seemed like the pandemic was nearing its end. At the time, we thought that in these stories, we had captured physicians' reflections on the darkest days of the pandemic. Clearly, we could not have been more wrong. Revising this chapter in the spring of 2022, we are now all too aware of the toll that fourth-wave Covid continues to take and the new frustrations it brings. While most of the world outside of the hospital seems to have moved on, hospitals must continue navigating surges and the (potential) scarcity of ICU beds. Patients, both those infected with Covid and those impacted by the lack of healthcare capacity, are suffering and dying, and healthcare workers continue to struggle. Stories of those struggles continue to be published in nearly every issue of the medical journals that provide space for them. Narratives like these will be an important space to watch as the individuals practicing medicine navigate the months and years to come and attempt to heal from and come to terms with the injuries they have endured, the horrors they have witnessed, and the mistakes they have made during the course of the pandemic. We hope this analysis serves as a rhetorical resource that archives one piece of the complex reality we all continue to navigate.

NOTES

1. Marcin Chwistek, "Are You Wearing Your White Coat? Telemedicine in the Time of the Pandemic," *JAMA* 324, no. 2 (2020): 149.
2. Other HCPs and experts also publish these kinds of narratives. However, physicians' narratives are the most commonly published within medical journals. Rita Charon and Martha Montello, "Introduction: Memory and Anticipation: The Practice of Narrative Ethics," in *Stories Matter: The Role of Narrative in Medical Ethics*, ed. Rita Charon and Martha Montello (New York: Routledge, 2002), x; Tracy Moniz et al., "Voices from the Front Lines: An Analysis of Physicians' Reflective Narratives About Flaws Within the 'System,'" *Journal of Medical Humanities* 42 (2021); Tracy Moniz, Lorelei Lingard, and Chris Watling, "Stories Doctors Tell," *JAMA* 318, no. 2 (2017).
3. James W. Pennebaker, "Writing about Emotional Experiences as a Therapeutic Process," *Psychological Science* 8, no. 3 (1997).
4. Moniz et al., "Voices."
5. See Lora Arduser, "Agency in Illness Narratives: A Pluralistic Analysis," *Narrative Inquiry* 24, no. 1 (2014); Carol Berkenkotter, *Patient Tales: Case Histories and the Uses of Narrative in Psychiatry* (Charleston: University of South Carolina Press, 2019); M. Remi Yergeau, *Authoring Autism* (Durham, NC: Duke University Press, 2018). See also, Malea Powell, "2012 CCCC Chair's Address: Stories Take Place: A Performance in One Act," *College Composition and Communication* 54, no. 2 (2012): 390.
6. Judy Z. Segal, "Breast Cancer Narratives as Public Rhetoric: Genre Itself and the Maintenance of Ignorance," *Linguistics and the Human Sciences* 3, no. 1 (2007): 6.
7. Rita Charon, *Narrative Medicine: Honoring the Stories of Illness* (Oxford: Oxford University Press, 2006), vii.
8. Emily Winderman and Jamie Landau, "From HeLa Cells to Henrietta Lacks: Rehumanization and Pathos as Interventions for the Rhetoric of Health and Medicine," in *Rhetoric of Health and Medicine As/Is: Theories and Approaches for the Field*, ed. Lisa Melonçon, S. Scott Graham, Jenell Johnson, John A. Lynch, and Cynthia Ryan (Columbus: Ohio State University Press, 2020), 60–79.
9. Some scholars have distinguished between "story" and "narrative," referring to narrative as the broader templates that give shape to unique, individual stories. We use the terms interchangeably, as both narrative and story are used within the community to refer to the texts we analyzed. For further discussion, see Arthur Frank, *Letting Stories Breathe: A Socio-Narratology* (Chicago: University of Chicago Press, 2010).
10. Moniz et al., "Voices."

11. *NEJM*'s "Perspective" section features a mix of genres including narratives, opinion pieces, and research briefs. We collected all publications within *NEJM*'s "Perspective" and then, by consensus, determined which publications were first-person narratives. These journals published narratives for years prior to the pandemic; Covid marked a difference in that the narratives focused predominantly on the unique experiences manifested by Covid, but other genre conventions of the Covid narratives were consistent with previously published narratives.
12. Tedros Adhanom Ghebreyesus, "Director-General's Opening Remarks at the Media Briefing on Covid-19," *World Health Organization*, March 11, 2020.
13. We deemed this an in situ approach following Endres et al., who describe in situ rhetoric as "an all-encompassing sensual experience that happens in a particular time and place and through particular bodies." Danielle Endres, Aaron Hess, Samantha Senda-Cook, and Michael K. Middleton, "In Situ Rhetoric: Intersections between Qualitative Inquiry, Fieldwork, and Rhetoric," *Cultural Studies ↔ Critical Methodologies* 16, no. 6 (2016): 516.
14. Winderman and Landau, "From HeLa," 67.
15. For example, Cynthia Tsai, "Personal Risk and Societal Obligation Amidst Covid-19," *JAMA* 323, no. 16 (2020): 1555.
16. Lisa Rosenbaum, "Once Upon a Time... the Hero Sheltered in Place," *New England Journal of Medicine* (*NEJM*) 383, no. 2 (2020): e5.
17. For an in-depth discussion of rhetorics of essentiality/disposability, particularly regarding "frontline" worker language, see Marina Levina's chapter in this volume.
18. Bernard E. Trappey, "Running on Fumes," *JAMA* 324, no. 12 (2020): 1157.
19. Jane deLima Thomas, "Pandemic as Teacher—Forcing Clinicians to Inhabit the Experience of Serious Illness," *NEJM* 383, no. 4 (2020): 307.
20. Elizabeth J. Rourke, "Waiting," *NEJM* 382, no. 23 (2020): 2185.
21. Louise Aronson, "Age, Complexity, and Crisis—A Prescription for Progress in Pandemic," *NEJM* 383, no. 1 (2020): 4–6.
22. Allison Bond, "Socially Distanced Medicine," *JAMA* 323, no. 23 (2020): 2383.
23. Susan R. Hata, "The Ritual of the Table," *NEJM* 383, no. 14 (2020): 1301.
24. Rachel R. Hardeman, Eduardo M. Medina, and Rhea W. Boyd, "Stolen Breaths," *NEJM* 383, no. 3 (2020): 198.
25. Anna DeForest, "The New Stability," *NEJM* 383, no. 18 (2020): 1709.
26. Sara DiCaglio raises similar questions in her chapter in this collection.
27. Renata Thronson, "Lost Space," *JAMA* 323, no. 20 (2020): 2019.
28. Heather Kovich, "Rural Matters—Coronavirus and the Navajo Nation," *NEJM* 383, no. 2 (2020): 106.

29. Simone V. Benatti, "Love in the Time of Corona," *Annals of Internal Medicine* 172, no. 9 (2020): 628.
30. Richard E. Leiter, "Reentry," *NEJM* 383, no. 7 (2020): e141(1).
31. Christina Dimopoulos, "Calling a Code," *Annals of Internal Medicine* 174, no. 2 (2021): 268.
32. Glenn K. Wakam et al., "Not Dying Alone—Modern Compassionate Care in the Covid-19 Pandemic," *NEJM* 382, no. 24 (2020): e88(1).
33. Simone Vais, "The Inequity of Isolation," *NEJM* 394, no. 8 (2021): 690.
34. Rana LA Awdish, "The Liminal Space," *NEJM* 383, no. 4 (2020): e17(1).
35. Arjun Gupta, "Plans and Pandemics," *NEJM* 383, no. 8 (2020): e53.
36. Uri Ladabaum, "Life After May 25," *Annals of Internal Medicine* 173, no. 11 (2020): e141.
37. Hardeman, Medina, and Boyd, "Stolen Breaths," 198.
38. Christopher Thomas Veal, "At the Intersection of Fear, Grief, and Love," *Annals of Internal Medicine* 173, no. 10 (2020): 849.
39. Kovich, "Rural Matters," 105.
40. Silvia Castelletti, "A Shift on the Front Line," *NEJM* 382, no. 23 (2020): 283(1).
41. Thomas J. Doyle, "Covid-19, Prisons Visits, and the Value of a Cup of Coffee," *Annals of Internal Medicine* 173, no. 8 (2020): 667.
42. DeForest, "New Stability," 1709.
43. We recognize that intersecting public crises/contexts as well as discrimination/social oppression are inherently political, and we do not mean to ignore them in our references to political discourse here. We are, instead, trying to distinguish them from explicit mentions of government, political elections, policies, and the context of disinformation that became rhetorically significant throughout 2020.

Covid and Fatphobia

How Rhetorics of Disposability Render Fat Bodies
Unworthy of Care and Life

Hailey Nicole Otis

"On February 5, I saw that New York had updated its eligibility guidelines for COVID-19 vaccines. One of the newly acceptable comorbidities was obesity; anyone with a BMI over 30 could get vaccinated after February 15. That included me," writes Juliana Kaplan. "In a strange twist of fate, a measure based on the fatphobic BMI—and on the heels of fatphobic messaging throughout the pandemic—brought me nothing but joy."[1] Kaplan's joy about getting vaccinated is matched by many other folks in larger bodies (hereafter referred to as "fat").[2] I know this because of both my own experience as a fat person who was prioritized for Covid vaccination and as a member of many fat-focused social media groups who witnessed feelings of relief and elation emanating from others' posts in the early days of vaccine rollouts. However, not all fat people felt overjoyed about getting prioritized for Covid vaccines. Many fat folks felt shame and even unworthiness in response to their early vaccine access.[3] In the face of such mixed feelings, many fat activists and other fat-positive public figures took to social media to convey the following message: that fat people should absolutely not feel ashamed and, instead, should jump at the chance to get an early vaccine because they are victims of medicalized fatphobia. Medicalized fatphobia has put fat people at a higher risk for complications (including death) from Covid and a whole host of other diseases and, therefore, fat people deserve the chance to protect themselves via early vaccination.[4]

Medicalized fatphobia—a constellation of anti-fat attitudes and actions enacted by medical professionals as well as by laypeople based in flawed, discriminatory notions of "health"—does not exist in a vacuum; indeed, it shapes and is shaped by popular/public discourse around fat bodies. At the intersection of medical and popular discourse emerges what I term "rhetorics of disposability," which are discourses that render vulnerable bodies (in this case, fat bodies) unworthy of care and life. Rhetorics of disposability are a form of what Allison Rowland calls "zoerhetorics" in that they transvalue and contrive livability for certain groups depending on where those groups fall on the biopolitical hierarchy.[5] Against the backdrop of the global Covid pandemic, rhetorics of disposability occur (yet also shift and evolve) within various rhetorical contexts, including public health campaigns, popular discourse, and healthcare triage procedures. This essay uses the case study of medicalized fatphobia during the Covid pandemic to speculate on the defining features of rhetorics of disposability. I argue that rhetorics of disposability render vulnerable bodies unworthy of care and life by positioning them as a drain on resources, promoting logics of personal responsibility, blaming/scapegoating the vulnerable group, and trivializing death, harm, and suffering of that group. Moreover, rhetorics of disposability become material in the ways that they are coded into specific kinds of tangible practice—in this case, tangible medical practice.

To understand how rhetorics of disposability produce such rhetorical and material consequences, I first provide a working definition of medicalized fatphobia and then theorize "rhetorics of disposability." Next, I analyze how rhetorics of disposability toward fat bodies unfold within the Covid pandemic in three distinct contexts: public health messaging, popular discourse as represented on Twitter, and state crisis standards of care guidelines. I conclude with a brief discussion of the significance of rhetorics of disposability, what distinguishes them, their potential applicability across various dynamics of marginalization, and how we, as rhetoricians, can intervene in and interrupt such discourses to humanize vulnerable groups and bodies.

Medicalized Fatphobia

Medicalized fatphobia is a specific and contextualized instantiation of the broader social phenomenon that many fat activists and scholars of fat studies have identified as *fatphobia*, the pathological fear and hatred of fatness and fat bodies enacted at the level of the social. More specifically, fatphobia encompasses all of the social and cultural practices that serve to cement thinness as both the norm and most desirable form of embodiment as well as those that stigmatize, dehumanize, and enact bias and violence against people who inhabit fat bodies. Fatphobia can also be thought of in terms of anti-fatness, fat stigma, and inequity for those in fat bodies. Though fatphobia takes on specific contours in specific historical moments, its existence as a social condition has persisted over time in Western contexts, since at least the late nineteenth century. Alternatively conceived of through lenses such as "fat panic" and fat oppression, fatphobia constructs a marginalized existence for fat people, emplacing them in webs of power that rob them of agency and humanity; question their morality, intelligence, and autonomy; and deprioritize their health and well-being.

The Medicalization of Fatness

Medicalized fatphobia essentially represents the convergence of "fatphobia" with "medicalization." Medicalization can broadly be understood as "the process by which some aspects of human life come to be considered as medical problems."[6] Rhetoricians have defined medicalization as "a process in which the expertise of science and medicine (and the public vocabularies that support such expertise) is valued over lived and experiential knowledge and used to categorize aspects of social life as disease or abnormality."[7] In particular, it positions "both technical and lay publics" as possessing "the rhetorical tools to consistently constitute [insert condition here] as a medical condition."[8] Medicalization is, at its core, a rhetorical phenomenon—a way of reframing a variety of embodied experiences as medical issues to serve particular rhetorical goals and agendas. Raquel M. Robvais's discussion earlier in this volume exemplifies how the medicalization of Blackness acts as a pre-existing condition in service of white innocence.

Peter Conrad clarifies the rhetorical nature of medicalization, distinguishing that "the key to medicalization is definition. That is, a problem is defined in medical terms, described using medical language, understood through the adoption of a medical framework, or 'treated' with a medical intervention."[9] Medicalized fatphobia, then, is a result of medicalized fatness, which represents the rhetorical processes through which fatness itself comes to be understood as illness and disease. One key way that medicalized fatphobia has proliferated is through the language of "obesity" and its subsequent power as a diagnosis.[10] The medicalization of fatness via the language of "obesity" creates a binary in which thin automatically equals healthy and fat necessarily equates to ill health even though fat people, thin people, and everyone between exist across the diverse spectrum of health, wellness, and ability.[11] Ultimately, "obesity epidemic discourse" functions as a "technique of neoliberal governance" that positions all people as responsible for their individual health (and therefore ignores a variety of structural and systemic factors that influence one's attainability of health), while specifically establishing fat people as needing to strive for thinness to overcome their moral failings.[12] Medicalized fatness is one, perhaps expected, result of the neoliberalization of health. However, medicalized fatness also produces unique forms of medicalized fatphobia that come in two primary forms: fatphobia enacted by medical professionals and fatphobia enacted in popular discourse that relies on medicalized logics. These two manifestations of medicalized fatphobia mutually shape each other.

Forms of Medicalized Fatphobia: Healthcare and Popular Discourse

Medicalizing fatness allows medical professionals to treat fat people as necessarily diseased, even if they do not experience any symptoms or manifestations of illness. This allows such professionals to "prescribe" weight loss as "treatment" for disease even though a robust body of research suggests that significant weight loss is both unattainable and unsustainable for the vast majority of people.[13] The medicalization of fatness has also led to medical professionals blaming many (if not all) fat patients' ailments on their weights, which results in misdiagnosis, late detection of disease, and fat people avoiding seeking medical help.[14] Ultimately, medicalized fatphobia at the hands of medical professionals threatens fat people's health, longevity, and even their lives. Thus, medicalized fatphobia is but one of the structural/social determinants of health that the editors of this volume argue we must attend to in order to track the residues of zoerhetorical hierarchies. In the case of the Covid pandemic, specifically, medicalized fatphobia and the threats to health and treatment that fat people experience because of it are precisely why people in fat bodies deserve priority vaccine access.

Medicalized fatphobia as it occurs in popular discourse uses the medicalization of fatness—the labeling of fatness as the disease of "obesity"—as a justification for enacting anti-fatness. This takes many forms, including shaming fat people for their weight (thinly veiled as "concern" for their health), making assumptions about the health and ability of fat bodies, and—as is particularly notable for this essay—assigning disproportionate responsibility to fat people for societal problems such as rising healthcare costs, the proliferation of certain diseases, as well as the damage inflicted by global pandemics.

It is important to note that medicalized fatphobia shifts and evolves over time and in response to historical context. For example, medicalized fatphobia in the late 1990s and early 2000s was shaped by the capitalist interests of a for-profit healthcare system that could make money off bariatric surgery and shame people into willingly accepting such "treatment" by framing it as their patriotic duty against the backdrop of global terrorist threats.[15] Medicalized fatphobia in the present moment is shifting and evolving to respond to the current most pressing global threat: the Covid pandemic. In this moment of fear of virus, contagion, illness, disability, and death, medicalized fatphobia has once again assigned disproportionate responsibility to fat people for the effects of the pandemic.[16] However, in this moment, medicalized fatphobia has also taken on a slightly new shape—it has produced rhetorics of disposability that render fat (and other vulnerable groups) unworthy of care and life in the context of the pandemic.

The Living Dead: Biopolitics of Disposability

Building on both Henry Giroux's theory of "biopolitics of disposability" as well as recent rhetorical scholarship on disposable bodies, I contend that rhetorics of disposability create a constellation of discourses that ultimately renders vulnerable bodies unworthy of care and life. Though, in this essay, I am predominantly interested in how rhetorics of disposability emerge at the intersection of popular and medical discourse in ways that affect fat bodies specifically (and can therefore be seen as a *product* of medicalized fatphobia), this concept is much broader than any one axis of identity/marginalization and can be applied to a variety of contexts and forms of vulnerability. To understand how disposability operates rhetorically, I first trace the nuances of "disposability" as a concept and cultural force.

Conceptually, *disposability* connotes a sense of excess—both that which is so excessive, it is reducible to waste as well as that which is widely available and, in such a sense, excessive. Disposability takes on particular valences when applied to bodies, specifically human bodies. Ranjana Khanna distinguishes that "disposable people appear as matter or raw material, always at hand, in the manner of a standing reserve."[17] Disposable bodies are marked by a sense of otherness that renders them less than human, if not inhuman, akin to waste and needing to be discarded, resulting in them ultimately evolving "into a living state of worthlessness."[18]

Henry Giroux concurs, identifying a "politics of disposability in which diverse individuals and populations are not only considered redundant and disposable, but barely acknowledged as human beings."[19] Giroux's "biopolitics of disposability" emphasizes questions about "who is going to die and who is going to live" and highlights how the state has "given up on the sanctity of human life for those populations rendered 'at risk' by global neoliberal economies."[20] Giroux specifically examines biopolitics of disposability as they come to bear on poor, racialized bodies in the context of the aftermath of Hurricane Katrina. This context is telling as I draw connections to the disposability of fat bodies in the current Covid context because Hurricane Katrina was another cultural moment in which fat bodies were also rendered disposable and left to die—lest we forget the many fat patients left behind in New Orleans's hospitals during the hurricane, deemed too troublesome to evacuate because of their weight. The result of biopolitics of disposability, whether during natural disasters like Hurricane Katrina or global pandemics like Covid, is a "a transnational economic and political framework" in which these disposable people "are already seen as dead . . . the living dead."[21] This construction of certain groups as "already dead"—deemed inhuman so as to be excluded from the sanctity of human life—is key to how biopolitics of disposability operate rhetorically in public discourse.

Disposability as Rhetorical

Rhetoricians have taken a recent interest in examining how notions of disposability function within discourse to both justify and perpetuate harm toward marginalized groups, including trans folks, Native women, and racialized others. Leland Spencer argues that biopolitics of disposability "render certain populations invisible, or worse, worthy of symbolic and material annihilation."[22] Disposable bodies are conceptualized from a variety of angles, as those "excluded from public view and liable for prosecution for existing in public space," "capable of being destroyed without repercussion," as well as those that are "used and then subject to disposal—lives discarded."[23] Lisa Flores clarifies that disposability is a fundamentally rhetorical phenomenon often "premised in law, labor, and legality."[24] Marina Levina echoes this point in her discussion in this volume about disposability being the rhetorical outcome for those whose labor is deemed "essential" amid the Covid pandemic.

If disposability is fundamentally rhetorical, then, the question arises: what are its distinctive features as a discourse?

In this essay, I use the case of medicalized fatphobia in the context of the global Covid pandemic to speculate on the defining features of rhetorics of disposability, especially as they operate at the intersection of medical and popular discourses. In the scholarship, rhetorics of disposability function to render certain bodies as excessive, invisible, and destroyable. I build upon this conversation to argue that rhetorics of disposability—as a tool of the larger biopolitics of disposability—ultimately render vulnerable bodies unworthy of care and life.

Rhetorics of Disposability in the Covid Pandemic: Shifting across Rhetorical Contexts

When the first news articles emerged pointing to "obesity" as a risk factor for Covid, it was only a matter of time until blame, disgust, and attitudes of disposability would take a hostile turn toward people in fat bodies. Such attitudes and beliefs permeated a variety of rhetorical contexts, including public health campaigns and conversations on public platforms such as Twitter and were then coded into tangible medical practice via healthcare triage procedures. In the following sections, I analyze public health messaging in the form of the CDC's web page on "Obesity, Race/Ethnicity, and COVID-19," popular discourse in the form of tweets from CNN and CNBC about the relationship between Covid and "obesity," as well as state crisis standards of care documents. These texts serve as fragments of a larger anti-fat rhetoric of disposability in the context of a pandemic that shapes attitudes and treatment toward fat people. I use the tools of rhetorical criticism to stitch together the fragments of this discourse so that my audience can see—and so that I can evaluate—how the discourse shifts and evolves across rhetorical contexts.

Public Health Messaging

In April 2020, the CDC published an early release report "noting that 48% of patients then hospitalized with Covid-19 had a Body Mass Index (BMI) in the 'obese range' (compared with 42% of Americans as a whole."[25] In March 2021, the CDC published a second report solidifying the connection between Covid and "obesity" with an updated sample of Covid patients that exhibited a 50.8 percent "obesity" prevalence. Though the report acknowledges a variety of limitations of the study, including potential healthcare professional bias and a nonrepresentative sample, the results made waves across the United States, resulting in news headlines such as: "CDC study reveals connection between obesity and COVID," and "CDC data strengthens link of obesity, severe COVID."[26] These CDC reports can be read in the context of what many have labeled a "failure of public health messaging about COVID-19."[27] Indeed, the public messaging around Covid, especially in the United States, has been criticized by a variety of experts, including physicians and scholars of health communication, for making possible the spread of misinformation, igniting mistrust in marginalized populations, and causing stress and confusion.[28]

The CDC's public health messaging is certainly not as blatantly anti-fat and stigmatizing as some other countries' like, for example, Public Health England's "Better Health" campaign, which urged UK citizens to "lose weight to beat coronavirus (COVID-19) and protect the NHS [National Health Service]."[29] However, both artifacts use similar rhetorical topoi that ultimately position "fat people [as] the problem" and emphasize the monetary cost of "obesity" on the country's healthcare system.[30] These topoi are most immediately visible on the CDC's website. In this section, I engage in a close textual analysis of the CDC's web page on "Obesity, Race/Ethnicity, and COVID-19."[31] This is the CDC's primary and most accessible messaging on Covid and "obesity"—indeed, it is the first result in a Google search of the terms "CDC," "Covid," and "Obesity." The web page (which was last edited in March of 2021) first overviews the role of "obesity" as a risk factor for Covid, including touching on racial/ethnic disparities in "obesity" prevalence numbers, before presenting sections on "What Can Be Done" and "Steps to Take Now" to mitigate the effects of the pandemic supposedly amplified by "obesity" rates. I ultimately contend that the CDC's public health messaging advances rhetorics of disposability by positioning fat people as a drain on resources and by promoting logics of personal responsibility for fat people in the context of the pandemic.

Positioning Fat People as Drain on Resources

The first paragraph of the CDC's web page on "Obesity, Race/Ethnicity, and COVID-19," albeit only three sentences long, draws on both aforementioned topoi of disposability. It first establishes "obesity" as a "common, serious, and costly disease," starting off with a strong connection to monetary cost as a drain on resources. It then goes on to state that "everyone has a role to play in turning the tide against obesity," previewing the emphasis on personal responsibility that colors much of the rest of the web page. Considering the first topos of disposability—positioning a vulnerable group as a drain on resources—the web page moves pretty quickly from labeling "obesity" as "costly" to a short section titled "Adult Obesity is Increasing" that details that adult "obesity" prevalence is high and has increased in recent years. This is paired with a color-coded "Adult Obesity Prevalence Map" that visualizes high "obesity" prevalence with a dark crimson color. Not only does the color assigned to high "obesity" prevalence conjure associations with blood and death, the argument forwarded here that "adult obesity is increasing" paired with the earlier statement that "obesity" is "costly" work together to produce the logical conclusion that the monetary costs of "obesity" are rising. In the US context, where costs of healthcare are already of serious concern, it is easy to see how rising costs of "obesity" can translate into accusations of people with "obesity" being seen as a drain on monetary resources.

Monetary resources are not the only resources of concern gestured to by the CDC's web page. The next section of the web page, titled "Obesity Worsens Outcomes from COVID-19," provides data about the "greater risk" that those with "excess weight"—note the framing through the term "excess" here—suffer in relation to Covid. This section exhibits a heavy focus on "risks of hospitalization" as well as "intensive care unit admission, [and] invasive mechanical ventilation."[32] Indeed, the word *hospitalization* occurs three times in this short, six-bullet-point section, and the word "ventilation" occurs twice. These terms, rather than calling to mind the human suffering linked to Covid-related illness, conjure associations with hospital resources, which have been deemed scarce within the context of the pandemic. By rhetorically linking "obesity" to overreliance on what we have come to know as scarce hospital resources, this web page encourages audiences to see fat people as a possible threat to receiving proper Covid treatment/resources.

Promoting Logics of Personal Responsibility

A second topos the CDC webpage draws upon to advance rhetorics of disposability toward fat people in the context of Covid involves relying on logics of personal responsibility. As mentioned, the webpage begins drawing on topoi of personal responsibility from the very first paragraph with its statement that "everyone has a role to play" in relation to the problem of "obesity" and Covid. And, though the webpage dedicates a significant amount of space to "What Can Be Done," which purports to emphasize the role that the CDC and its "partners, states, and communities" can do to promote good health, as mentioned above, that same section still positions fat people as the problem in relation to the "severity" of the pandemic. This section even gestures to various "social determinants of health," listing factors such as "poverty, education, and housing." However, it proves wholly unwilling to recognize context-specific factors such as weight stigma and systemic fatphobia that a wealth of studies have shown to affect health outcomes for people in larger bodies.[33] This ensures that the blame remains firmly on the backs of fat people, rather than considering other factors for poor health (both broadly but also in specific relationship to Covid) than body size.

The remainder of the web page—and the section that takes up the most space—details "Steps to Take Now," which is where the argument for personal responsibility really thrives. From the very first sentence, which begins with the reminder that "systemic change takes time," the webpage absolves state actors like the CDC from any real accountability; it is the equivalent of saying "we promise we are working on the problem even though you cannot see and we cannot guarantee any tangible results." "Systemic change takes time" is followed by the prompt that "as does long term weight loss," which cements weight loss as the responsibility for all fat people if they are to be on the right side of the fight against Covid. The section then goes on to describe a variety of steps "individuals can [take to] help protect themselves and their families during this pandemic" from eating healthy to being active to getting adequate sleep and coping with stress.

Of course, all of the above actions are sound general advice; however, the CDC articulates each health behavior (healthy eating, exercise, sleep, and coping with stress) in terms of "help[ing] with weight loss" or "preventing weight gain." Weight loss is equated to health—as it almost always is in the context of "obesity" discourse—and is presented as the solution to the various problems brought on by the Covid pandemic. Audiences are offered a variety of tangible ways to start working toward weight loss so as to "protect themselves and their families," while the CDC skirts any accountability for the various actions they claim to be pursuing earlier on in the webpage such as "making healthy foods more available" and designing communities more intentionally to promote exercise. As these arguments congeal, the conclusion becomes clear: if one does not want to be part of the problem that is the pandemic, one must take on the personal responsibility of weight loss as that is the only way to guarantee protection. Not only is this conclusion riddled with problematic neoliberal logics of individual responsibility, it also overlooks the fact that weight loss, especially sustainable weight loss, is unachievable for most people, an assertion supported by a wealth of peer-reviewed research.[34]

Positioning a vulnerable group as a drain on resources and promoting logics of personal responsibility for that same vulnerable group emerge as two distinguishing features of rhetorics of disposability. Positioning the group as a drain on resources allows them to be viewed as excessive—as "too much" for the system and needing to be done away with. Making them personally responsible for their excessiveness robs them of their humanity in the current moment, yet promises a return of that humanity so long as they are able to conform to normative expectations about bodies (in this case, if fat people are to magically become thin, they will no longer be excessive or a burden and can re-realize their humanity and potentially avoid disposability). However, such a promise is a farce. Not only is weight loss notoriously unachievable for most fat people, it is impossible in the short span of time occasioned by a pandemic. Together, these two topoi, as deployed in the CDC's public health campaign, position fat people as "the living dead" of the pandemic, awaiting to be cast aside by state actors, excluded from the sanctity of human life, and rendered utterly disposable.[35]

Popular Discourse

Early in the pandemic, politicians, pundits, and even some scientists discussed the relationship between body weight/BMI and complications from the virus as if it was a foregone conclusion. Statements like that of France's chief epidemiologist—which indicated concern for "our friends in America" because "those who are overweight really need to be careful"—abounded before there was ever any data to support a connection to weight.[36] When it was determined that people with higher BMIs would receive vaccine priority in many states, anti-fatness took form in public figures complaining about this decision. Take Fox 5 news anchor Blake McCoy's since-deleted tweet as an example: "I'm annoyed obese people of all ages get priority vaccine access before all essential workers . . . Vaccinate all essential workers. Then obese."[37] Throughout the pandemic, popular discourse has advanced rhetorics of disposability toward fat people in distinct ways.

To identify key argumentative themes, or topoi, that animate anti-fat rhetorics of disposability as they occur in popular discourse about Covid, I turn to the following two tweets and their corresponding re-tweets and responses:

- A tweet posted by CNN's official Twitter account on March 4th, 2021 that reads "the risk of death from Covid-19 is about 10 times higher in countries where most of the population is overweight, according to a report released Wednesday by the World Obesity Forum" paired with an image of two fat, feminine-presenting people with only their neck to torso area in frame (this form of photography that cuts fat people off at the head has been labeled and critiqued as the "headless fatty" stereotype).[38]
- A tweet posted by CNBC's officially Twitter account on March 8th, 2021 that reads "CDC study finds roughly 78% of people hospitalized for Covid were overweight or obese" paired with a picture of two EMTs loading a fat, older white man on a stretcher into an ambulance.[39]

Both tweets link to long-form news stories based on the tweeted headlines. These two tweets are representative of much of the news discourse around fatness and Covid—headlines emphasizing the presumed relationship between fatness (coded as "obesity") and Covid-related complications like hospitalization and death. Their responses, then, serve as representative examples of popular discourse around these topics that reveal how rhetorics of disposability function in public conversation about Covid and fatness. In this section, I explore how popular discourse, as represented on Twitter, advances rhetorics of disposability by drawing on topoi of blaming/scapegoating a vulnerable group (in this case, fat people) and trivializing their death, harm, and suffering.

Blaming/Scapegoating Fat People

The first topos that these tweets draw on to promote anti-fat rhetorics of disposability is blaming fat people for the negative effects of the pandemic. This topos involves critiquing measures such as lockdowns, social distancing, and masks as only benefiting fat (also coded as "unhealthy") people and, therefore, pointless. Examples include tweets responding to CNBC's post such as "we shut down the economy so fat people can be protected . . . impressive," and "but sure, put all the healthy people under house arrest and staple masks on their faces because some people can't be bothered to eat healthy and exercise." Another similar tweet asked "so why are the rest of us being punished for their laziness[?]" The implicit argument here is that protecting fat people is not a worthy goal, certainly not worthy of even minimally affecting the quality of life of thin (coded as "healthy") people.

This topos of blame also takes form as using fat people—and the data around "obesity" and Covid—to promote misinformation about the virus and protective measures. For example, one tweet response to the CNN post sarcastically states, "So let's promote lockdowns, stay at home orders, Netflix and Doritos for a year instead of exercise, sunshine, healthy diets? Those 'experts' made a bad situation worse." A similar response to the CNBC post reads "& yet the CDC just keeps pushing masks and vaccines. As if exercise, nutrition, sunlight, fresh air, & vitamins don't exist and make a difference." Both of these tweets position choices like healthy diets/nutrition and exercise as somehow being able to fight a virus better than masks, vaccines, and stay-at-home orders. Another response to the CNBC tweet assured others that "if you are elderly or obese be extra careful, everyone else live your life like normal." As these tweets echo the shifting of blame to fat people for the severity of the virus, they also communicate an unwillingness to engage in measures to protect others while using fat people as a scapegoat or justification for that unwillingness. Blaming and scapegoating cultivates a sense of disposability toward fat people by implying that if there were no fat people, the pandemic would be less severe. This ultimately reveals that fat people are more useful as pawns in a political game to promote misinformation and are rarely seen as vulnerable, marginalized humans suffering at the hands of a deadly virus.

Trivializing Fat Death and Suffering

A second way that that popular discourse as represented via the CNN and CNBC tweet responses draw on *topoi* of disposability is by trivializing fat death (and, more broadly, harm of fat bodies). Indeed, many of the responses to the CNN tweet, the topic of which is higher Covid-related death rates for fat people, take a cruelly humorous tone through statements such as "thinning the herd... a regrettable pun" and "COVID is a chubby chaser." Responses to the CNBC tweet similarly trivialize harm toward fat bodies (since the tweet itself is about higher rates of hospitalization for fat Covid patients) through equally cruel statements such as "SAVE THE WHALES," "so, chastity mask for the fatties," and "wow guess I'm pro-covid now." Another way that the responses trivialize fat death and harm toward fat bodies is through statements like "lol shocking," "geee you don't say," and "no shit, REALLY" which, once again, forward fat people's demise as a foregone conclusion.

Perhaps the most insidious ways that these Twitter conversations trivialize fat death is by drawing connections between the death or hospitalization of fat Covid patients and natural selection. Examples abound: "The purest form of natural selection, Darwin would be so proud," "Darwin Strikes again," and "maybe unhealthy people dying off is an example of survival of the fittest?" Some tweets just simply state "natural selection" as a brief, but impactful response. These tweets, in their callousness, endorse Covid's potential as a form of Darwinism/natural selection that results in fat death and suffering. Indeed, the easiest way to construct a vulnerable group as disposable is to portray their demise as a good thing—a worthy goal.

Blaming/scapegoating a vulnerable group (in this case, fat people) and trivializing their death, harm, and suffering emerge as two more distinguishing features of rhetorics of disposability. Deploying these argumentative commonplaces constructs fat bodies as existing in a "living state of worthlessness," ready to be used as political pawns to spread misinformation and then readily discarded.[40] Most, insidiously, these *topoi*, as forwarded in popular discourse, position fat bodies as "worthy of symbolic and material annihilation"—their deaths not only a foregone conclusion, but also a goal worth accomplishing.[41]

Crisis Standards of Care

A question that emerges during almost any global medical crisis is that of limited medical resources. Guidance on how to allocate both critical supplies and treatment are typically outlined in state Crisis Standards of Care (CSC) documents, which pre-date Covid, but have gained an unprecedented amount of attention because of the pandemic. CSC documents/guidelines allow states and other regulatory bodies to detail any "substantial change in usual healthcare operations and the level of care it is possible to deliver, which is made necessary by a pervasive (e.g., pandemic influenza) or catastrophic (e.g., earthquake, hurricane) disaster."[42] The Covid pandemic arrived at a time when health practitioners have begun to understand that stigma, bias, and discrimination exacerbate (and even cause) health risks for fat people, especially in the context of medical care, which one might hope would shape the guidance provided in CSC documents. Instead, however, CSC documents contribute to what we have historically seen as "a lower standard of treatment as part of a vicious cycle for PwO [persons with 'obesity'] experiencing the healthcare system."[43] Pandemic allocation decisions highlight "the terrible injustices in the world that we try and ignore" and, as Dr. Sara Kirk, a professor of health promotion at Dalhousie University, warns, "once the dust has settled after the pandemic, we may see that people were offered less treatment because of their weight."[44]

The singular goal of CSCs to promote utility and efficiency is typically bolstered by some kind of ethical framework based on the idea of maximizing the number of "lives" or "life-years" saved. Indeed, this is one foundational way that anti-fatness is implicitly written into CSC documents—diagnoses such as "morbid obesity" are defined by their presumed connection to decreased life-span, therefore ensuring that fat people categorized through this medical framework will never be seen as having many "life-years" to save. CSCs have also promoted a sense of disposability toward fat people by broadly painting "serious comorbidities" as a reason for knocking people lower on the priority list since fatness (coded as "obesity") is automatically seen as a comorbidity. Beyond these relatively broad examples, sometimes "obesity" is explicitly written into CSC guidelines as a factor that "may weigh against the most advanced lifesaving care" for a patient, as is the case in New York State's CSC guidelines.[45]

Fortunately, in the context of the pandemic—as medical practitioners are just starting to scratch the surface of accounting for medical bias/discrimination toward a variety of marginalized people at the broader policy level—the United States witnessed many revisions to more traditional CSC guidelines to ensure that allocation of resources does not promote discrimination against protected identities. For example, California revised its first set of Covid CSC guidelines, which were published early in the pandemic and initially emphasized "saving the most life-years" and deprioritizing people with "serious comorbid illness."[46] Ultimately, California shifted its guidelines to promote equity for marginalized patients, including "weight/size" as one of the factors that cannot affect "healthcare decisions, including allocation of scarce resources."[47] Though many states have revised their guidelines to include a similar statement of equity, California is the only one to explicitly include weight.

Excluding Weight as Equity Consideration

One way that disposability of fat bodies is coded into Covid CSCs is, indeed, the *exclusion* of weight/size from considerations of equity/social justice as written into most states' guidelines. New York's guidelines prohibit allocation decisions based on "demographic factors like race, ethnicity, sexual orientation, socio-economic status, education, religion, ability, and quality of life," noting that "members of marginalized groups face stigma and discrimination, which can be exacerbated in public health emergencies characterized by fear and distrust."[48] Alabama's guidelines state that "resource allocation decisions should not be based on . . . race, sex, color, national origin, disability, age, socio-economic status, perceived quality of life, perceived social worth, or past or future use of medical resources; ability to pay; [or] age, on its own."[49] New Mexico's guidelines, in their section on "justice," prohibit allocation decisions based on race, gender, ethnicity, religions, social status, location, education, income, ability to pay, "disability unrelated to prognosis," immigration status, or sexual orientation.[50] Massachusetts's guidelines add "perceived social worth," "incarceration status," and "homelessness" to its unique list of factors to exclude.[51]

Though all of the factors/marginalized identities listed above are crucial ethical considerations as they relate to the allocation of resources and absolutely should not factor into whether someone receives care, it is notable that body size/weight/BMI fails to make an appearance on states' lists of equity considerations, with the exception of California. Leaving weight off these lists ignores fatphobia as a form of systemic marginalization, leaving fat people vulnerable to medical bias and discrimination. This omission upholds rhetorics of disposability by obscuring fat peoples' need for protection under considerations of equity and social justice. It obfuscates their position as a victim of the healthcare system's biases, leaving them susceptible to being harmed and discarded throughout the course of the pandemic.

Reliance on Clinical Judgment

Another issue that arises in conjunction with the biases of the healthcare system and healthcare professionals is that of "clinical judgment." Indeed, another common rhetorical move among state CSC documents is to leave treatment decisions ultimately up to "clinical judgment," which can be defined as "an interpretation or conclusion about a patient's needs, concerns, or health problems, and/or the decision to take action (or not), use or modify standard approaches, or improvise new ones as deemed appropriate by the patient's response."[52] When written into CSC documents, clinical judgment is essentially a mechanism that allows the overseeing medical provider to make the ultimate care and treatment decisions for their patients amid a crisis such as a pandemic based on what is assumed to be sound and maximally objective reasoning. Alabama's CSC guidelines establish that providers must "follow sensible triage decisions based on his/her sound clinical judgment and avoid triage decisions based on factors that are not fair and equitable."[53] Massachusetts's guidelines clarify that its ethical framework must be balanced with "with application of clinical judgment."[54] And, though California's CSC guidelines do not necessarily use the word *clinical*, they do state that "physicians and nurses make triage decisions based on their best judgment, through individualized determinations using objective medical evidence."[55]

Reliance on clinical judgment, specifically, or the judgment of healthcare providers, broadly, is written into the majority of individual state's CSC guidelines. This may not immediately present as a problem; however, "clinical judgment" becomes a particularly sinister concept when considered alongside the pervasive anti-fat bias that exists among healthcare professionals.[56] If healthcare professionals are to use their assumed sound discretion to help determine who gets care and resources during a pandemic, yet they also likely possess strong anti-fat bias, anti-fatness is thus subtly coded into the structure of CSCs. Healthcare professionals' anti-fatness is permitted to flourish, leading to harm and perhaps even death of fat people, which can then be blamed on "obesity" as a comorbidity itself. The denial of medicalized fatphobia's harm to fat people and their health is a problem in all medical contexts, but is especially menacing in the context of a global pandemic in which life or death decisions likely have to be made swiftly, demonstrating the "biopolitical commitment ... to 'let die'" when it comes to disposable fat bodies.[57]

Moreover, the CSC guidelines, both in their exclusion of body size as a protected status as well as in their reliance on "clinical judgment," are more about how *not* to make a decision; in other words, their specificity recedes right at the moment they are supposed to be useful. In this way, CSC guidelines reveal their darker and more pragmatic purpose—to evade liability for things like discrimination lawsuits rather than to provide guidelines for ethical care. Ultimately, CSC guidelines eliminate the possibility of real accountability when it comes to decisions made for the allocation of resources in ways that directly harm fat patients and render them vulnerable to medical neglect.

Conclusion

Rhetorics of disposability toward fat people emerge as a contemporary manifestation of medicalized fatphobia, which has shifted and evolved to respond to the current most pressing global threat: the Covid pandemic. In this essay, I have demonstrated how medicalized fatphobia takes form as a practice enacted by both medical professionals (through CDC public health messaging and CSC documents) as well as through popular discourse that relies on medical logics (as witnessed in the public tweet responses and conversations analyzed above). Parsing out the distinguishing features of rhetorics of disposability can help scholars better understand how medicalized fatphobia operates uniquely in the context of a global pandemic (and, hopefully, challenge and disrupt its rhetorical impacts) while also emphasizing the need to examine how rhetorics of disposability operate in a variety of contexts to harm other vulnerable groups, especially those that exist at various intersections of marginalized identities.

Throughout the course of this analysis, I have uncovered four defining features of rhetorics of disposability: (1) positioning a vulnerable group as a drain on resources, (2) promoting logics of personal responsibility for vulnerable groups in the context of social problems, (3) blaming/scapegoating a vulnerable group for social issues, and (4) trivializing death, harm, and suffering of a vulnerable group. These features reveal the common types of arguments deployed across a variety of rhetorical texts and contexts to construct fat bodies as disposable, ultimately rendering them unworthy of care and life in the context of a global pandemic. My hope is that, by identifying these argumentative commonplaces or topoi, scholars and activists are better equipped to identify, critique, and challenge them in our scholarship, teaching, and personal lives.

Though this chapter focused on rhetorics of disposability that render specifically fat bodies unworthy of care and life, I imagine that the topoi of disposability identified above operate zoerhetorically in ways that cut across dynamics of power, privilege, and oppression, and can ultimately be applied to a variety of marginalized groups. Indeed, we can glean from the work of Giroux and various rhetorical scholars who theorize disposability that politics and discourses of disposability work across lines of race, class, and gender/sexuality to render a variety of marginalized bodies excessive, invisible, and destroyable in US culture.[58] Moreover, recent work on the intersection of anti-fatness and anti-blackness—most notably that of Sabrina Strings—illuminates the interrelated nature of anti-fatness and anti-blackness.[59] The intersection of these dynamics brings into view the ways in which anti-fat rhetorics of disposability might also serve a larger project of anti-blackness. For, when Black bodies and fat bodies are equated as they have been in much of Western culture, one way to ensure the elimination of Black bodies while obscuring the violent racism of such a project is to target fat bodies for annihilation. Indeed, rhetorics of disposability justify material annihilation. Disposability is certainly not an inherent property of fat bodies, nor is it applied to fat bodies singularly. A fertile area for future rhetorical scholarship involves examining how the four topoi of disposability proffered here do (or do not) hold up when applied to situations in which different types of marginalized bodies are implicated.

Another dynamic of rhetorics of disposability made visible by this specific case study is that such discourses become material in the ways that they are coded into specific kinds of tangible practice. In the context of the Covid pandemic, I revealed how anti-fat rhetorics of disposability are coded into tangible medical practice via CSC guidelines. However, rhetorics of disposability are neither confined to the Covid pandemic, nor exclusively anti-fat; rather, they ultimately target a variety of marginalized groups across a variety of cultural contexts. This means that there is a vast range of possible ways that such rhetorics are coded into tangible practice that result in harm and suffering for those various marginalized groups. Therefore, as we broaden our scholarly lenses out to consider the various ways vulnerable groups are rhetorically constructed as disposable, I hope that we can interrupt the harm and suffering of those groups as we start to gain a clearer picture of the types of practices that cause material harm. Rhetorics of disposability render vulnerable groups unworthy of care and life; thus, it is our job as critical rhetoricians to investigate how and where these discourses proliferate and advance more ethical ways of thinking and speaking about bodies rooted in a shared sense of humanity and solidarity with those deemed disposable.

NOTES

1. Juliana Kaplan, "I Got the COVID-19 Vaccine Because I'm Fat. You Should Too," *Insider*, March 8, 2021.
2. I use the word "fat" rather than a variety of euphemisms for larger bodies to align myself with fat activist movements that have worked to reclaim the word by imbuing it with a sense of neutrality and challenging the stigma associated with the word.
3. Nicole Lyn Pesce, "Am I a Jerk for Getting a COVID-19 Vaccine if I Feel Healthy and Work from Home?," *MarketWatch*, March 27, 2021.
4. Matthew J. Townsend, Theodore K. Kyle, and Fatima Cody Stanford, "COVID-19 and Obesity: Exploring Biologic Vulnerabilities, Structural Disparities, and Weight Stigma," *Metabolism: Clinical and Experimental* 110 (2020); S. M. Phelan et al., "Impact of Weight Bias and Stigma on Quality of Care and Outcomes for Patients with Obesity," *Obesity Reviews* 16, no. 4 (2015): 319–26.
5. Allison Rowland, *Zoetropes and the Politics of Humanhood* (Columbus: Ohio State University Press, 2020), 16.
6. Antonio Maturo, "Medicalization: Current Concept and Future Directions in a Bionic Society," *Mens Sana Monographs* 10, no. 1 (2012): 122.
7. Robin E. Jensen, "Improving Upon Nature: The Rhetorical Ecology of Chemical Language, Reproductive Endocrinology, and the Medicalization of Infertility," *Quarterly Journal of Speech* 101, no. 2 (2015): 330.
8. Jensen, "Improving Upon Nature," 331.
9. Peter Conrad, *The Medicalization of Society: On the Transformation of Human Conditions*

into Treatable Disorders (Baltimore, MD: John Hopkins University Press, 2007), 6.
10. In this essay, I use quotation marks around the word "obesity" to delegitimize its status as a diagnosis/disease and indicate its harmfulness and instability as a discourse.
11. Hailey Nicole Otis, "Tess Holliday's Queering of Body-Positive Activism: Disrupting Fatphobic Logics of Health and Resignifying Fat As Fit," *Women's Studies in Communication* 43, no. 2 (2020): 161.
12. Julie Guthman, "Neoliberalism & The Constitution of Contemporary Bodies," in *The Fat Studies Reader*, ed. Esther D. Rothblum, Sondra Solovay, and Marilyn Wann (New York: New York University Press, 2009), 194.
13. Traci Mann et al., "Medicare's Search for Effective Obesity Treatments: Diets Are Not the Answer," *American Psychologist* 62, no. 3 (2007): 220–33.
14. Christine Aramburu, Alegria Drury, and Margaret Louis, "Exploring the Association Between Body Weight, Stigma of Obesity, and Health Care Avoidance," *Journal of the American Academy of Nurse Practitioners* 14, no. 12 (2002): 554–61.
15. See Peter Kennedy, "The Contradictions of Capitalist Healthcare Systems," *Critique* 43, no. 2 (2015): 229; and Courtney Bailey, "Supersizing America: Fatness and Post-9/11 Cultural Anxieties," *The Journal of Popular Culture* 43, no. 3 (2010).
16. Shelley Wood, "Obesity and COVID-19: Theories and Blame Fill the Scientific Void," *TCTMD.Com*, April 21, 2020.
17. Ranjana Khanna, "Disposability," *Differences* 20, no. 1 (2009): 194.
18. Melissa W. Wright, *Disposable Women and Other Myths of Global Capitalism* (New York: Routledge, 2006), 4; Françoise Vergès, "The Age of Love," *Transformation* 47 (2001): 11.
19. Henry A. Giroux, "Beyond the Biopolitics of Disposability: Rethinking Neoliberalism in the New Gilded Age," *Social Identities* 14, no. 5 (2008): 604.
20. Henry A. Giroux, "Reading Hurricane Katrina: Race, Class, and the Biopolitics of Disposability," *College Literature* 33, no. 3 (2006): 171.
21. Lesley Gray and Carol MacDonald, "Morbid Obesity in Disasters: Bringing the 'Conspicuously Invisible' Into Focus," *International Journal of Environmental Research and Public Health* 13, no. 10 (2016): 1029. Giroux, "Reading Hurricane Katrina," 186.
22. Leland G. Spencer, "Bathroom Bills, Memes, and a Biopolitics of Trans Disposability," *Western Journal of Communication* 83, no. 5 (2019): 554.
23. Spencer, "Bathroom Bills," 543; Valerie N. Wieskamp and Cortney Smith, "'What to Do When You're Raped': Indigenous Women Critiquing and Coping through a Rhetoric of Survivance," *Quarterly Journal of Speech* 106, no. 1 (2020): 73; Lisa A. Flores, *Deportable and Disposable: Public Rhetoric and the Making of the "Illegal" Immigrant* (University Park:

Penn State University Press, 2020), 8.
24. Flores, *Deportable*, 9, 149.
25. Virginia Sole-Smith, "How Fatphobia Is Leading to Poor Care in the Pandemic," *Elemental*, January 11, 2021; Shikha Garg et al., "Hospitalization Rates and Characteristics of Patients Hospitalized with Laboratory-Confirmed Coronavirus Disease 2019—COVID-NET, 14 States, March 1–30, 2020," *Morbidity and Mortality Weekly Report* 69, no. 15 (2020): 458–64.
26. Dylan Abad, "CDC Study Reveals Connection Between Obesity and COVID-19 Hospitalizations," *ABC27 News*, May 6, 2021; Damian McNamara, "CDC Data Strengthens Link of Obesity, Severe COVID," *WebMD Health News*, March 9, 2021.
27. Meeta Shah, "The Failure of Public Health Messaging about COVID-19," *Scientific American*, September 3, 2020.
28. Jennifer Rainey Marquez, "A Failure to Communicate," *Georgia State University Research Magazine*, December 2, 2020; Shah, "Failure."
29. Public Health England, "New Obesity Strategy Unveiled as Country Urged to Lose Weight to Beat Coronavirus (COVID-19) and Protect the NHS," press release, Department of Health and Social Care, July 7, 2020.
30. Gina Tonic, "Why the Government's Anti-Obesity Strategy Won't Work," *VICE*, July 28, 2020.
31. Centers for Disease Control and Prevention (CDC), "Obesity, Race/Ethnicity, and COVID-19," *CDC.gov*, March 22, 2021. The invocation of race in a document that is primarily about Covid and "obesity" rates is notable and, unfortunately, outside the scope of this particular chapter. The conflation of race and "obesity" in this document perpetuates the myth of Blackness as a disease property by associating it with various comorbidities, as discussed by Raquel M. Robvais earlier in this volume.
32. CDC, "Obesity."
33. Angelina Sutin et al., "Perceived Discrimination and Physical, Cognitive, and Emotional Health in Older Adulthood," *American Journal of Geriatric Psychiatry* 23, no. 2 (2015): 171–79.
34. See Mann et al., "Medicare's Search," 220–33.
35. Giroux, "Reading Hurricane Katrina," 186.
36. Christy Harrison, "Covid-19 Does Not Discriminate by Body Weight," *Wired*, April 17, 2020.
37. Adrianna Rodriguez, "'Weight Isn't Always within Your Control': Why Some States Are Prioritizing Obesity Patients for the COVID-19 Vaccine," *USA TODAY*, March 8, 2021.

38. CNN, "The Risk of Covid-19 Is About 10 Times Higher," Twitter post, March 4, 2021, https://twitter.com/CNN/status/1367418555612995587.
39. CNBC, "CDC Study Finds Roughly 78% of People Hospitalized," Twitter post, March 8, 2021, https://twitter.com/CNBC/status/1368976290703945737.
40. Wright, *Disposable Women*, 2; Flores, *Deportable and Disposable*, 8.
41. Spencer, "Bathroom Bills," 554.
42. Institute of Medicine (U.S.) Forum on Medical and Public Health Preparedness for Catastrophic Events, "Summary of Guidance for Establishing Crisis Standards of Care for Use in Disaster Situations: A Letter Report," *Crisis Standards of Care: Summary of a Workshop Series* (Washington, DC: National Academies Press, 2010), https://www.ncbi.nlm.nih.gov/books/NBK32748/.
43. Allison Daniel, "There Are Many Reasons Why Obesity Puts People at Risk of Becoming Critically Ill from COVID-19," *Healthy Debate*, April 27, 2020.
44. Daniel, "Many Reasons."
45. Mike Baker and Sheri Fink, "At the Top of the Covid-19 Curve, How Do Hospitals Decide Who Gets Treatment?," *New York Times*, March 31, 2020.
46. Maria L. La Ganga, "Fat Shaming, BMI and Alienation: COVID-19 Brought New Stigma to Large-Sized People," *Los Angeles Times*, May 9, 2021.
47. California Department of Public Health, "California SARS-CoV-2 Pandemic Crisis Care Guidelines," Concept of Operations, Health Care Facility Surge Operations and Crisis Care (Sacramento: State of California Health and Human Services Agency, June 2020).
48. NYC Health, "COVID-19 Pandemic Patient Surge: Preparing for Crisis Care," City of New York, April 26, 2020, https://www1.nyc.gov/assets/doh/downloads/pdf/imm/covid-19-patient-surge-crisis-care.pdf.
49. "Alabama Crisis Standards of Care Guidelines," Alabama Department of Public Health, August 31, 2020, https://www.alabamapublichealth.gov/cep/assets/alabamacscguidelines2020.pdf.
50. "New Mexico Crisis Standards of Care Plan," New Mexico Department of Health, 2018, https://www.nmhealth.org/publication/view/plan/4877/.
51. Massachusetts Department of Public Health, "Crisis Standards of Care: Planning Guidance for the COVID-19 Pandemic," The Commonwealth of Massachusetts April 7, 2020, https://d279m997dpfwgl.cloudfront.net/wp/2020/04/CSC_April-7_2020.pdf.
52. Christine A. Tanner, "Thinking like a Nurse: A Research-Based Model of Clinical Judgment in Nursing," *Journal of Nursing Education* 45, no. 6 (2006): 204.
53. "Alabama Crisis."

54. Massachusetts Department of Public Health, "Crisis Standards."
55. California Department of Public Health, "California SARS-CoV-2."
56. See B. A. Teachman and K. D. Brownell, "Implicit Anti-Fat Bias Among Health Professionals: Is Anyone Immune?," *International Journal of Obesity* 25, no. 10 (2001): 1525–31; Janice A. Sabin, Maddalena Marini, and Brian A. Nosek, "Implicit and Explicit Anti-Fat Bias Among a Large Sample of Medical Doctors by BMI, Race/Ethnicity and Gender," *PLOS ONE* 7, no. 11 (2012): https://doi.org/10.1371/journal.pone.0048448.
57. Giroux, "Reading Hurricane Katrina," 180.
58. Giroux, "Reading Hurricane Katrina," 171–96; Flores, *Deportable*; Spencer, "Bathroom Bills," 542–59.
59. Sabrina Strings, *Fearing the Black Body: The Racial Origins of Fat Phobia* (New York: New York University Press, 2019).

Covid and Intersex

In/Essential Medical Management

Celeste E. Orr

INTERSEX PEOPLE, PEOPLE WITH BIOLOGICAL TRAITS THAT DEFY THE TRADItional male-female sex binary, face unique, disproportionally negative challenges during the Covid pandemic. Mainstream media and academia have devoted little attention to the issue, which is unsurprising given the long-standing silence and interphobic stigmatization faced by members of the intersex community. Though activist organizations like interACT: Advocates for Intersex Youth and Intersex Human Rights Australia offer recognition and resources, many intersex folks avoid Covid testing or treatment because of the ways that medical institutions have already harmed and traumatized them in the name of "cure."

Doctors around the world routinely subject intersex infants and children to various procedures—such as genital surgeries, also known as intersex genital mutilation (IGM)—hoping intersex people will better conform to the male-female sex/gender binaries. The ways in which intersex characteristics manifest can vary (e.g. genital, hormonal, genetic, chromosomal), and medical interventions vary accordingly. Prior to the pandemic, most North American doctors claimed interventions on intersex people to be "essential" because intersex variations constitute an "emergency";[1] that is, intersex traits are supposedly disabled, disordered, or diseased and ought to be eradicated at all costs. Intersex activists and Intersex Studies scholars have long demonstrated that these nonconsensual interventions are medically unnecessary, executed for discriminatory reasons, and constitute "medical abuses."[2] This position gained traction when, during Covid, many medical procedures were redesignated as "inessential" and postponed in order to curb the spread of the virus. As I followed and participated in debates around what should be deemed in/essential during the pandemic and witnessed the promotion of using telehealth to expand access to essential health services,[3] I wondered, how has in/essential rhetoric impacted IGM practices and rates during Covid? Furthermore, given the scant public commentary on the issue, how can the presence of something be examined in the absence of information?

During my search for information on the topic, I found only *one* statement about whether intersex medical management is being treated as in/essential. The statement was released in August 2020 by the Southern African gender equality nongovernmental organization (NGO), Gender Links (GL), and quotes Professor Solwayo Ngwenya, the acting chief executive officer of Mpilo Central Hospital in Zimbabwe: "The surgeries for intersex patients are deemed elective in nature, meaning their conditions are not life-threatening, hence not emergencies, so they are suspended" during Covid.[4] This suspension is significant for intersex people in Zimbabwe *and* to the broader, transnational intersex rights movement. Before I attend to this significance, I must digress: the supposed elective nature of these surgeries is not corroborated by two factors. First, Mpilo Central Hospital admitted they evaluated intersex people as young as *three weeks old* in 2019.[5] A three-week-old infant is *far* from being able to elect surgery. Additionally, Mpilo Central Hospital is not alone in previously advocating for and performing early surgeries. Medical professionals around the world often advocate for "surgeries, usually '*between 12 and 24 months of age*.'"[6] Nevertheless, the fact that surgeries are halted in Zimbabwe because of Covid and the language used by Ngwenya—these surgeries are "elective," "not emergencies," inessential—can bolster ongoing intersex human rights initiatives across the globe, namely banning nonconsensual intersex medical management like IGM.

Remarking on this suspension, Crystal Hendricks, coordinator for Intersex South Africa, claims, the suspension of surgeries "is not only happening in Zimbabwe alone but across the globe."[7] I unfortunately cannot corroborate Hendricks's claim; medical and health professionals, organizations, and institutions are not remarking publicly. The lack of commentary about this medical practice during the pandemic is unsurprising: it is incredibly controversial; there is a culture of silence around intersex issues that maintains interphobia and "naturalizes" the sex/gender dyads; there are no globally accepted medical guidelines concerning intersex medical management; and young intersex people have been at risk for decades because of the tendency of medical professionals to favor "normalizing" procedures. Yet I am confident Hendricks is right. I conjectured similarly early in the pandemic.[8]

Few countries, institutions, organizations, or medical professionals have publicly addressed this issue because doing so would put medical professionals and institutions in a tricky situation. If medical or health institutions publicly deemed IGM essential during the pandemic they would have likely been then met with a barrage of anti-interphobic critiques from intersex activists and Intersex Studies scholars, the general public, and over-worked, traumatized medical professionals concerning spreading the virus and depleting medical resources. Alternatively, if they deemed IGM *in*essential, these institutions would confirm what intersex activists and Intersex Studies scholars have been saying for decades: these nonconsensual surgeries are inessential. Either way, then, Zimbabwe's statement offers an opportunity to dislodge the privileged narrative that intersex traits are pathological aberrations in need of immediate "cure." Zimbabwe's suspension presents a means to pressure other medical institutions to break their silence, raise awareness about interphobic violence, and underscore intersex management as a human rights issue. As fewer intersex infants and children are subjected to surgery during the pandemic, medical institutions may not—and *should not*—go back to regarding IGM as a routine postpandemic practice. Narratives and debates surrounding what constitutes "essential medical care" during the pandemic, offer an opportunity to rethink the supposed essential nature of intersex medical management moving forward.

Thus, this chapter contributes to the "partial archive of the unfolding pandemic," as the editors note, *and* to the archiving of anti-interphobic work of activists and academics more broadly but does so in a unique fashion. I conceptualize this project as offering a *penumbral reading* of intersex issues during Covid;[9] that is, I turn attention to the ghostly, shadowy silences that accompany and enshroud the very limited public record about the issue. In essence, I sought to read the silence trailing what little information on the topic exists. A penumbral reading reveals how oppression and violence are maintained via remaining quiet, shadowy, unseen; the idea of in/essential medical care need not even be addressed when the group impacted is so marginalized, ignored, and rendered invisible. If the shadow of violence is behind one, unknown and suppressed—if the penumbra cannot be seen by the subject—then the violence can continue. Hence, this chapter aims to make the shadowy ghost of how interphobia underpins intersex people's experiences with the pandemic visible. To do so, I attend to the scant literature about this topic and build on said literature to pressure more medical institutions to break their silence on the in/essential nature of nonconsensual medical interventions devoted to maintaining compulsory modes of being.

Compulsory Dyadism and Intersex Medical Management

People with intersex traits undermine "compulsory dyadism," the cultural mandate that people cannot have intersex variations and challenge the sacrosanct male-female sex binary.[10] Given this cultural violation, intersex traits are referred to as *Disorders* of Sex Development (DSD) by medical professionals and are routinely conflated with diseases (e.g. cancer).[11] Given this characterization, I argue, intersex traits are simultaneously construed as violating "compulsory able-bodiedness."[12] The ideologies of pathologization and cure prompt and "justify" unnecessary and non-consensual interventions on infants and children, such as hormone replacement therapies (HRT) and surgical interventions (e.g. gonadectomies, vaginoplasties, phalloplasties, clitorectomies/clitoroplasties). In our ableist culture, any trait, embodiment, or identity deemed disabled, diseased, or disordered must be avoided, "cured," or eradicated because such traits are apparently disposable and unviable.

Additionally, intersex individuals violate "compulsory heterosexuality."[13] Many intersex folks are pathologized and surgeries are deemed essential because their biologies do not facilitate heterosexual, penis-in-vagina sex. Intersex people, therefore, are construed as (pathologically) queer, conjuring images of "sickness, dirtiness, and immorality."[14] Indeed, there are numerous accounts of intersex individuals sociomedically assigned female being encouraged to "get a boyfriend soon" postoperation, even when they are still "bleeding and in pain."[15] Doctors imply they should be comforted by the fact that a "normal" sized penis can fit into their medically de/re/constructed vaginas. The logics of compulsory dyadism, able-bodiedness, and heterosexuality are intertwined and often indistinguishable from each other. Intersex folks undermine compulsory dyadism; in turn, their biologies challenge compulsory heterosexuality; they are simultaneously pathologized and construed as violating compulsory able-bodiedness.[16]

To be clear, intersex variations in and of themselves rarely cause genuine medical or health issues. However, given that intersex people's biologies challenge compulsory modes of being, they are framed as medical emergencies and "appropriate *objects* [emphasis added] of medical intervention."[17] In a horribly ironic twist, the "curative" interventions medical professionals perform typically cause short- or long-term body-mind disabilities such as chronic pain, urinary issues, loss of sexual sensation, depression, anxiety, and incontinence.[18] These issues are often compounded because surgery is rarely a one-time occurrence;[19] surgeries tend to fail. There are many accounts of intersex people being subjected to well over a dozen surgeries during their lifetime.[20]

Moreover, medical practitioners have a long history of withholding medical diagnoses and records from intersex patients, advising parents/guardians to never disclose diagnoses or tell their intersex children why medical interventions took/take place. That is, medical professionals are "self-silencing" or encouraging parents/guardians to self-silence; there is a "rhetorical quieting" happening to ensure interphobic violence remains out of public consciousness and discourse. J. Logan Smilges, writing of rhetorical quieting, explains "quieting" "should not be confused with 'quietness,' which could be taken to mean passivity."[21] Remaining silent can be and often is an active choice. There is just as much power in silence as there is in speech; silence communicates a lot and defers power.[22] In this instance, it communicates shame and reveals that doctors exercise discursive and literal power over intersex people; intersex variations are apparently so shameful they should be hidden and not spoken about. And yet, intersex people *hear* the overwhelming quiet—they feel, experience, and embody the shadow of violence that remains silent—and respond in various ways: many spend years seeking out their medical records; others testify to strained familial bonds; some seek out intersex activist collectives; many explain the shame they endured and seek to remake what intersex means and how doctors respond to intersex traits.[23]

Given the discriminatory, nonconsensual, disabling, and silencing nature of prevailing medical protocol, activists and scholars have been advocating against these medical procedures for decades; they are, to borrow from Jonathan Alexander and Jacqueline Rhodes, "[articulating] resistance to regimes of sexualized normalization" that "disrupt and reroute ... discursive power."[24] Some influential NGOs have also supported these efforts. For example, the United Nations (UN) and WHO condemn IGM. The former classifies IGM as torture.[25] The latter urges doctors to defer surgeries until intersex people are old enough to consent.[26]

Unique and Disproportional Impact of Covid on Intersex People

While the fact that intersex people are inordinately negatively impacted by Covid has not infiltrated mainstream news or conversations, intersex activists, some NGOs, and a couple of medical associations have noted ways intersex people are struggling because of the pandemic. For example, Christina P. Tadiri and colleagues explain that gender and sex traits—including intersex traits—play a role in one's "infectious disease risk and outcomes, and severe acute respiratory syndrome coronavirus 2 appears to be no exception."[27] One's sex characteristics may influence their immune response. Hence, robust testing and data collection are imperative to preventing people from being disproportionately impacted. Moreover, the UN's Department of Global Communications reports that intersex people (and LGBT people) "are among the most vulnerable during" Covid.[28] The aim of this section is to outline the ways intersex people are negatively impacted by the pandemic, struggling against a culture of silence, and rendered disposable and unimportant. My claims, in part, echo Hailey Nicole Otis's observations earlier in this book that medicalized people—Otis specifically writes about the pathologization of fat people—are deemed disposable; their lives are sacrificial. I address body-mind health risks, economic strain, fear of seeking out medical care, and navigating interphobic family dynamics during stay-at-home orders.

As activist and scholar Morgan Carpenter explains, some people with intersex traits have underlying health risks that Covid may compound. Carpenter draws readers' attention to three examples. I explain them in turn and add examples to illustrate intersex people's risk during Covid. I must note, the health risks cannot be resolved by nonconsensual cosmetic interventions; indeed, some of the health risks I outline below stem from medically unnecessary, cosmetic procedures. First, Carpenter notes that some intersex people with chromosomal variations "can sometimes have cardiovascular issues."[29] Second, some intersex folks "are at risk of metabolic syndrome."[30] Third, Carpenter draws our attention to people with congenital adrenal hyperplasia (CAH), a diagnosis that falls under the DSD umbrella. This example requires more context.

People with CAH have a chronic adrenal condition in which one's adrenal glands do not produce enough cortisone. Cortisone aids the body in responding to stress or trauma. Mineralocorticoids (hormones that maintain water and salt balance) and androgens (steroid hormones) may also be affected. I must note, however, that not all people with CAH have intersex variations. CAH rarely causes intersex variations in people with XY chromosomes (assigned male). CAH sometimes causes intersex traits in XX individuals (assigned female). Thus, intersex traits can sometimes signal an underlying medical issue to address. The difference between XX and XY folks is because CAH is associated with higher levels of prenatal testosterone and may, consequently, "masculinize" an assigned female fetus. An assigned male's "masculine" traits (i.e., phallic structure) are not deemed intersex because said traits are expected and deemed normal. Assigned female intersex folks with CAH are presumed incongruous and often subjected to IGM. To clarify, these surgeries are *not* needed to manage CAH, but when intersex traits are identifiable, surgery often occurs. That said, people with CAH—including those with intersex characteristics—are vulnerable to Covid complications or death because they "face severe risks associated with stress and infection."[31]

I underscore: genital surgeries are *not* necessary to manage any of the medical issues Carpenter outlines. In fact, my next two examples—HRT and mental health disabilities—illustrate the health dangers that often come with medical intervention, dangers that Covid compounds. Many intersex people are coerced/forced into unnecessary, lifelong HRT regimens to ensure their physical characteristics align with their sociomedically assigned sex/gender. Additionally, intersex individuals who were subjected to sterilizing gonadectomies (removal of testes, ovaries, or ovotestes) must remain on HRT for their entire lives because the procedure removed their source of endogenous hormones. The problems here are manifold. During Covid, many intersex people (as well as trans, genderqueer, and nonbinary folks) have run out of or have been worried they will run out of vital HRT prescriptions because of federal, state, or provincial restrictions deeming these life-saving/-sustaining prescriptions inessential.[32] Some intersex people *need* HRT to live and a lack of access to HRT puts these people in danger. This dependency, however, can be paradoxically detrimental to one's long-term health and wellbeing. In addition to the fact that continued use of HRT increases one's risk of developing, for example, osteoporosis, it puts one at an increased risk of developing certain types of cancers (e.g. prostate, breast/chest, testicular).[33] We cannot ignore the ironic fact that supposed medical treatment puts intersex people in this grave medical situation, a situation that Covid worsens. It was clear early in the pandemic that people with underlying health conditions like cancer are particularly vulnerable when infected because of their compromised immune systems.

Many intersex people report experiencing mental health disabilities such as suicidal ideation, anxiety, and depression. Intersex folks are clear that these mental health disabilities have been caused by medical intervention and surveillance as well as interphobia broadly speaking, *not* because they have intersex traits. In their Australia-based study, Tiffany Jones and colleagues report that "42% of [intersex] participants had thought about self-harm and 26% had engaged in it; 60% had thought about suicide and 19% had attempted it."[34] Amy Rosenwohl-Mack and colleagues' US-based study concerning intersex people's mental health reports that "More than half of participants (53.6%) described their mental health as fair/poor ... 61.1% reported ever having been told they had a depressive disorder, 62.6% an anxiety disorder, and 40.9% PTSD," and "61.7% of the sample screening positive for clinically significant depressive symptoms in the past week."[35]

A couple months into the pandemic, it was clear that "people living with long-term mental health problems will remain vulnerable over the coming months."[36] Those who are vulnerable have been and still remain so over three years later and the fact that mental health disabilities (e.g., anxiety, depression, substance abuse) have been on the rise because of the pandemic has been proven time and time again. According to Nirmita Panchal and colleagues' US-based study, over 40 percent of adults surveyed in January 2021 reported various mental health issues, stemming from, for instance, loneliness, job and income loss, illness and deaths, and a lack of child care.[37] The authors underscore that racialized people, young adults, people who experience job loss, parents/guardians, and essential workers are among the most impacted. Others also rightly note that senior people's mental health is precarious during the pandemic, particularly queer, racialized, and disabled seniors, those experiencing poverty, and those living in (isolated) care facilities.[38] Additionally, LGBTQ folks are "psychologically vulnerable" to mental health disabilities, especially during Covid.[39] LGBTQ youths isolated in unsupportive environments and queer people whose gender-affirming care has overwhelmingly been deemed inessential are particularly vulnerable. And, as I illustrate, so are intersex people, but the culture of silence around them prevents most people from recognizing and attending to this fact. Indeed, the "I" that is often attached to the LGBTQ acronym remains in the shadows.

Concerns with people's mental health will remain a long-term issue that will not be resolved when the pandemic subsides. Indeed, "History has shown that the mental health impact of disasters outlasts the physical impact."[40] Moreover, oppressive material realities—living in a capitalistic world that breeds economic precarity; living in a racist, colonial, sexist, queerphobic, cisgenderist, fatphobic, ableist, sanist, and interphobic world—inevitably cause mental health disabilities that require radical systemic change. The popular neoliberal advice that one simply needs to access mental health care (as if doing so is destigmatized and always easy to do), phone a friend (assuming one has a friend willing to offer this emotional labor), or download a meditation app (are you kidding me?) will not do.[41] Mental health disabilities are not inherently a person's "problem" to solve individually as many Disability and Mad Studies scholars attest, but are rather "cultural and political [phenomena]."[42]

Assuming intersex people's mental health disabilities have exacerbated during the pandemic is prudent. And the barriers to receiving affordable and destigmatizing mental health care is concerning for intersex people. Not only are mental health disabilities and seeking out mental health care stigmatized to varying degrees,[43] and not all mental health care providers offer anti-interphobic (or anti-oppressive) mental health care, as I explain in more detail below, but also intersex people are more likely to be economically precarious and experience poverty. Hence, gaining access to mental health care may be economically prohibitive. It is inevitable that intersex people's mental health disabilities have worsened amid Covid. Yet, continuing the culture of silence around intersex issues, these issues have been overwhelmingly overlooked during Covid.

Intersex people are more likely to live in poverty and "tend to work casual day jobs that have dried up amid lockdown measures."[44] To understand why intersex people are more likely to live in poverty and work in precarious positions one must look to education and interphobic job discrimination. While there is little research around intersex people and education, Jones and colleagues' study demonstrates that intersex people are much less likely to have positive educational experiences: "Only a quarter of participants rated their overall education experiences positively and there were many reports of bullying based on physical or other aspects of having a variation."[45] Many intersex individuals report, for instance, being bullied by peers and teachers, their education experience was interphobic (e.g., sex and biology education), a sense of shame around their bodies, and not being provided antidiscriminatory counseling services. As a result, intersex people are more likely to leave school and less likely to pursue education. Jones and colleagues' study confirms that 18 percent of the intersex people surveyed "had only had a primary school education."[46]

Consequently, many intersex people struggle to become economically secure in a precarious, capitalistic, neoliberal job market that increasingly demands advanced degrees. Additionally, intersex individuals report experiencing interphobic job discrimination, particularly if their intersex characteristics are visible (e.g. an intersex woman having supposedly excessive facial or body hair due her hormones).[47] Lack of education coupled with interphobic job discrimination while on the capitalistic job market, in part, explains why intersex people are disproportionally likely to live in poverty and experience economic precarity. This precarity is rooted in interphobia and is compounded by, for example, racism, sexism, queerphobia, ableism, sanism, and fatphobia. And, of course the Covid pandemic has only exacerbated these issues, leaving countless people—particularly the most marginalized—destitute because they have lost their jobs, cannot work due to illness, are in debt from accrued medical bills, and so on.

And yet, intersex activists are determined, performing largely unrecognized labor to support intersex people. Bria Brown-King (2020), a program coordinator at interACT, recognizes the ways intersex folks are impacted by the pandemic and offers advice and recourses on interACT's web page.[48] Drawing attention to the fact that intersex people face interphobia inside the home, Brown-King notes many intersex people are likely "navigating challenging family dynamics" during lockdown.[49] Indeed, many intersex people report parents inflicting intense gendered social conditioning that is extremely stressful, particularly if they do not identify with the sociomedically assigned gender/sex.[50]

Many intersex youths are also subjected to various nonconsensual medical "treatments" prescribed by doctors that parents administer at home, such as HRT and vaginal dilation that are unwanted and, as with the latter, constitute sexual assault. Vaginal dilation "involves dilating assigned girl children and adolescents with hard dildo-like instruments whose vaginas are deemed too small or shallow to accommodate a prospective 'normal' sized penis."[51] Dilation can be prescribed for months or *years*. While doctors often perform vaginal dilation, parents—typically mothers[52]—are tasked with dilating their children at home. Mothers, "are compelled to perform this abusive, traumatizing act because, (1) mothers are disproportionately expected to make decisions about and 'care' for their children... and (2) dilation will not be read as sexual abuse if performed by the mother rather than the father due to gender norms."[53] While I outline below that I maintain IGM interventions have reduced during the pandemic, dilation (and HRT) are interventions that can and likely did continue during the pandemic. While there are no available statistics on this matter—unsurprisingly, given that statistics concerning intersex patients are rarely (if ever) publicly released "because disclosure of such information discloses human rights violations"[54]—it is reasonable to assume that parents were instructed to dilate their children at home more during the pandemic as compared to prepandemic for three reasons. First, this procedure need not take place in a doctor's office, hospital, or clinic. Hence, second, there was already a precedent for doctors to instruct parents to administer this prescription at home; and, third, countless medical appointments/consultations have been taking place over the phone/computer during the pandemic to prevent exposure to Covid. Undoubtedly, many intersex people are navigating challenging family dynamics during the pandemic, dynamics that can be profoundly physically and psychologically traumatizing.

Brown-King and Carpenter also underscore that seeking out medical care, including Covid testing and treatment, might be distressing given that many intersex people have experienced medical trauma.[55] Given this history, some intersex folks report avoiding doctors for years, which often compounds illness and disabilities.[56] Additionally, many intersex individuals avoid doctors because medical professionals often coerce intersex patients to undergo unnecessary procedures, such as dehumanizing genital examinations/displays that constitute sexual assault and abuse.[57] Consequently, Brown-King reminds intersex individuals that "it's okay to say, 'no' to unnecessary tests and medical examinations. Testing for Covid shouldn't require questions about genitalia or sex traits."[58]

Some of the concerns and negative impacts of Covid outlined thus far are encapsulated in Alex David's testimony: despite their underlying health conditions, David explains they are "worried about going to the hospital for any issues" because of their traumatic experiences with IGM (David notes they have PTSD).[59] David continues, "My specialist told me if I caught COVID-19, it would be potentially deadly."[60] Given these issues and harmful impacts of Covid on intersex people, interACT executive director Kimberly Zieselman, to borrow the editors' of this collection expression, "exemplifying the ameliorating possibilities of resistance," implores US Congress to "Include Intersex People in COVID-19 Relief" in an open letter.[61] Like Zieselman, intersex activists around the world have been working to draw people's attention to intersex human rights issues and intersex people's struggles for decades, and that did not subside during the pandemic. This activist work is indispensable given that, as the discussion above illustrates, intersex people's struggles have only exacerbated during the pandemic: "If the coronavirus hits hardest at the margins, among the most marginalized are those born intersex."[62] While a few folks attend to this reality, the fact that intersex people are so marginalized is clear given the lack of mainstream medical commentary around intersex people's hardships during the pandemic. Intersex people deserve better; their struggles should never be rendered invisible.

Intersex Medical Management, Covid, and In/Essential Medical Care

M (pseud.) laments: "During the pandemic... no one speaks of intersex persons."[63] M is right. While I draw readers' attention to the smattering of pieces that address how intersex people are navigating the pandemic above, there is a lack of attention paid to intersex issues, particularly around how medical professionals are (not) proceeding with intersex medical management during Covid. Even influential organizations invested in people's wellbeing, who advise on what is or what should be deemed in/essential care, *and* condemn IGM did not publicly urge people, countries, or doctors to view/classify nonconsensual surgical practices enacted on intersex people as inessential during the pandemic. For example, the UN and WHO offer no recommendations or comments about in/essential medical care for intersex people—a silence that leaves intersex people vulnerable to violence.

As noted, Zimbabwe is unique for publicly explaining that surgeries performed on intersex people have been halted during the pandemic. Before I outline the implications of this suspension, I address what the lack of commentary regarding whether surgical interventions enacted on unconsenting young intersex people are deemed in/essential during the pandemic tells us. Amid countless publicized debates and published guidelines about what should be deemed in/essential medical care, why did the routine surgical procedures intersex infants and children are subjected to go largely unmentioned during the pandemic? While knowledge about intersex people and issues are growing due to the work performed by intersex activists and Intersex Studies scholars, this knowledge is not entirely mainstream. As a result, it is unsurprising that this matter was not actively addressed. The lack of public concern with whether "normalizing" surgical intervention for intersex folks is deemed in/essential during the pandemic is a reflection of the dearth of public knowledge about interphobic medical violence and intersex human rights issues.

The lack of commentary around this medical practice during the pandemic is unsurprising for many more reasons: IGM is a controversial topic and is, therefore, often avoided; there are no globally accepted medical guidelines concerning intersex medical management; intersex infants and children are typically at risk because of the tendency for medical practitioners to favor "normalizing" procedures to maintain compulsory modes of being; and there is a culture of silence around intersex people, experiences, and issues to, in part, maintain the illusion that compulsory dyadism, heterosexuality, and able-bodiedness are "normal" and "natural." I want to elaborate on this culture of silence. As noted, medical professionals and institutions are tight-lipped when it comes disclosing information about intersex diagnoses and surgical procedures; there is a long history of medical practitioners withholding diagnoses and records from patients; medical professionals have advised parents to not disclose diagnoses or tell their intersex children why medical interventions take place; and intersex children have been discouraged from talking about their bodies, diagnoses, and medical experiences. Lying and silence have been a part of intersex medical management for decades and, as we know, silence is incredibly powerful and can lead to violence being ignored. The failure of doctors, organizations, and institutions to publicly address how intersex people are or are not being surgically "treated" during the pandemic cannot be construed as an oversight, but a continued investment in maintaining this culture of silence and ensuring the maltreatment of intersex people remains out of public consciousness. The lack of commentary communicates medical professionals' and institutions' investment in maintaining "their jurisdiction over intersex."[64]

In April 2020, I remarked, despite heated debates around what is deemed in/essential medical care (e.g., abortions), "There have been no formal statements concerning the medical management of intersex infants and children since the COVID-19 outbreak."[65] Since penning that piece, I have come across one country or medical professional, organization, or institution to remark on the in/essential nature of enacting nonconsensual surgeries on intersex people during Covid. In early August 2020, Lungelo Ndhlovu reports on behalf of GL, during the pandemic "Surgeries for intersex people in Zimbabwe have been indefinitely postponed."[66] Ndhlovu quotes Ngwenya, the acting chief executive officer of Mpilo Central Hospital in Zimbabwe: "The surgeries for intersex patients are deemed elective in nature, meaning their conditions are not life-threatening, hence not emergencies, so they are suspended" during the pandemic.[67]

Remarking on the suspension of intersex surgeries in Zimbabwe, Hendricks, the coordinator for Intersex South Africa, claims, "the suspension of intersex operations due to COVID-19 is not only happening in Zimbabwe alone but across the globe."[68] I unfortunately cannot substantiate Hendricks's claim given that medical and health professionals, organizations, and institutions across the globe are self-silencing; there is a rhetorical quieting happening. As noted, Smilges, writes of rhetorical quieting that quieting "should not be confused with 'quietness,' which could be taken to mean passivity."[69] There is just as much power in silence as there is in speech; silence communicates a lot.[70] In this instance, silence communicates that these professionals, organizations, and institutions do not want to draw attention to the fact that IGM rates have decreased because, if they do, they admit IGM was never really essential.

Yet, I am confident Hendricks is correct in stating that Covid has halted IGM procedures because countries worldwide reported disruptions to, for example, medical resource supplies, life-saving care and surgeries, noncommunicable disease diagnoses and treatments, and blood transfusions.[71] As we know, and as underscored by Molly Margaret Kessler, Michael Aylward, and Bernard Trappey in this volume, medical professionals around the world were not simply struggling to "keep up" with limited resources; they were and remain confronted with fear, anxiety, and stress. They were confronting the trauma of witnessing mass deaths and overwhelmed hospital morgues. And we can only anticipate the long-term consequences medical professionals will deal with because of this sustained trauma. Continuing to routinely perform genital surgeries on intersex infants and children so they can better approximate compulsory modes of being during this crisis seems inconceivable.

Even though I was disheartened that I could only find one country to publicly address the matter, I am hopeful that activists and scholars around the world can leverage the fact that Zimbabwe postponed surgeries because of Covid, specifically by underscoring the discursive shift used to justify this suspension. Unlike dominant medical narratives that portray intersex variations as emergencies, life-threatening, disordered, diseased, or disabled, Ngwenya's language echoes and confirms what intersex people, activists, and scholars have been correctly stating for decades: intersex traits are not life-threatening and not emergencies; IGM is inessential; these life-altering surgeries should not take place on nonconsenting infants and children for discriminatory purposes. In short, these linguistic and policy shifts are momentous during the pandemic and can have significant impacts postpandemic as well.

Unlike other medical interventions that have been deemed inessential in various parts of the world and have been leveraged to support discriminatory policies and ideologies (e.g. sexist, antiabortion and cisgenderist, anti-gender-affirming policies and ideologies), the implications of deeming intersex surgical interventions inessential during the pandemic is uniquely positive. The medical establishment's investment in compulsory dyadism has unequivocally communicated to intersex people that they do not fit and, therefore, need to be "fixed" and rendered invisible—a culture invested in compulsory modes of being is not expansive enough to recognize and celebrate intersex people's beauty, differences, and knowledges. Due to this violent oppression, the pandemic has been particularly traumatic for intersex people. Moreover, some intersex activists note that the pandemic impedes on advancing their activist work.[72]

And yet, strangely positive things happened: fewer intersex infants and children have been subjected to IGM during the pandemic, *and* Zimbabwe set a linguistic precedent by explicitly naming these procedures elective, inessential. To be sure, this is not a legal precedent, but this linguistic precedent still holds power insofar as those of us invested in intersex human rights can appeal to it. I recognize doing so could be interpreted as troubling because, in essence, one is appealing to a problematic figure within intersex activism and Intersex Studies scholarship, a medical professional, to confirm what intersex folks have been saying for decades. That said, there is utility in doing so because one can point to this precedent to put pressure on other medical professionals, organizations, and institutions to explain whether they have been treating IGM as in/essential and why. Not only that, the silence of other medical professionals, institutions, and organizations seem that much louder when one lone voice actively stakes a claim on the in/essential nature of IGM; those who have remained silent can be pressured to also vocalize a claim; indeed, as the editors' of the book note, "talk," and I emphasize silence here as well, "[matters] to the status of public life." While some intersex activist work has understandably been stalled because of the pandemic, it will not be stalled forever, and appealing to this precedent can become another tool both activists and scholars can appeal to in advancing intersex human rights.

By drawing attention to this positive, I in no way suggest it outweighs any trauma endured pre-, during, or postpandemic. As I have illustrated, intersex people suffered greatly during this pandemic. I also do not want to understate the significance of a global decline in IGM procedures and a country formally stating these procedures have been halted because they are inessential. Without a doubt there is much work that remains to be done to secure justice and reparations for intersex people across the globe. As activists and scholars invested in intersex human rights issues and outlawing IGM continue this invaluable work, this strangely positive thing can be appealed to to bolster arguments against IGM and narratives that claim intersex characteristics constitute life-threatening emergencies warranting immediate, nonconsensual, mutilating surgical intervention.

Conclusion

To be clear, this chapter is no way undermining the invaluable work medical professionals are doing right now to deal with the pandemic; indeed, as Kessler, Trappey, and Aylward's contribution to this book demands, people ought not simply recognize this traumatizing labor, but understand how these medical practitioners have been dehumanized and objectified and push back against said dehumanization and objectification. Medical personnel were and are in great danger, risking their lives for the global community often without enough resources. Indeed, many have experienced unspeakable trauma and many have died. I am also not claiming that only essential medical care ought to be available to people when the pandemic subsides. However, I am inviting everyone to think critically about, reflect on, and actively oppose the supposed essential nature of these *nonconsensual, irreversible, cosmetic* interventions on intersex infants and children.

To reiterate, the pandemic is a reason to delay these surgeries because they are not imperative to one's health or wellbeing. When the pandemic subsides, there is an opportunity for the medical community and general population to resist the silence, violence, and violence in silence revealed by this penumbral reading via vocally and publicly contesting the supposed necessity of irreversible, nonconsensual, cosmetic interventions on intersex individuals. So many scholars, activists, and cultural critics have noted that we cannot go back to "business as usual" after the pandemic. The pandemic clearly reveals that said business places marginalized populations and the environment in danger. As fewer intersex infants and children are being subjected to the surgical knife during the pandemic, all of us must work to ensure that the medical institution does not go back to subjecting intersex infants and children to cosmetic procedures postpandemic.

NOTES

1. Katrina Karkazis, *Fixing Sex: Intersex Medical Authority, and Lived Experience* (Durham, NC: Duke University Press, 2008), 96.
2. Emi Koyama, "Medical Abuse of Intersex Children and Child Sexual Abuse," in *Introduction to Intersex Activism: A Guide for Allies*, comp. Emi Koyama (Portland, OR: Intersex Initiative Portland, 2003), 2.
3. Janis Border and Celeste E. Orr, "Abortion Is Always Essential Medical Care," *Impact*

Ethics, May 18, 2020. Centers for Disease Control and Prevention, "Using Telehealth to Expand Access to Essential Health Services During the COVID-19 Pandemic," *COVID-19 Archive Content*, June 10, 2020.
4. Solwayo Ngwenya qtd. by Lungelo Ndhlovu, "Intersex Surgeries Halted During Covid-19," *Gender Links*, August 7, 2020.
5. Ndhlovu, "Intersex Surgeries Halted."
6. Markus Bauer and Daniela Truffer, "Intersex Genital Mutilations: Human Rights Violations of Children with Variations of Sex Anatomy," NGO Report on the Answers to the List of Issues (LoI) in Relation to the Initial Periodic Report of Germany on the Convention on the Rights of Persons with Disabilities (CRPD), 2015, 30.
7. Crystal Hendricks in Ndhlovu, "Intersex Surgeries Halted."
8. Celeste E. Orr, "COVID-19: Intersex and 'Essential' Medical Care," *Impact Ethics*, April 15, 2020.
9. I thank the editors of this collection for helping me think through this concept and refine my understanding of reading silence.
10. Celeste E. Orr, *Cripping Intersex* (Vancouver: University of British Columbia, 2022); Celeste E. Orr, "Exorcising Intersex and Cripping Compulsory Dyadism" (PhD diss., University of Ottawa, 2018).
11. See Orr, *Cripping Intersex*; Georgiann Davis, *Contesting Intersex: The Dubious Diagnosis* (New York: New York University Press, 2015).
12. Orr, *Cripping Intersex*. Robert McRuer, "Compulsory Able-Bodiedness and Queer/Disabled Existence," in *The Disability Studies Reader*, 4th ed., ed. Lennard J. Davis (New York: Routledge, 2013), 369.
13. Adrienne Rich, "Compulsory Heterosexuality and Lesbian Existence," *Signs* 5, no. 4 (1980): 631; Orr, *Cripping Intersex*.
14. Orr, *Cripping Intersex*. J. Logan Smilges, "White Squares to Black Boxes: Grindr, Queerness, Rhetorical Silence," *Rhetorical Review* 38, no. 1 (2019): 81.
15. Daniela Truffer, "It's a Human Rights Issue," *Narrative Inquiry in Bioethics* 5, no. 2 (2015): 112.
16. Orr, *Cripping Intersex*.
17. Robert Sparrow, "Gender Eugenics? The Ethics of PGD for Intersex Conditions," *American Journal of Bioethics* 13, no. 10 (2013): 34.
18. Orr, *Cripping Intersex*.
19. "Evidence Brief: Inform Your Practice Because LGBTQ Health Matters," Rainbow Health Ontario, www.RainbowHealthOntario.ca, August 2011, 1; Orr *Cripping Intersex*.
20. Orr, *Cripping Intersex*.

21. Smilges, "White Squares," 80.
22. Cheryl Glenn, *Unspoken: A Rhetoric of Silence* (Carbondale: Southern Illinois University Press, 2004).
23. See Katelyn Dykstra, "Charting Intersex: Intersex Life-Writing and the Medical Record," in *Bodies in Transition in the Health Humanities*, ed. Lisa M. DeTora and Stephanie M. Hilger (London: Routledge, 2019), 35–44; Kimberly Zieselman, "Invisible Harm," *Narrative Inquiry in Bioethics* 5, no. 2 (2015): 124; Celeste E. Orr and Amanda D. Watson, "'Usually the Mother': Dilation and the Medical Management of Intersex Children," in *From Band-Aids to Scalpels: Experiences in/of Medicine*, ed. Rohini Bannerjee and Karim Mukhida (Bradford: Demeter Press, 2021), 65–83; Karkazis, *Fixing Sex*.
24. Jonathan Alexander and Jacqueline Rhodes, "Queer Rhetoric and the Pleasures of the Archive," *Enculturation* 1, no. 13 (2012).
25. Office of the High Commissioner for Human Rights, "Intersex Awareness Day—Wednesday 26 October," *United Nations*, October 24, 2016.
26. World Health Organization, *Sexual Health, Human Rights and the Law* (Geneva: WHO Press, 2015).
27. Christina P. Tadiri et al., "The Influence of Sex and Gender Domains on COVID-19 Cases and Mortality," *Canadian Medical Association Journal* 192, no. 36 (2020): E1041.
28. Department of Global Communications, "UN Supports LGBTI Community During COVID-19 Pandemic," United Nations, June 15, 2020.
29. Morgan Carpenter, "Intersex People and COVID-19," Intersex Human Rights Australia.
30. Carpenter, "Intersex People."
31. Carpenter, "Intersex People."
32. Amie Bishop, *Vulnerability Amplified: The Impact of the COVID-19 Pandemic on LGBTIQ People* (New York: OutRight Action International, 2020).
33. Orr, *Cripping Intersex*; Karen A. Walsh, "'Normalizing' Intersex Didn't Feel Normal or Honest to Me," *Narrative Inquiry in Bioethics* 5, no. 2 (2015): 119–22.
34. Tiffany Jones et al., *Intersex: Stories and Statistics from Australia* (Cambridge: Open Book Publishers, 2016), 3.
35. Amy Rosenwohl-Mack et al., "A National Study on the Physical and Mental Health of Intersex Adults on the U.S.," *PLOS ONE*, 15, no. 10 (2020): 7, 8.
36. Kelly Winstanley et al., "Rising to the Challenges of COVID-19: The Front Line and Support for People with Long-Term Mental Health Problems and the Response of Northern Healthcare," *British Journal of Mental Health Nursing* 9, no. 3 (2020): 1.
37. See Shoshana Magnet and Celeste E. Orr, "Feminist Loneliness Studies," *Feminist Theory* 23, no. 1 (2022): 3–22. Nirmita Panchal et al., "The Implications of COVID-19 for

Mental Health and Substance Use," *Kaiser Family Foundation*, February 10, 2021.
38. Ontario Senior Pride, "Long-Term Care, COVID-19 and Ontario's 2S-LGBTQ+ Seniors: A Call to Action," October 14, 2020.
39. John P. Salerno, Natasha D. Williams, and Karina A. Gattamorta, "LGBTQ Populations: Psychologically Vulnerable Communities in the COVID-19 Pandemic," *American Psychological Association* 12, no. S1 (2020): S239.
40. Panchal et al., "Implications."
41. See Magnet and Orr, "Feminist Loneliness Studies," 8–9.
42. See Brenda A. LeFrançois, Robert Menzies, and Geoffrey Reaume, eds., *Mad Matters: A Critical Reader in Canadian Mad Studies* (Toronto: Canadian Scholars' Press, 2013). Ann Cvetkovich, *Depression: A Public Feeling* (Durham, NC: Duke University Press), 1.
43. LeFrançois, Menzies, and Reaume, *Mad Matters*.
44. Rachel Savage, "Isolation for Intersex People: Coronavirus Revives Trauma," *Reuters*, April 23, 2020.
45. Jones et al., *Intersex*, 4.
46. Jones et al., *Intersex*, 4.
47. Jones, et al., *Intersex*, 131, 151.
48. Bria Brown-King, "Intersex Resources in the Time of COVID-19," *interACT*, https://interactadvocates.org/intersex-covid-19/.
49. Brown-King, "Intersex Resources."
50. See Sean Saifa Wall, "Standing at the Intersections: Navigating Life as a Black Intersex Man," *Narrative Inquiry in Bioethics* 5, no. 2 (2015): 117–19; Karkazis, *Fixing Sex*.
51. Orr and Watson, "Usually the Mother," 73.
52. Koyama, "Medical Abuse."
53. Orr and Watson, "Usually the Mother," 66.
54. Morgan Carpenter, "Public Consultation on Protection Against Violence and Discrimination Based on Sexual Orientation and Gender Identity," United Nations, January 25, 2017 (Geneva, Switzerland).
55. Brown-King, "Intersex Resources"; Carpenter, "Intersex People."
56. See Sherri A. Groveman, "Sex, Lies and Androgen Insensitivity Syndrome," *Canadian Medical Association Journal* 154, no. 12 (1996): 1832–33.
57. See Koyama, "Medical Abuse"; Orr and Watson, "'Usually the Mother'"; Orr, *Cripping Intersex*.
58. Brown-King, "Intersex Resources."
59. Alex David qtd. by Savage, "Isolation for Intersex People."
60. Savage, "Isolation for Intersex People."

61. Kimberly Zieselman, "Congress: Include Intersex People in COVID-19 Relief," *interACT*, April 9, 2020.
62. Savage, "Isolation for Intersex People."
63. Pushpesh Kumar and Debomita Mukherjee, "Subordinate and Marginalised Masculinities and the COVID-19 Pandemic," *Engage* 56, no. 11 (2021).
64. Davis, *Contesting Intersex*, 54.
65. Orr, "COVID-19: Intersex and 'Essential' Medical Care."
66. Ndhlovu, "Intersex Surgeries Halted."
67. Ngwenya qtd. by Ndhlovu, "Intersex Surgeries Halted."
68. Hendricks in Ndhlovu, "Intersex Surgeries Halted."
69. Smilges, "White Squares," 80.
70. Glenn, *Unspoken*.
71. International Federation of Red Cross and Red Crescent Societies, *COVID-19 Outbreak 9-Month Update* (2020), https://reliefweb.int/sites/reliefweb.int/files/resources/MDR00005OU21.pdf.
72. Bishop, *Vulnerability Amplified*, 61.

PART 3

Remedy and Resistance

Covid and Shared Black Health

Rethinking Nonviolence in the Dual Pandemics

DiArron M.

DURING THE 2020 LOCKDOWNS, SOCIAL MEDIA KEPT ME UPDATED ON COVID'S impact on my close circles. The news kept me abreast of Covid's larger picture. Amid this terrifying and unprecedented reality, a sad normality competed with Covid for headlines. Ahmaud Arbery was murdered by white racist vigilantes in my home state. Police murdered Breonna Taylor in her sleep. They also lynched George Floyd in the middle of the streets while a helpless crowd could do nothing but record the badged thugs. Then something happened. Uprisers took to the streets. In response, Atlanta's mayor appeared on the news to reprimand the uprisers for neglecting *nonviolence*. I was disappointed and hurt. With all the violence that had been perpetrated against Black people just that year, why was now the time to call for *nonviolence*? Is *nonviolence* an idea that exclusively polices Black responses to violence? I asked myself: what is *nonviolence* in a world where Black people can be killed for sleeping?

    I felt that the uprisers wondered the same thing. The mayor, the uprisers, and I were negotiating questions of anti-black violence and Covid within the context of a communal discourse. We were undeniably connected by the exigencies of the moment and the reverberations that would emanate from our responses. Even if our perspectives and strategies were not shared, our future physical, emotional, social, and political health would be. The conversations being held in homes, Zoom meetings, and so forth about Covid's disproportionate impact on Black people's physical health, and the uprising against the centuries-old anti-black threat to all manners of Black health both exemplified that interconnectedness. Our words and our actions negotiated our shared Black health.

Therefore, I joined the uprisers in downtown Atlanta to show any hegemonic power that we were willing to take justice even if we had to do it by less acceptable means. We were met with police in riot gear and eventually the National Guard. We had no guns. We had no intention of harming people. Still, I had a rifle brandished in my face. What had we done wrong? Had we murdered someone on a run? In their sleep? In the middle of the street? No. We were doing something that the hegemonic force deemed much worse. We were protesting anti-black violence *violently*.

The summer 2020 uprisings that erupted across the globe were prompted mostly by the national and international coverage of a pandemic of Black lynchings. George Floyd's video-captured murder by Minnesota Police seemed to be the final straw. In the weeks that followed, people flooded the streets of other major cities. According to the Armed Conflict Location & Event Data Project (ACLED), an overwhelming number of these uprisings resembled the *nonviolent* protests made popular in American consciousness during the American civil rights movement. Others featured property damage and commandeering resources from corporations. Reports at the time suggested that many Americans believed this to be the action of outside agitators.[1] The uprisings also came a little over two months after the United States went into lockdown, transpiring at a period when the public had very little knowledge of how the virus spread. Despite this danger, people took to the street. For many like myself, the threat of Covid was less intimidating than anti-black predatory policing practices and the crime industrial complex. That, coupled with emerging reports that Black communities are disproportionately impacted by Covid, made it clear that Black people were enduring two pandemics: Covid and anti-black racism.[2]

City, state, and national officials across the country scrambled to restore *peace*. Atlanta was one of those places, and Mayor Keisha Lance Bottoms was one of those officials. Regardless of whether the *violence* was perpetrated by fed-up protesters or outside opportunists, the immediate response from Atlanta officials (and elsewhere) was policing what they assumed was the Black response. Alongside Mayor Bottoms, Atlanta rappers T. I. and Killer Mike, and activists Dr. Joe Beasley, Rev. Dr. Bernice King, and Derrick Boazman, spoke at the press conference. In a little under thirty minutes, this group mounted a collective effort to tell the uprisers to "go home!"

In this chapter, I examine Mayor Bottoms's May 29, 2020, press conference posted to YouTube by 11 Alive, Atlanta's local NBC affiliate. Trapped in this press conference is a discourse about *violence*: how it is defined, if/when it is permitted, and by whom it is acceptable. Beyond that, the discourse broaches deeper conversations regarding Black agency and shared Black health. Shared Black health is specifically concerned with how our responses to anti-blackness impact our collective well-being. Similar to what Angela Nurse and Diane Keeling describe as Black Collective Corporeal Condition later in this volume, shared Black health is where Black people communally negotiate risk management. Here, we take into account our past, present, and future as we broker our responses to anti-black phenomena. This press conference argues that the uprisers' approach to remedy the anti-blackness pandemic is dangerous. Rebuking the upriser's tactics, the press conference asserts that the uprising's deviation from *nonviolence* poses a more significant threat to the shared Black health than anti-blackness itself. I frame the press conference's intentions in terms of shared health to gain a more complete understanding of two things. First, what does the rhetoric of shared Black health in the press conference disclose about the evolving practice of policing Black people? Second, what might be the implications for shared Black health if *nonviolent* strategies are the *only* acceptable means of resistance? However, the question remains: why examine this uprising text as a health text? To answer that question, I first provide a brief overview of some of the ways people at the time used health rhetoric to make sense of the 2020 uprisings.

The Rhetoric of Health from on the Ground, a Justification

Following George Floyd's lynching, the horrible irony of his death was not lost on many people. Invoking the manner of Floyd's death as a metaphor, Rachel R. Hardeman, Eduardo M. Medina, and Rhea W. Boyd explained that "Despite potential risks of exposure to Covid-19, demonstrators are laying bare the deep pain that persists for Black people fighting to live under the crushing weight of injustice that has long been at our necks."[3] A statement posted by the Washington University in St. Louis Department of African American Studies explains that, "'I can't breathe' captures not only the last words of our beloved, but also speaks the truth of so many in the Black community who are made most vulnerable to and suffer with covid-19."[4] Additionally, Rashid Shabazz remembers that "Jerome Adams, the U.S. surgeon general, has . . .

blamed Black people for dying from Covid-19 at higher rates than others, ignoring the chokeholds of presidential inaction, environmental racism, and inequities in the healthcare system that are killing us."[5] Kimberly D. Manning counters Adams claim, noting that "years of disenfranchisement and missed economic opportunities forced large numbers of our [Black] patients and loved ones out on the front lines to do essential jobs."[6] Rosemary Enobakhare and Oliver Brooks juxtapose the two pandemics: "Reports released [in May 2020] revealed the [Covid] mortality rate for Black Americans is nearly three times higher than the rate for white people. Meanwhile, being murdered by the police is a leading cause of death for young Black men in America."[7] In these cases, Covid acts as a metaphor for anti-black racism and vice versa. As Eric King Watts illuminates, "the pandemic has reanimated the real viral infection plaguing society: racism."[8] Like Covid, anti-blackness is a pandemic.

The relationship between Covid and anti-black racism, however, goes beyond metaphor. Covid also contributes to the pandemic of anti-blackness. Almost a year after the uprising, the APM Research Lab reports that "Black Americans suffered the greatest losses in the month of April 2020—especially in cities where the pandemic first raged."[9] This report reveals that just a month before the uprisings, Black citizens were experiencing the greatest Covid-related losses. To that end, "the devastating effects of the Covid global pandemic on US Black communities helped to fuel mass outpourings of righteous anger and powerful demands for freedom and justice on city streets across this country."[10] Cato T. Laurencin and Joanne M. Walker further explain: "The interplay [between racism and Covid] acts in a number of ways. The direct and indirect consequences of racist policing can vary from direct trauma to PTSD-type symptoms, to effects such as medical mistrust and mistreatment that *create* the ultimate pre-existing condition among those so often quoted for Blacks as being predisposed to covid-19 infection" (emphasis mine).[11] Covid actively contributes to the anti-blackness pandemic by perpetuating pre-existing racial disparities. At the time of the 2020 uprisings, awareness of Covid's disproportionate effects on the Black community stood parallel with the onslaught of the centuries-long Black public lynchings, of which George Floyd's death was simply the latest.

The uprisings, then, can be understood as people's attempt to remedy the anti-blackness disease. Long before Covid normalized masks and social distancing, anti-blackness standardized Black suffering and death as American staples. In the case of Covid, many hoped that a vaccine might help return the world "to normal."[12] People took to the streets, perhaps hoping that the vaccine of uprising would change normal. As Ersula J. Ore notes, "A return to normalcy is a return to more Breonnas and more Georges."[13] Unlike Covid, anti-blackness has diseased America for centuries. Viewing the uprisings as a remedy illuminates a hope for an existence in which people like George Floyd, Breonna Taylor, Ahmaud Arbery, and countless others would still be alive. Chloe Banks asserts, America's normalized resistance rhetoric entails a public memory "where the Civil Rights movement is framed as being worthy of remembrance according to socially acceptable discourse on nonviolent advocacy."[14] One of the most pivotal things that the uprising vaccine sought to accomplish is stepping out of this frame of acceptability to extend Black agency. The press conference addresses the viability of that vaccine. The dissonance between the speakers and the uprisers arises from distinct perspectives of acceptable resistances to anti-blackness. Both positions draw from communal wisdoms gathered over the course of Black histories and a shared Black health. To better contextualize all these elements, I turn to Afrocentric thought.

Afrocentric Collectivism

Many scholars of Afrocentricity have given attention to the collectivist values within Black cultures. The forefather of Afrocentrism, Molefi Kete Asante, asserts that "the African view of communication is an example of a human behavior affected by a strong collective mentality in which the group was more important than the individual."[15] Later in that same work, he explains that "within the Afrocentric culture, one sees a distaste for individual achievement that is not related to collective advancement."[16] Mwalimu J. Shujaa argues that "a comprehensive Afrocentric philosophical statement" founded in Afro-centered epistemology makes possible "individual transformation that makes an Afrocentric collective consciousness viable."[17] Similarly, A. Wade Boykin explains that " the notion that duty to one's social group is more important than individual privileges and rights" guides this communal perspective.[18] Taking Mekada Graham's Afrocentric approach to social work as an example, Afrocentric work "encompass[es] the values and cultural heritage of Black people as action-oriented strategies for social change," which includes "the interdependence of collective and individual identity."[19] To that end, Leslie R. Carson finds principles of collectivism "reflected in neighborhood or community interventions aimed at increasing the emotional well-being and physical safety of its members."[20] Within the Afrocentric paradigm, collectivism at least in part, emerges from and operates within the reality of Black life that is revealed in part through our experiences with anti-blackness. The ways we negotiate our responses to anti-blackness and any reclamation of agency oftentimes take on a collective tone. Questions of a *violent or nonviolent* response are navigated for the purpose of our shared Black health.

Shared Black Health

Shared Black health, then, is conceptually born out of the Afrocentric value of collectivism. In *Afrocentricity: The Theory of Social Change*, Asante asserts that in Afrocentric thought "*Ethos* is the collective personality of the people."[21] Kimberly C. Harper asserts that identity is "an extension of ethos."[22] Therefore, "the Afrocentric response to ethos determines what is in the best interest of African people at a given time, and then creates, nationalizes, and justifies the symbols which validate our interests."[23] Shared Black health steps into this space and speaks directly to "our reaction [to] the forces surrounding us."[24] Leaning into the "African conception of the interconnectedness of all things," shared Black health honors the ultimate interconnectedness of Black fates. It speaks to the urge that might cause a Black person to hope that a crime being covered on the local news was not perpetrated by another Black person. It is embedded in the hope a Black person might feel at the sight of a Black elected official, celebrity, doctor, etc. Shared Black health is the understanding that any foci of Black activity can produce ripples of impact for the Black people surrounding it, be that positively or negatively. The Covid pandemic provides a poignant example. The disease's disproportionate effect on Black people speaks to how social, political, economic, and cultural factors can converge to threaten not just individual Black people but Black people conceived as a collective whole. Shared Black health acknowledges Asante's assertion that "we must respond to the external forces, there is no escaping that responsibility."[25] Shared Black health, then, is a particularly useful frame for studying Black responses as we anticipate feedback and retaliation from outside forces. It asks what fears, hopes, values, and histories do our responses lean into and why? How do we navigate the anti-blackness pandemic in a way that will ensure what we value? Safety, agency, liberation, and so on. It is important to note that from its origin, Afrocentric liberation has been bound to Black agency. Asante explains that "Afrocentricity is a paradigmatic intellectual perspective that privileges African agency within the context of African history and culture transcontinentally and trans-generationally."[26] Elsewhere, Asante explains that "By agency is meant an attitude toward action originating in African experiences."[27]

Speaking to the interconnectedness of collectivism, liberation, and agency, Ronald L. Jackson explains "a 'warrior' in the struggle for human liberation is powerless without the armor of cultural consciousness and self-consciousness."[28] That cultural consciousness is defined and redefined through the collective Black body. Here, the collective Black body leans into wisdoms gathered throughout our histories to safely navigate toward our future. Or, as Asante puts it, "Ancestors do in fact gather to inspire us and bring us victory."[29] The ideas, strategies, solutions, and so on that emerge from the material-discursive space that is the collective Black body comprise shared Black health. In the case of Mayor Bottoms's press conference, the foci to which shared Black health speaks is the 2020 uprisings. Here, the shared wisdom that the collective Black body draws from is born out of histories of violence against Black people and the kind of white vigilantism that claimed lives like Ahmaud Arbery's.

White Violence, Nonviolence, and Black Resistance

As The Library of Congress's brief article *The Murder of Emmett Till* indicates, within American public and Black collective memory, the decision of Emmet Till's mother, Mamie Till, to hold an open casket funeral for her beaten and disfigured adolescent son played a huge role in sparking the civil rights movement of the 1960s.[30] Through that act, young Till became a poster child for a relationship of violence perpetrated by white hegemony onto Black people that is several centuries long. With Dr. Martin Luther King Jr. becoming the president of the Southern Christian Leadership Conference and the face of the movement in the 1960s, the message and strategy of *nonviolence* became etched into the American psyche. King's *nonviolent* strategy fell in line with a long-standing tradition of moral suasion that the Black community has employed as a measure to accomplish shared Black health for more than four centuries. As Jim Casey explains, moral suasion is "the appeals to [white] morality, in support of the cause for Black freedom and civil rights."[31] Importantly, rather than being absent of violence, King's nonviolent strategy sought to highlight and magnify white serving hegemonic violence against Black people.

While some marches and rallies of the 1960s occurred without expressions of such violence, many did not. Look no further than the events that transpired on the Edmund Pettus Bridge on March 7, 1965. Though the Black protesters did not burn cars or buildings, they were met with the full force of the Alabama Police Department's anti-black racism. As Cheryl Janifer LaRoche's exposition of nineteenth-century figure and underground railroad operative William Whipper illuminates, the price for Black resistance has always been white hegemonic violence.[32] Whipper, a successful Black lumberman in Philadelphia in the early 1800s used his access to the Atlantic Ocean and his lumberyards to bring formerly enslaved Black people to freedom. As LaRoche explains, Whipper's lumberyards were targeted for burning on two separate occasions. In Whipper's (and countless others) case, white hegemonic violence occurs regardless of how *violent or nonviolent* the resistive action is.

However, by highlighting the overt and excessive violence of white people, *nonviolent* protest strategies hope to juxtapose the white hegemonic violence with the collective Black body's *nonviolent* response. As Banks poignantly explores, the rhetoric of *violence and nonviolence* established in the 1960s has, in recent times, been used by pundits like Bill O'Reilly to frame the actions of contemporary movements such as BLM as *violent* and juxtaposed to more acceptable and successful *nonviolent* means of resistance.[33] This take on *nonviolence* ignores and trivializes the kind of violence that initiated the circumstances that made the 2020 uprisings necessary. Violence is a presidential administration withholding life-saving information about a virus, setting the stage for it to break out into a pandemic, then subsequently encouraging its supporters not to take the pandemic seriously. Violence is when both of Georgia's senators (at the time) moved around their stocks and financial holdings before alerting their constituents of the deadly virus. Violence is police lynching's systematically being overjustified in the press and beyond, and underprosecuted in the courts.

Canonizing the strategy of nonviolence employed during the civil rights movement as absent of violence and exclusively acceptable contributes to what Amanda Nell Edgar and Andre E. Johnson describe as a "misremembering" of the 1960s civil rights movement, and this misremembering comes at the detriment of Black agency.[34] Because shared Black health is by its nature discursive, such misremembering can lead to responses built upon historic fallacies that were born out of the very anti-blackness we respond to. The press conference engages shared Black health to police a collective Black body by reifying the anti-black resistive norm of *nonviolence* and framing the uprisings as a nonviable vaccine for anti-blackness. Here, the speakers rebuke and redirect uprisers' actions, defining them as *violence*. In doing so they position this *violence* as a threat to shared Black health. My analysis explores how they engage collectivism to present the 2020 uprisings as a more dangerous disease than anti-black racism. For them, the people's vaccine presents a greater threat to shared Black health than the virus itself.

Policing the Collective Black Body

The press conference begins with Mayor Bottoms engaging in the shared Black health conversation. She says, "We're talking about how you're burning police cars in the streets of Atlanta, Georgia, Go home! Go home!"[35] In this short statement, she lays the groundwork for what the press conference would seek to accomplish. Criticizing what the speakers would continuously define as *violence*, she rebukes the uprisers. She then employs Atlanta as a sort of emblem being unfairly subjected to that *violence*. Finally, she seeks to redirect the uprisers by telling them to go home. From here, the speakers seek to articulate what forms of protests qualify as healthy for the collective Black body and which do not. To do so, they strike different tones. Killer Mike and T. I., for example, try their best to appear understanding and sympathetic. Derrick Boazman and Mayor Bottoms, on the other hand, are more openly frustrated and rebuking. Despite these differences, all parties agree. The uprisings are an unhealthy form of resistance. They also present a danger to Black liberation and are unhealthy for the collective Black body. The press conference frames the connection between the uprisings and shared Black health. Ultimately, its rhetoric falls into three categories: (1) defining and rebuking *violence*; (2) framing Atlanta as a silo of Black progress because of historic *nonviolence*; (3) redirecting uprisers "back" to *nonviolence*.

Defining and Rebuking Violence

For the speakers, the uprisers' tactics of burning things and commandeering resources are a distinct type of *violence* that threatens shared Black health and must be addressed primarily and immediately. The press conference thereby isolates the uprisings from the legions of Black lynchings and Covid-related developments that propelled them. Having separated these two interconnected issues, they address the uprisers' *violence* while only mentioning white hegemonic violence in passing. By dedicating the whole of the press conference to the uprisers, they paint the uprisings as the true acts of *violence*. Having defined the uprisings as a more dangerous form of *violence*, they rebuke the *violence* by establishing the uprisings as ultimately ineffective, framing the uprisers as immature, and seeking to delegitimize the uprisings as senseless *violence*.

The Uprising as Ineffective

Speaking third, following Mayor Bottoms and T. I., Killer Mike explains that though he "don't want to be here," he is "duty-bound to be here to simply say that it is your duty not to burn your own house down for anger with the enemy . . . to fortify your own house, so that you may be a refuge in times of organization." Here, the activist-rapper insists that burning down Atlanta's downtown area will prevent further progress. By framing the city as the upriser's "home," he attributes ownership of the city (particularly the buildings and vehicles actually owned by corporations and city police) to the uprisers. The uprisers' tactics, then, are a form of self-inflicted *violence* that will ultimately hurt the Black people. For Mike, the uprisings are a dangerous remedy because they damage Black people's ability to "organize," which seems to be the bedrock of what he suggests they do. Later he says, "We have an opportunity now. Because I'm mad [about George Floyd's lynching], I don't have any advice. But what I can tell you is to sit in your homes tonight instead of burning your home to the ground. You have time to properly plot, plan, strategize, and organize and mobilize in an effective way." Though Mike takes a softer approach, his statement stands as a clear rebuke of the upriser's strategy. It also conveniently ignores how violent and rampant gentrification is boxing Black people out of ownership in the area in question. For him, plotting, planning, strategizing, and organizing are the "effective" ways to resist, as opposed to the strategies the uprisers have deployed.

To that end, Mayor Bottoms later reinforces the uprisings as counterintuitive to organizing. She says, "If you want a peaceful protest, go home. Organize and come back on a peaceful day. This is not a peaceful night." Here, she builds upon the foundation established by Mike and others. However, she goes a step further by tying "peaceful" to organizing. Perhaps working from Joe Beasley's earlier assertion that "because we in a crowd, the adrenaline's pumping. You didn't really mean to get in trouble. You came out, but in fact, when you're following the crowd, whatever the crowd does—who you're with, you're going to be a part of it," Mayor Bottoms assumes that the uprisers want a *peaceful* demonstration. Working from that assumption, she places *peaceful* and organizing in one camp, and the uprisings in an opposing and mutually exclusive camp. Assuming a shared understanding of *peace*, as well as the supremacy of organizing as a resistive approach, she urges the uprisers to go home because their approach is ultimately doomed to be ineffective. In doing so, she and Mike attempt to place the uprisings outside of the Afrocentric value of collectivism. Through this lens, the commandeering of resources, for example, is viewed as individual advancement divorced from the more important collective achievement. Fittingly, both Beasley and Bottoms assume that the uprisers do not fully grasp the gravity of their actions. This assumption falls in line with another of the speakers' rebuke: uprising is an immature approach to resistance.

The Uprisings as Immature

Through Mike's rebuke of the uprisings as ineffective, organizing is presented not only as an effective measure, but also a mature way of treating anti-blackness. Therefore, the upriser's response is immature. This widespread assertion in the press conference becomes most apparent in insistences that uprisers are children. To this end, Mike says, "So that's why children are burning [things] to the ground. They don't know what else to do." Similarly, Rev. Dr. Bernice King says, "We have to listen to the cries that are coming out of the hearts and the souls of my young brothers and sisters and all of the others that are in the streets of America right now and in our city." Though she is calling for authorities to listen to the uprisers' voices, she does so in a way that delegitimizes their actions. Importantly, she ascribes the uprisings to her "young brothers and sisters," tying the uprising action to younger, less mature players who have yet to fight and defeat the "demon" of *violence*, as she has. For her, these vulnerable and uncalculated young people must be reminded that "everybody is not on the same page. There are people who will try to incite a race war in this country. Let's not fall into their hands and into their trap." Here, she presents the uprisers as youths being manipulated to assist in the opposition's agenda to start a race war. Further, Derrick Boazman says, "I joined with the mayor when I saw young people who are hungry and thirsty to know what freedom tastes like. And so I saw a lot of teenagers out there." While acknowledging the uprisers' "hunger and thirst" for "freedom," he takes care to advance the narrative that the uprisers are "young people" and "teenagers." It is important to note that youth culture often drives social change. However, none of the speakers who mention the demographic they believe to compose the uprisings mentions the upriser's youth for that reason. Rather, they present the uprisers' actions as a primitive form of resistance, lacking the refinement and maturity needed to create legitimate change. For them, these are children with legitimate concerns behaving in an illegitimate way. The speakers present this *violence* as the backlash of children deprived of freedom. The speakers assemble to rebuke the children's *violence* and bring them back in line with the time-honored wisdom and maturity of *nonviolence*. To this end, Derrick Boazman provides the sternest rebuke.

The Uprisings as Violence

Boazman begins his statement saying, "Let me say as one who was born and raised in this city and have led a many protests myself, what we saw tonight should disturb all of us." In one swoop, he establishes his credentials as a legitimate protester and the uprisings as "disturbing." He continues, "I don't know what the intent was tonight. We had what was a *peaceful* protest that descended into something that none of us can be proud of." First alluding to the marching and chanting that preceded the activities of that night, he establishes the "peaceful protest" as the legitimate resistance that preceded the abomination of resistance that has drawn his ire. Later, he says that "the Atlanta police department ought to be commended. They showed an extraordinary amount of restraint." Completely affirming the right of the police to respond brutally to uprisings designed to resist police brutality, he commends the Atlanta police for resisting the urge to violate and kill Black people. This statement works not only to delegitimize the uprisings but also to legitimize a view of acceptable and unacceptable *violence* used to justify the death of people like Kendrick Johnson, Atatiana Jefferson, and Botham Jean, while constraining Black agency in response to that violence. It is worth noting that within twenty-four hours, Atlanta Police violently dragged Messiah Young and Taniah Pilgrim from their vehicle, and less than two weeks later, Atlanta Police murdered Rayshard Brooks.[36] For Boazman, it is the uprisers, and not police and white hegemonic violence that need complete and direct rebuke. This rebuke engages shared Black health to name the uprisings as violence.

To that end, he says, "Let's be very real here. Some of the people who were down there tonight did not come for brother Floyd. They did not come for Ahmaud Arbery. They came there with the intent to be destructive. They came there with an agenda to create havoc. What does shattering a car window, breaking into a restaurant . . . how does that move the margin closer towards freedom?" Disconnecting the uprisers from the larger movement for Black lives, he presents them as opportunists whose focus was destruction, havoc, and *violence*. He then subjects them to a list of rhetorical questions about the effectiveness of their resistive strategies, culminating with a question of how they will bring about liberation. For him, the answer is clear and should be clear to any real liberation fighter. Therefore, "what we saw tonight was destruction and it was for destruction purposes." Boazman concludes his scathing reading of the uprisings saying, "What we saw down here in the last hours or two has nothing to do with those brothers who are crying out from the grave from freedom. It had everything to do with people who really don't care about this city, and don't care about real freedom and real justice." For Boazman, what needs to be indicted first and foremost is the idea of the uprisings as remedy. This *violence* is "for destruction purposes." It is unsanctioned and unacceptable. It is, therefore, illegitimate *violence*.

Though other speakers do not rebuke with nearly as much vitriol as Boazman, they build their rebuke on the same foundation: the illegitimacy of the uprisings. Without considering Black agency, the press conference draws upon shared Black health to rebuke the uprisers' tactics. Whether it is Killer Mike asserting that the uprisings will damage Black ability to organize, Mayor Bottoms insisting on *peace* as the sole way to approach white hegemonic violence, or Derrick Boazman rebuking the uprising as wholly for destructive purposes, all of the speakers tap into a long tradition of collectivism in Black culture, but transgress Afrocentric agency through their message. They do so by adopting the Eurocentric view of Black agency in resistance as pathological. To this end, they work against what Asante describes as our "responsibility" to "respond to the external forces" in a way that is true to our "sanity" and our collective "consciousness."[37] For them, an anti-blackness vaccine designed to preserve and advance shared Black health would never employ such strategies, especially in a place like Atlanta.

Atlanta as Black Progress

In addition to issuing rebukes, every speaker takes time to highlight what they perceive as a disregard for Atlanta as evidence of the uprisers' threat to shared Black health. As T.I. explains, "This city don't deserve this." In fact, the speakers present Atlanta as the perfect example of the type of progress *nonviolent* resistance manifests. The uprisings, then, serve as the antithesis of that progress, threatening shared Black health in the process. If Atlanta is burned, the strides that the city has made—that Black people have made—burn as well. Here, Atlanta becomes the seat of historical and contemporary progress toward Black liberation. What happens to Atlanta happens to the collective Black body. To this end, the speakers present Atlanta in two lights: (1) a landmark of Black history and (2) a bastion of Black success and progress.

Historical Atlanta

Throughout the press conference, the speakers make countless references to Atlanta's history of Black greatness and advancing shared Black health. After describing himself as "the son of an Atlanta city police officer," and, through tears, the cousin of "an Atlanta city police officer," and "an east point city police officer," Killer Mike discusses Atlanta's history of Black police officers. He says, "I got a lot of love and respect for police officers, down to the original eight Black police officers in Atlanta, that even after becoming police, had to dress in a YMCA, because white officers didn't want to get dressed with niggas. Here we are 80 years later." While this statement precedes remarks legitimizing the upriser's anger toward police brutality, Mike's brief history of Black policing in Atlanta alludes to what he frames as progress within the Atlanta police department. By discussing the hardships of the original eight officers and then bringing his audience into the modern day "80 years later," Mike provides an outlook on how far policing in Atlanta has come.

Taking Atlanta's historical achievements outside of policing, Rev. Joe Beasley says, "I grew up here in North Atlanta—83 years ago, so I've really seen a change... I appreciate Mayor Bottoms for asking me to come to stand with the group because change is here. I remember very well that we couldn't even venture into this building. But now the mayor is the mayor of this city." Here, Beasley reminds the audience that Atlanta, which did not previously allow Black people into the capitol building, now has its fifth Black mayor. Such statements leave the audience to wonder how such strides came about. Throughout the press conference, speakers tie Atlanta's historic progress to the 1960s civil rights movement. They present the civil rights movement as a seemingly perfect contribution to shared Black health and as a model that must not be deviated from.

In public memory, there is no greater face of the 1960s civil rights movement than Rev. Dr. Martin Luther King Jr. Fittingly, every speaker besides Derrick Boazman mentions Dr. King directly. T. I. says, "People like Dr. King, Maynard Jackson, Ambassador Young have paved the way for us." Killer Mike adds, "I'm responsible to be here because it wasn't just Dr. King and people who dressed nicely who marched and protested to progress this city and so many other cities." Speaking of the upriser's tactics, Mayor Bottoms says, "This is not how we changed the world with the leadership of Dr. Martin Luther King Jr." No mere mention of the good reverend doctor could match his presence, however. While he could not be physically present, his legacy was fully in attendance.

Rev. Dr. Bernice King spoke on her father's behalf during the press conference, at one point even saying, "So in the name of Martin Luther King Jr.—from the soils of Atlanta, Georgia—and from the five-year-old girl who lost her daddy to gun violence—senselessly, at the hands of law enforcement—let's do this the *peaceful* and *nonviolent* way to deal with the evils and the conditions of our time." More than anyone, Rev. Dr. Bernice King ties Atlanta to the civil rights movement. She reminds the audience that her father "was a son of this state and this city, born on the soils of this city on Auburn Ave." Through her very presence and reminding of her father's Atlanta native status, she establishes the city as sacred. Returning to Mike's insistence that the uprisers are "burning your own home," the message becomes clearer. Atlanta is more than the city. It is Black history. It is, in many ways, the culmination of Black struggle—Black *nonviolent* struggle. The press conference argues that the work of people like Dr. King made it possible to have a Black Mayor and Black police officers. However, Atlanta is sacred not only because of its history, but also because of its contemporary accomplishments.

Progressive Atlanta

Somewhat infamously, T.I. ends his speech by saying, "But, we can't do this here. This is Wakanda. This sacred—must be protected." As insensitive as calling Atlanta "Wakanda" amid the uprisings might be, T.I.'s sentiment seems to be shared among the speakers. T.I., in particular, attempts to drive home Atlanta's sacredness, spending almost all of his time discussing how the city provides opportunities for Black people. He first says, "Atlanta is the place where people like me, Killer Mike, other artists, creators, other people who come from our culture, and other people who rise up out of the wreckage of the struggle that we all experience, just by being born a certain color in this country." Leaning into his position as one of Atlanta's main hip-hop ambassadors, T.I. explains that the city provides opportunities for people in the throes of poverty and racism. He argues that his and Mike's success in rap serves as a testament to Atlanta's ability to advance Black people. To that end he says, "Atlanta is a place where we can set an example of prosperity, and we've done that for generations." Beyond being an example for other cities, T.I. regards Atlanta as a refuge for Black people. He says, "When everything else goes away ... when you don't get treated right in New York, when you don't get treated right in L.A., when you can't get treated right in Detroit, when you don't get treated right in St. Louis, when you don't get treated right in Alabama—Atlanta has been here for us." While T.I. does not elaborate on how exactly Atlanta has earned the progressive status he ascribes to it, Killer Mike and Mayor Bottoms do.

Killer Mike explains, "Atlanta's not perfect but we a lot better than we ever were, and we a lot better than cities are." For example, "In this city, officers have done horrendous things and they have been prosecuted." This was not the fate for Garrett Rolfe and Devin Brosnan, who murdered Rayshard Brooks. Beyond that, Killer Mike explains that Atlanta "got good enough to destroy cash bond. You don't have to worry about going to jail for something petty. We got smart enough to decriminalize marijuana." Additionally, Mayor Bottoms explains that Atlanta "closed our doors to ICE. We are in the process of closing our city jail and converting it into a center of equity, health, and wellness." Further, under her leadership, "we have 'At-Promise Centers' going up across this city where our police recruits go in and volunteer with the kids in the community so that their first encounter with them is not when they're chasing them down the street." For them, Atlanta does not deserve to be burned because, as Derrick Boazman says, "the beauty of this city that's called Atlanta is that we always had the Atlanta way of doing things," which for the speakers is tied to Black progress. That is why Killer Mike says, "If we lose Atlanta, what else we got?"

By establishing Atlanta as the seat of historic and contemporary Black progress, the press conference presents the city as a proxy for the collective Black body. The city's fate, then, is a matter of shared Black health. T.I. argues that it is the place that Black people go to escape. As Mike repeatedly emphasizes, Atlanta is "your home." For them, Atlanta houses the collective Black spirit that drove the civil rights movement. It leads other cities in innovative strategies and policies for helping Black people escape the clutches of anti-black racism. Just as Covid acts as both a metaphor for and contributor to anti-black racism, the speakers present Atlanta as both metaphor for, and contributor to, shared Black health. Framing the uprisings, then, as *violence* against Atlanta, presents them as a threat to shared Black health. As I argue, the press conference frames the uprisings as the musings of immature youth, subjecting the city to senseless damage. From this perspective, the 2020 uprisings are a vaccine that not only does more harm than good, but actually damages the body more than the disease itself. However, neither Atlanta's history or its modern-day strides toward progress prevented Garret Rolfe and Devin Brosnan from murdering Rayshard Brooks only to be reinstated to his position within a year.

Imagining Atlanta as the seat of Black progress did very little, if anything, to squelch the anti-blackness pandemic. Rather, by presenting Atlanta in this way, the press conference seeks to incite a fear of loss response from the uprisers. It asks the uprisers to consider the potential ripple of white hegemonic violence that might be produced from their actions. The audience is left to wonder not about liberation, but what might be lost if the uprisings continue. If *nonviolence* leads to progress as depicted through Atlanta, what might the uprisings lead to? What strides might be reversed? What pain might be inflicted upon the collective Black body? What will be the impact on shared Black health? That is why Mayor Bottoms describes the uprisers as "disruptive," adding that "we are all angry. [George Floyd's lynching] hurts. This hurts everybody in this room. But what are you changing by tearing up a city? You've lost all credibility tonight." For me, the question becomes credibility in whose eyes? To whom should Black resistance appeal? From whom should the collective Black body seek credibility? The press conference's answers to that question lie in the way it seeks to redirect the uprisers toward their perspective of shared Black health.

Redirection toward Nonviolence

While the speaker's tones throughout the press conference are not always unified, they redirect the uprisers toward *nonviolent* action with a uniformed voice. Killer Mike petitions, "I want you to go home. I want you to talk and tell your friends. I want you guys to come up with real solutions." For him, real solutions include things like filling out the census and "making sure you exercise your political bully power and go into local elections beating up the politicians you don't like." He tells the uprisers that if "you got a prosecutor that sent your pawtna to jail and you know it was bullshit, put a new prosecutor in there. Now is your election to do it." Along those same lines, Derrick Boazman tells the uprisers to "go home and learn what this democracy is all about." For Mayor Bottoms, the uprisings are not meaningful resistance. They are "something else. And this isn't about justice. If you're breaking out windows and you're running down the street with liquor in your hands, whose memory is that honoring?" This statement follows her invocation of Dr. King. Here, she argues that his memory and legacy are on the line. For her, his memory and legacy calls people into *peaceful* and *nonviolent protests*. For me, that is a major reason that Rev. Dr. Bernice King is present.

Rev. Dr. Bernice King carries the bulk of the load in pushing the *nonviolent protest* agenda. If her presence as representative to her father's legacy and message are not enough, her words drive the message home. She says, "The *nonviolent* way is the way because the means and the end have to be consistent. We will never get to the end of justice and equity, and true peace—which is not merely the absence of tension but the presence of justice—unless we do it through *nonviolent* means." King puts into words what the press conference as a whole implies: There is no meaningful response to anti-black racism other than *nonviolent* means. The only way to protect and advance shared Black health is *nonviolence*. Unlike what the uprisers are doing, "*nonviolence*," when done correctly, brings about "results," because "change never comes through *violence*. It is not a solution." Rather, much like a faulty vaccine, *violence*, here defined as the upriser's strategy, "creates more problems" for the collective Black body.

Conclusion and Invitation

Throughout this chapter, I have strategically italicized words such as *nonviolence*, *nonviolent*, and *peaceful*. These words maneuver through this whole press conference uninterrupted and uninterrogated. Each insistence for *nonviolence* fails to acknowledge the inherent and assigned violence of the *nonviolent protest* strategy. Though this was our ancestors' and elders' strategy, it is imperative that we acknowledge that it is only *a* strategy. I decided to participate in the uprisings because I saw a group of people challenging the discursive Black experience with nonviolence as an exclusive means of resistance. Rather than dishonoring the history of where *nonviolence* has gotten us, we questioned if it can get us where we are going. Both resistance and liberation are keepsakes inherited by new generations that must decide how to move forward. Each generation is tasked with striking the balance of honoring the struggles, efforts, strategies, and progress of previous generations, while adjusting and, when need be, critiquing those efforts and strategies to answer new struggles and produce new progress.

For me the uprising's turn toward agency was equally if not more encouraging than the press conference's turn toward policing was discouraging. By shedding *acceptable* means of resistance, the uprisers provided a vital critique of the idea that there must be more Black death before *non-nonviolent* options can be considered.

By employing shared Black health, my analysis allows us to investigate the rhetorics and discourses that permeate Black responses to anti-blackness. Beyond allowing us to investigate 2020's phenomena of the dual pandemics, shared Black health frames Black liberation efforts as a discourse about the fears, hopes, values, and histories that govern our responses.

In responding, the press conference's speakers make a mistake similar to that of the Global Health Security Index in accessing the United States' "capability to prevent and mitigate epidemics and pandemics" (see this volume's introduction). Rather than presenting overt American exceptionalism, they opted to exceptionalize a resistance strategy predeemed as acceptable by America. In doing so, they urge their audience to operate from the same dangerous rhetorical place from which the Global Health Security Index operated. The insistence that Black responses to white serving hegemonic violence remain *nonviolent* only designates white hegemonic violence as acceptable and Black agency as pathological. This chapter is certainly not a call for violence. It is an unequivocal call for an unbridled Black agency. It is a call to continue to engage shared Black health to find ways to honor our ancestors while not turning their strategies and perspectives into a resistance prison. It is a call to interrogate what our discourses about violence say about our collective view of Black action, liberation, and shared Black health and our urge to police these interconnected elements. After all, Black people bear the brunt of the pandemic of anti-blackness and any other pandemic that comes along to illuminate anti-blackness. It is Black people, therefore, who must fully engage our agency in our response.

NOTES

1. "Demonstrations & Political Violence in America: New Data for Summer 2020," Armed Conflict Location & Event Data Project, updated September 2020, https://acleddata.com/2020/09/03/demonstrations-political-violence-in-america-new-data-for-summer-2020/.
2. Shelby Lin Erdman, "Black Communities Account for Disproportionate Number of Covid-19 Deaths in the U.S., Study Finds," CNN Health, May 6, 2020.
3. Rachel R. Hardeman, Eduardo M. Medina, and Rhea W. Boyd, "Stolen Breathes," *New England Journal of Medicine* 383 (2020): 197.
4. Department of African American Studies, "Statement on Anti-Black Violence and a Global Pandemic," Washington University in St. Louis, June 15, 2020.

5. Rashid Shabazz, "We Can't Breathe: COVID-19 and Police Injustice Are Suffocating Black People," *The Root*, May 29, 2020.
6. Kimberly D. Manning, "When Grief and Crises Intersect: Perspectives of a Black Physician in the Time of Two Pandemics," *Society of Hospital Medicine* (2020): 566.
7. Rosemary Enobakhare and Oliver Brooks, "Why Anti-Blackness Is America's Perpetual Pandemic," *Blavity News*, June 5, 2020.
8. Eric King Watts, "The Primal Scene of COVID-19: 'We're All in This Together,'" *Rhetoric, Politics & Culture* 1, no. 1 (2021), 18.
9. Elisabeth Gawthrop, "The Color of Coronavirus: COVID-19 Deaths by Race and Ethnicity in the U.S.," *APM Research Lab*, March 5, 2021.
10. Department of African American Studies, "Statement on Anti-Black Violence and the Covid-19 Global Pandemic," *University of Illinois Urbana-Champaign*, June 2, 2020.
11. Cato T. Laurencin and Joanne M. Walker, "A Pandemic on a Pandemic: Racism and COVID-19 in Blacks," *Cell Systems* 11, no. 1 (2020): 10.
12. John Cohen, "The Long Road: Early Signs Suggest COVID-19 Vaccines Are Having an Impact, but Questions Abound about the Path to Normal," *Science*, February 16, 2021.
13. Matthew Houdek and Ersula J. Ore, "Cultivating Otherwise Worlds and Breathable Futures," *Rhetoric, Politics & Culture* 1, no.1 (2021), 87.
14. Chloe Banks, "Disciplining Black Activism: Post Racial Rhetoric, Public Memory, and Decorum in News Media Framing of the Black Lives Matter Movement," *Journal of Media and Cultural Studies* 32, no. 6 (2018): 713.
15. Molefi Kete Asante, *The Afrocentric Idea* (Philadelphia: Temple University Press, 1998), loc. 882–83 of 1340.
16. Asante, *Afrocentric Idea*, loc. 882–83 of 1340.
17. Mwalimu J. Shujaa, "Afrocentric Education, in *Encyclopedia of Black Studies*, ed. Molefi Kete Assante and Mambo Ama Mazama (Newbury Park, CA: Sage Publishing, 2004), 64.
18. A. Wade Boykin, "Communalism: Conceptualization and Measurement of an Afrocultural Social Orientation," *Journal of Black Studies* 27, no. 3 (1997): 409–18.
19. Mekada Graham, "Afrocentric Social Work, in *Encyclopedia of Black Studies*, eds. Molefi Kete Assante and Mambo Ama Mazama (Newbury Park, CA: Sage Publishing, 2004), 71.
20. Leslie R. Carson, "'I Am Because We Are': Collectivism as a Foundational Characteristic of African American College Student Identity and Academic Achievement," *Social Psychology of Education* 12, no. 3 (2009): 327–44.
21. Molefi Kete Asante, *Afrocentricity: The Theory of Social Change* (Chicago: African American Images, 2003), 29.
22. Kimberly C. Harper, *The Ethos of Black Motherhood in America: Only White Women Get*

Pregnant (Lanham, MD: Lexington, 2021), 49.
23. Asante, *Afrocentricity*, 29.
24. Asante, *Afrocentricity*, 35.
25. Asante, *Afrocentricity*, 35.
26. Molefi Kete Asante, *The Afrocentric Manifesto* (Cambridge, UK: Polity Press, 2007), 2.
27. Asante, *Afrocentricity*, 3.
28. Ronald L. Jackson II, "Afrocentricity as Metatheory: A Dialogic Exploration of it's Principles," in *Understanding African American Rhetoric*, ed. Ronald L. Jackson II and Elaine B. Richardson (Oxford: Routledge, 2003), 117.
29. Asante, *Afrocentricity*, 28.
30. Library of Congress, "The Murder of Emmett Till," Collection: Civil Rights History Project, https://www.loc.gov/collections/civil-rights-history-project/articles-and-essays/murder-of-emmett-till/.
31. Jim Casey, "Social Networks of the Colored Convention 1830–1864," in *The Colored Conventions Movement*, ed. P. Gabrielle Forman, Jim Casey, and Lynn Patterson (Chapel Hill: University of North Carolina Press, 2021), 268.
32. Cheryl Janifer LaRoche, "Secrets Well Kept: Colored Conventioneers and Underground Railroad Activity," in *The Colored Conventions Movement*, ed. P. Gabrielle Forman, Jim Casey, and Lynn Patterson (Chapel Hill: University of North Carolina Press, 2021), 252.
33. Banks, "Disciplining Black Activism," 713.
34. Amanda Nell Edgar and Andre E. Johnson, *The Struggle Over Black Lives Matter and All Lives Matter* (London: Lexington, 2018).
35. Unless otherwise specified, all further cited evidential references come from "T.I., Killer Mike Join Mayor Keisha Lance Bottoms in Condemning Violence in Atlanta Protests," 11Alive, May 29, 2020, https://www.youtube.com/watch?v=vOvB29-1FK4.
36. Kate Brumback, "6 Atlanta Police Officers Charged After 2 College Students Were Pulled from Their Car During George Floyd Protests," *Chicago Tribune*, June 2, 2020.
37. Asante, *Afrocentricity*, 35–36.

Covid and Masking

Race, Dress, and Addressivity

Angela Nurse and Diane Keeling

ON APRIL 4, 2020, AARON THOMAS TWEETED, "I WANT TO STAY ALIVE BUT I also want to stay alive."[1] As SARS-CoV-2 began to sweep across the United States, little was known about how the virus was transmitted or what could be done to prevent infection. Initially, there was significant debate about whether the public should wear masks, whether this would help or hinder the spread of the virus, despite the longtime practice of masking in Asian countries. Even when consensus eventually emerged in public health messaging that face coverings could help prevent transmission of Covid, it was unknown whether wearing a mask would protect the mask wearer from others or if it would only protect others from the mask wearer who might transmit the virus to them.

Messaging that promoted mask wearing as good for public health ignited a frenzy of N95 mask purchases. However, there was already a shortage of surgical masks for healthcare workers created by US exports to other countries.[2] For most, medical masks were not an option. Instead, pandemic-cautious people began to create their own ad hoc masks using any available cloth material: bandannas, handkerchiefs, scarfs, old clothes. Social pressure was mounting to cover one's face in public, and mask wearers were lauded by many as good biocitizens—altruistic, responsible individuals, conscious of community, and acting for the larger social good.[3] To wear a mask was to protect others and possibly oneself.

Resisting the blanket framing of mask wearing as the healthy choice, Aaron Thomas crafted a tweet that resonated with over one hundred thousand Twitter users on April 4, 2020: "I don't feel safe wearing a handkerchief or something else that isn't CLEARLY a protective mask covering my face to the store because I am a Black man living in this world. I want to stay alive but I also want to stay alive."[4] Thomas's message called attention to the precarity of wearing a mask in an anti-black racist society.[5] A "protective mask" (i.e., surgical) might emplace Thomas's "black(ened) body" within a medical discourse, while displacing a racist one. He closes his message with *antanaclasis*, a figure of speech that repeats a phrase whose meaning changes in the second instance. This figure of repetition expresses the way Black folks and people of color lived through two pandemics, negotiating different forms of death-accelerating violence in the United States.[6] Both SARS-CoV-2 and racism each have life-threatening consequences in social interactions. I want to stay alive (viral violence) but I also want to stay alive (racist violence).

For many Black men during the pandemic, masking in the present was conditioned by at least two swirling discursive histories: a neoliberal health discourse of personal responsibility and a racist discourse attacking the Black Collective Corporeal Condition. A neoliberal public health solution to Covid was to mask up, which created the potential of racist violence against Black men, whose presumed criminality and dangerousness was heightened by wearing a mask. Black men were caught between the history of violence perpetrated against them for their presumed criminality and danger when wearing masks as well as the neoliberal imperative to wear a mask to protect against viral violence.

Black folks are not the only community who have dealt with the racist consequences of masking during the pandemic since masks cannot be understood separately from the bodies that wear them. For the Asian (AAPI) community, racist rhetoric from then-president Trump legitimized the long-standing belief that Asians are particularly infectious hosts of Covid. Wearing masks in the United States triggered anger, frustration, and an increase in hate crimes.[7] Prior to the Covid pandemic, Muslim women who practiced hijab through niqab reckoned with Islamophobia, anti-Muslim hate crimes, and a loss of freedoms.[8] While these violences persist, some Muslim women have also found "public life in the niqab much more pleasant" during the pandemic due to a "growing acceptance of face covering." They have even been referred to as "experts on face covering" better at "detecting human emotion."[9] For Black folks and all people of color who are incarnated into and with the world through histories of racial violence, we argue that masking is never just masking but requires rhetorical labor to navigate violent discourses that will potentially dress the body. We focus on Black men's narrative experiences published in various news periodicals and social media accounts to make our case. As the editors of this collection describe in the introduction, this is a partial archive of Covid assembled in order to demonstrate a particular experience that was circulating in public discourse during the beginning of the pandemic.

In early 2020, Black men received increased media coverage due to unjust police violence against them. The national spotlight fueled interest in how Black men experience racism. There was an exigence to pay attention to other harms they endure. Black men were highlighted on mediated platforms, and as SARS-CoV-2 spread they articulated concerns about how to protect themselves from racism and the virus. Attending specifically to their concerns about masking, this study considers the way Black men navigate swirling violent discourses in their deliberations about masking.

We examine masking as a form of address, as that which orients and emplaces discourse. Masking, then, orients and emplaces discourse during interactions. Address is conditioned by its addressivity, the immeasurable past instances in which mask wearing took place: who has worn masks, when have they worn masks, with whom were they wearing masks, what constituted masks, the reasons for masking, and the responses to the mask wearers. When an individual masks their face, as with any act of dress, the behavior is oriented by all previous iterations of masking. Addressivity binds the individual act to its discursive histories of practice, therein shaping the present as a particular spatial-temporal moment.

By applying a theory of addressivity, we are able to explain the way masking, as a form of address, requires rhetorical labor to activate history in the present.[10] Addressivity is a vortexual movement that pulls particular lived histories into the present and gives discourse a place to be directed. The act of directing discourse through address, we argue, is rhetorical labor. We attend to the way different discursive violences deepen rhetorical labor by creating a disorienting effect we call *the swirl*.[11] Swirling is an affective disorientation experienced in the anticipation of multiple discursive violences. If addressivity is meant to orient discourse by activating a history for the present, then swirling points to the competing violences that emerge and disorient as they bleed with different types of historical memory.

In this essay, we will demonstrate how the discourse of the Black Collective Corporeal Condition swirls with neoliberal public health discourse. This swirling deepens the rhetorical labor for Black folks and, as an example, provides a starting place for scholars to consider how other discursive violences might swirl together to tax some communities more than others. Between and among multiple discourses, there is no easy answer or obvious path to action; instead, navigating this complex terrain requires a delicate balancing act. Thus, we understand the swirl as having laborious features; some bodies do more work than others to thrive and survive. We proceed by first explaining the discursive formations of neoliberal health discourse and the Black Collective Corporeal Condition and then offer specific accounts of how their discursive violences swirl.

Neoliberal Public Health Discourse

In this section, we overview the discursive formation of neoliberal health discourse. This discourse emphasizes the ways individuals are expected to take personal responsibility for their health as biocitizens rather than initiating systemic changes that could address racial inequities in public health writ large. Here we focus on the way this discourse is critiqued but also adopted by Black men due to a lack of more equitable remedies. In the following sections, we turn first to a discursive tradition of corporeality in the Black community and then to the way both of these discourses swirl in the present moment of personal masking deliberation to create additional rhetorical labor for Black men.

In the United States, the discourse of public health dictates health imperatives, transforming pathologies "into a 'priority' or a 'problem.'"[12] This discourse responds "to issues of health that [a]ffect large populations" and "tends to be centered on concerns about prevention, containment, empowerment, and advocacy in relation to disease."[13] It is also neoliberal in practice. That is, US public health strategies are often positioned as an individual's responsibility. The state's role is to fuel fears of illness and produce anxieties that will lead to self-surveillance, "inciting the active monitoring of [one's] own health."[14] The individual is expected to be proactive at attaining health through practices of body modification and consumption that reduce risk and prevent illness. As *biocitizens*, individuals actively monitor their bodies through "self-observation, self-diagnosis, and self-treatment."[15] A biocitizen is marked as a "'good citizen' [when they are] autonomous, strong-willed, responsible, entrepreneurial, and relentlessly striving to improve."[16]

This neoliberal discourse of self-discipline and self-regulation shapes US public health messages about the Covid global pandemic. Through its emphasis on the individual, the messaging disregards the systematic forces and structural inequalities that fundamentally determine health and wellbeing, such as the discriminatory housing practices and policies that ghettoized neighborhoods, creating high rates of exposure to toxic pollution and inaccess to healthy food.[17] For example, note how the pandemic update to the "Action Plan to Reduce Racial and Ethnic Health Disparities" tasks individuals with taking care of themselves:

> CDC has published information for people who need to *take extra precautions*. Conditions like diabetes, hypertension, cancer, and other chronic health conditions that are prevalent at higher rates in some minority communities can elevate the risk for complications due to Covid-19. The published information offers guidance on how *those at highest risk can protect themselves*.[18]

The action plan presumes any individual, including "those at highest risk," can equally "take extra precautions" and "protect themselves," while ignoring structural and institutional contributions to conditions like "diabetes, hypertension, cancer." It presumes knowledge of the risk will itself sufficiently enable individuals to reduce the risk. These forms of public health initiatives are hollow, ineffective, and anxiety inducing, perpetuating chronic health conditions like hypertension.[19] Anyone who does not meet defined health standards is marked as an amoral, culturally deficient bio-Other regardless of the systemic barriers they face.[20] In fact, racialized cultural practices are often evoked as the cause of unhealthiness rather than the structural racism that delimits access to healthy options.[21]

Andrew Ricketts, a Black man from Harlem, describes his anxiety despite or even due to self-education during an early stage of the Covid pandemic. He is aware of the systemic inequalities facing Black folks as the virus spreads and also the way public health discourse "blames its victims at the same time." His actions nonetheless activate a neoliberal discourse and emplace biocitizenship. Before heading to the grocery store, he watches "a panic-inducing video about how droplets spread," educating himself on how to reduce health risks in public spaces. Instead of connecting his potential exposure to his social position as a Black American in the densely populated New York City, Ricketts takes responsibility for his wellbeing through a prescriptive course of actions. At the conclusion of his shopping trip, Ricketts decides on a protocol of "calming tea blends, hoping cinnamon and ginger" will "ease" his stomach."[22] Even in the face of systemic anti-black racism, many Black folks, like Ricketts, still attempt to be good biocitizens.

The Black Collective Corporeal Condition

In the previous section, we overviewed the discursive formation of neoliberal public health discourse during the pandemic. Next, we turn to a discussion of the Black Collective Corporeal Condition, a discourse developed by Black folks in response to white supremacist violence. While the terms are similar, the Black Collective Corporeal Condition has notable differences from DiArron M.'s conceptualization of the collective Black body discussed in the previous chapter. Where we focus on the conditioning of the Black body through interactional and discursive practices, DiArron M. focuses on an Africa-based shared orientation of collectivity that defines the Black experience. This section provides examples of how Black men contemplate whether to wear masks during the pandemic. After, we demonstrate the way this discourse swirled with neoliberal public health discourse to create additional rhetorical labor for Black men during the pandemic.

Embedded in the anti-black social system are tropes about Black folks as inferior, inhuman, and a problem. Despite the weight of the dominant discourse of Blackness, Black folks create space for an "alternative conception of being."[23] Through discursive processes, Black folks fashioned individual histories into a uniting narrative that nurtures community across time and space.[24] For example, by testifying and bearing witness to the various acts of racialized violence, Black folks create a discourse of the Black Collective Corporeal Condition as under attack.[25] This discursive tradition includes all the various ways Black lives have been *touched* by violence, either through the violent transportation and enslavement of their ancestors, lynching, dispossession of land, disruption of community, and sexual violence.[26] This sense of corporality foregrounds how Black folks determine risk. As Black folks mentally prepare for all of the possible outcomes of wearing a mask, they emplace this host of historical and contemporary violences of the collective corporeal condition. Some of their considerations include how the tropes about Black masculine bodies are positioned as dangerous, with a likelihood of gang association and predilection for crime.[27] Even as these racialized tropes are a type of violence, it is the activation of this discourse in the present that places Black folks at risk for lynching, racial profiling, and discrimination.

Kip Diggs, a Black Nashville marketing consultant, says "as an African American man, I have to be cognizant of the things I do and where I go, so appearances matter."[28] As Kip Diggs considers wearing a mask, he calls forth how the hypervisibility of Black people in predominantly white spaces puts him at risk.[29] To mitigate the effect his body can have in social situations with white folks, Diggs engages in self-regulation and disciplining behavior. He evokes knowledge and skills about the Black Collective Corporeal Condition, often shared during "the talk." "The talk" is a conversation typically between Black youth and a primary caretaker. It includes three dimensions: egalitarian messages, encouragement of mistrust, and preparation for bias. Egalitarian messages encourage children to gain skills that will help them thrive in the white-dominated spaces. The mistrust messages encourage children to be skeptical of the social order, ideology, and white folks. Preparation for bias offers strategies to use when encountering racist individuals and racist acts.[30] Central to the "the talk" are self-policing measures to "stay under the radar" and avoid drawing any attention to the body, sometimes colloquially called wearing a mask.[31] This includes wearing clothing that blends in with white folks, avoiding abrupt movements, regulating emotions, and generally being as inconspicuous as possible.[32]

As Diggs considers how bodily presence in the United States can impact future social situations, he draws on themes from the "the talk." For example, Diggs's cadre of masks are selected to mitigate the perceived threat and stigma induced by his racialization. He says, "I have pink, lime green, Carolina blue so I don't look menacing. I want to take a lot of that stigma and risk it as best I can."[33] Whether his efforts are a success depends on the specific set of conditions he encounters, but his active consideration of how his masked body will be experienced emplaces knowledge of the Black Collective Corporeal Condition into the present moment.

Where Diggs invests in self-regulation, Allen Hargrove expresses anxiety about any masking choice. As a 220-pound Black man with a self-described "football build," Hargrove's stature sparks concern for how he will be perceived wearing a mask.[34] His bodily awareness draws the many violences that have shaped the Black Collective Corporeal Condition into his present decision about masking. In fact, his presence and bodily size has the potential to activate or exacerbate the myth that Black bodies are dangerous "Bucks" that should be controlled.[35] As a controlling image, the "Buck" is an aggressive, hypersexual, threatening, and violent beast, constructed as biologically inferior. This controlling image provides the justification for brutality against Black men. For example, Black men are frequently presented as naturally and/

or culturally more aggressive and physical than white men in sports media coverage and therefore more dangerous and in need of white male domination.[36]

Relatively larger Black bodies can increase the likelihood of being perceived as a threat. When "you are big... they will automatically see you as a threat," writes Charles Coleman, a Black man responding to the murder of Eric Garner.[37] For Black men who are already perceived as dangerous bucks, being tall and having a large body deepens fear invoked by Black masculine bodies.[38] And while Black people are at a greater risk of being stopped by police than other racial groups, tall Black men face an even greater likelihood.[39] Gesturing to his height and stature while considering whether to wear a mask, Hargrove is pulling in all the potential ways the perception of his body has to incite racist violence. In evoking these aspects of the Black Collective Corporal Condition, Hargrove contracts the past and places the history of violence against Black men into his present consideration of dress. All of which leaves Hargrove with "a sense of anxiety wearing the mask."[40]

Swirl

On April 3, 2020, Kiese Laymon tweeted, "I had the Bane mask. Forgot I'm Black. And big. And ancestrally red-eyed. And of the United States. New mask is floral. Don't shoot. Naw, for real. Don't shoot."[41] At some moments, for some Black Americans, Covid was "not the scariest thing in their lives," and they were willing to participate in social gatherings to protest anti-black police violence "despite the risk of infection."[42] For other folks, alongside the barrage of anti-black violence is the visceral threat posed by Covid. For Black folks entangled within the Black Collective Corporeal Condition and the Covid pandemic, violent discourses of anti-blackness and neoliberal public health swirl together to create the rhetorical labor of discursive displacement. It is to this latter situation we now turn to understand the way multiple threats swirl.

A number of Black scholars speak to the entwined relationship between anti-black racism and the virus, as DiArron M. gestures to in the previous chapter. We provide three noteworthy examples that describe this entanglement: combined pandemics, health emergencies, and asymptomatic lethalities. First, Kimberly Manning, a physician, discusses the "Time of Two Pandemics" as "the intersection of the crisis of the Covid-19 pandemic, complete with its social isolation and inordinate impact on minorities, and the acuity of the grief felt by the most recent events of abject racism."[43] Second, public health educators describe this historic moment as one where "black people cannot breathe because we are currently battling at least two public health emergencies, and that is a conservative estimate."[44] Finally, T. J. Tallie, an African historian, compares the asymptomatic lethality of Covid to the asymptomatic lethality of "*all* white people." He explains, "for centuries, white people have had easy access to histories of racial power and deploy them, almost like a pathogen, against Black people." The appearance of a person as healthy while carrying Covid is similar to the appearance of a white person as not-racist while having access to white supremacist histories. Both appearances disguise their body's "always present deadly potential."[45] Amplifying Tallie's observations, we attend not only to the way people deploy histories of racial power and viral infection but also to the rhetorical labor involved in navigating histories that violently swirl the pandemics, health emergencies, and asymptomatic lethalities to remake a safe place of address.

We are all carriers of particular histories, both physical and virtual, and we access these histories to create, direct, and adapt discourse for address. Address is oriented and emplaced discourse that is capacitated through different configurations of touch. As bodies touch space-time, they enfold a past into the present and capacitate modes of address. For example, when a particular mask touches a particular face it is a mode of address whereby the touch activates a discursive time. Time is occupied in the present by contracting a past. In other words, the mask touches both the body and a history to make its address.

Address is situated in an ever-fleeting here and now, made present through a process of addressivity. Unlike address, addressivity is the condition upon which this presence emerges. The suffix "-ity" speaks to the *conditions* of address, the ceaseless quantity and sheer quality of the different kinds of history that can be enfolded infinitely into the present. As Nathan Stormer explains, addressivity is an incorporeal back and forth movement over the grounds of history to re-member a present as a place, a recursive touching of "the past in order to direct" and adapt an address.[46] Addressivity is the arena of contemplation and anticipation, where "discourse runs back over the past, again and again, in anticipation of the future."[47] Through this repetition, discourse obtains a "structure of feeling," a concept developed by Raymond Williams that Jeffrey A. Bennett elaborates on in this volume. A structure of feeling, or what is felt through patterns of thought, emerges in history and has a trajectory. For example, through a discourse of the Black Collective Corporeal Condition, Black men contemplate all the potential violences that may occur when a mask touches their face in moments leading to address. This will condition not only what will be touched but where and when it will be touched as an address. However, when the option of not wearing a mask has its own life-threatening consequences, when neoliberal health and anti-black racist discourses of masking swirl together, the labor of address is amplified.

The swirl speaks to the way a discursive solution to one violence is the cause of another violence: If Black folks wear the mask they may be subject to a racist violence; if they do not wear the mask they may be subject to a viral violence. There are no guarantees of safe address in the swirl of violent discourses. The swirl is disorienting as both discourses are borne and endure through different forms of death-accelerating violence, their deadly potential.

In US public health discourse, any threat posed by the virus activates neoliberal discursive solutions to avoid undue risk and provide protection. As potential good biocitizens, white people, for the most part, can displace the threat of the virus by capacitating the appropriate address—wearing a mask in public space. However, when the neoliberal public health discursive solution activates a different death-accelerating violence—racism—there is more work to be done, more threats to displace. The labor of rhetoric is to "search for a body in the present . . . to contract another place into the present so that [another] discourse may 'speak'" from a less risky place.[48] Black people must work to displace a new threat by capacitating an alternative discourse and reorienting the address. This creates more addressive work in preparing for the moment of masking.

This is the case for award-winning author Kiese Laymon, a "big [a]nd ancestrally red-eyed" Black man living in the United States. He describes his fear of being perceived as a threat when wearing a mask that was conveniently available to him. He writes, "I had the Bane mask," the mask worn by Batman villain Bane, which also looks like the N95 mask. However, he "forgot" he is Black and cannot wear a mask associated with villainy in an anti-black racist society. Instead, he adopts a red floral mask with large pink, yellow, and baby blue flowers.[49] After contemplating the emplacement of historical and contemporary violences of the Black Collective Corporeal Condition, he accommodates anti-black racism with a colorful garden patterned mask, attempting to avoid further violence. This labor is rhetorical work, that is, time and energy put toward emplacing his body differently. In the swirl, Black men anticipate outcomes and engage in preparation to reduce the risks posed by multiple discursive violences. Three further examples elaborate on this disorienting labor conducted by Black men.

As Black sociology professor Calvin John Smiley considers whether wearing a mask is safe, he invokes a different dimension of historical violences of the Black Collective Corporeal Condition. His concerns center around how Black masculine bodies are associated with gangs and labeled as thugs, trends that have emerged as mainstays in sports media and news programming.[50] This consideration underscores why Smiley and other Black men in a WhatsApp chat group collectively agree that "the standard darker blue or standard red colors were ones that we all kind of said, we're definitely not going to wear that," because of their associations with Crips and Bloods. In their discussion about whether to mask and how to mask, they express concern about how labels, such as a thug or gangster, are used to justify anti-black violence. The risk for being associated with gangs is increased police attention and racial profiling, which leaves Smiley wondering "do I wear this mask and potentially be stopped and profiled by the police? Or do I not wear it and risk my health and livelihood?"[51]

Smiley is caught in a swirl of discursive violences. When he states, "This really is a matter of health and people's lives, so we can't ignore it,"[52] it is evident he feels a sense of personal responsibility to mask in order to protect his own health and the health of the community. As he contemplates neoliberal discursive action he experiences addressive displacement, swirled between two divergent discursive formations. He is pulled into the historical potential of these violences and, feeling confined by either one or the other: "It's really a horrible decision to make."[53]

George Wesley, a Black freelance video editor and graphic designer, like Calvin Smiley, Kipp Diggs, and Allen Hargrove is aware of how white folks' perception of his body can place him at risk for violent encounters, particularly in overwhelmingly white social spaces.[54] Prior to entering a social space Wesley considers the possible racial demographics. His contemplation of racial demographics emplaces a host of violences done to Black folks in majority white spaces into his present consideration of whether to wear a mask—from the evils of the enslavement period, where Black folks were raped, worked, and beaten to death, to the discriminatory practices that uphold segregation, such as sundowning and violent removal of Black folks from their homes through the 1970s, to the legal murder of Black folks.[55] As he anticipates and considers future experiences, Wesley compresses the space between past racialized violences and the present moment. He would feel more comfortable wearing a mask in a location with diverse patrons but if the space is predominantly white, he says "I will take my mask down to make them feel comfortable, compromising my health."[56] His strategy is a performance of deference to any white folks in the vicinity, as he recognizes that his chances for survival are higher if he participates in the maintenance of the racial social order that privileges whites and subordinates Black folks.[57] Layered into Wesley's concern for racialized violence is the relationship between tropes about Black masculinity as dangerous beastly criminals and the practice of carrying concealed weapons.[58]

As Wesley considers the practice of wearing a mask, he states, "Am I going to risk my health or am I going to risk it all and pray that no one in this open-carry state mistakes me for a volatile?"[59] Embedded in his question are the various ways the presence of Black masculine bodies in majority white spaces enable "justifiable violence" against Black men. This then swirls with a neoliberal discourse about health risks. Wesley is keenly aware that the violence, aggression, and criminal intent projected onto his body by whites could be exacerbated by wearing a mask.[60] If white folks, who wield an enormous amount of power over Black folks in such social situations, feel any sort of threat, or insecurity, they have the latitude to wield that power in violent ways under the guise of protection.[61] Simultaneously, Wesley evokes neoliberal public health discourse as he expresses responsibility to protect his health and avoid catching Covid. He knows that not wearing a mask is risky behavior that might mark him as a weak-willed bio-Other who does not live responsibly.[62] In the swirl, there is no easy answer. As Wesley contemplates his address—"Black with a mask is a gamble"—but so too is not wearing a mask.[63]

As Gabriel Felix, a Black physician, contemplates wearing a mask, he discursively draws in the Black Collective Corporeal Condition. He says, "I wonder whether someone would call the police on me, a 'suspicious' Black man in a face mask."[64] Felix's concerns center around the presumption that Black men are predators and criminals, a trope that is often evoked to justify violent measures against Black people by white folks, particularly in predominantly white neighborhoods.[65] Felix evokes this violent history as he comments,

> The recent murder of Ahmaud Arbery, who was shot while jogging through a neighborhood outside Brunswick, Ga., serves as another reminder for me that, as a Black person, enjoying simple activities such as jogging outside requires preparing for the possibility of losing my life."[66]

Even as Black folks participate in the most mundane of activities, like jogging, their Black(ened) bodies are at risk for white violence.[67] By drawing in the violent history of anti-black lynching, Felix contracts the space between the past and the present.

Swirled into his concerns about how wearing a mask might incur racialized violence, Felix also evokes the neoliberal discourse of good biocitizenship. He states, "As a physician, I favor things that will help reduce the transmission of coronavirus infections." But as a Black man, I wondered how this order will affect people who look like me."[68] His sense of responsibility to prevent the spread of Covid by self-directed action—wearing a mask—places him at risk for a different type of harm: racialized violence. The neoliberal discursive solution disregards how racialized status impacts the effectiveness of masking as a protective device.

Conclusion

We opened this essay with a discussion of Aaron Thomas's antanaclasis: "I want to stay alive but I also want to stay alive." Thomas's tweet is about his decision not to wear a mask until a protective mask is available. Shortly after his post, @DeeboDown replied with a video article showing two Black men, Jermon Best and Diangelo Jackson, wearing protective masks as they were followed around an Illinois Walmart by a white cop. Best and Jackson record the officer telling them to take off their masks as he tracks them from behind. What @DeeboDown shares with @Aaron_Thomas through the discourse of the Black Collective Corporeal Condition is that whether he wears a protective mask, he will still be at risk of experiencing racism. Wearing a mask while Black emplaces his body with a history of violence.

In this essay, Black men resist the one-dimensional and neoliberal framing of masking as the healthy option, instead drawing attention to the ways that masking can also lead to bodily harm. The blanket neoliberal frame of mask mandates neglects the racial politics of masking and its implications when moving through social space. A mask is placed in a prominent location frequently used to ascribe race: the face. While neoliberal public health discourse focuses on how bodies are safer with masks, donning a mask is also rife with racial tropes that Black folks, in being familiar with the discourse of the Black Collective Corporeal Condition, are keenly aware of. The orientation of the address proposed by neoliberal public health discourse creates disorientation when it swirls with the Black Collective Corporeal Condition. Due to anti-black racism, there are increased risks associated with the types of masks worn, as well as how and when people wear them. The rhetorical labor is to make a place in the present that does not reiterate historical violences.

This research has taken seriously the dress in addressivity to understand the configuration of race and pandemic masks. Masking has disorienting spatiotemporal presencing-effects for Black folks, emerging from multiple messy histories swirling in a curvilinear temporality. Multiple here and nows are pulled to the present to unsettle a safe discursive relation. Negotiating the discursive violences is disorienting work. As the neoliberal imperative to mask is removed, so goes the disorientation from the swirl and a reduction of rhetorical labor. The risks of being infected by the virus are entangled with the risks of being subjected to racism, which troubles the presumption that masks are safe for everybody.

NOTES

1. Aaron Thomas's tweet received over sixteen-thousand retweets, 1,381 quote tweets, and over 118,300 likes. @Aaron_TheThomas, Twitter post, April 4, 2020, https://twitter.com/Aaron_TheThomas/status/1246493711032356866. Thomas's Twitter account is no longer active.
2. David DiSalvo, "I Spent a Day in the Coronavirus-Driven Feeding Frenzy of N95 Mask Sellers and Buyers and This is What I Learned," *Forbes*, March 30, 2020.
3. Geneviève Rail and Shannon Jette, "Reflections on Biopedagogies and/of Public Health: On Bio-Others, Rescue Missions, and Social Justice," *Cultural Studies ↔ Critical Methodologies* 15, no. 5 (2015): 327–36.
4. Aaron Thomas (@Aaron_TheThomas), Twitter post, April 4, 2020, https://twitter.com/Aaron_TheThomas/status/1246493711032356866.
5. Joe R. Feagin, *Systemic Racism: A Theory of Oppression* (London: Routledge/Taylor & Francis Group).
6. Kimberly D. Manning, "When Grief and Crises Intersect: Perspectives of a Black Physician in the Time of Two Pandemics," *Journal of Hospital Medicine* 15, no. 9 (2020): 566–67.
7. Jingqiu Ren and Joe Feagin, "Face Mask Symbolism in Anti-Asian Hate Crimes," *Ethnic and Racial Studies* 44, no. 5 (2021): 746–58; Hee An Choi and Othelia EunKyoung Lee, "To Mask or To Unmask, That Is the Question: Facemasks and Anti-Asian

Violence During COVID-19," *Journal of Human Rights and Social Work* (2021); Jo Hsu, "Containment and Interdependence: Epidemic Logics in Asian American Racialization," *QED: A Journal in GLBTQ Worldmaking* 7, no. 3 (2020): 125–34.

8. Susan Carland, "Isamophobia, Fear of Loss of Freedom, and the Muslim Woman," *Islam and Christian-Muslim Relations* 22, no. 4 (2011): 496–73; Abid Farhadi, "The Faces of Islamophobia," in *Countering Violent Extremism by Winning Hearts and Minds* (Tampa, FL: Springer, 2020), 82–112.

9. Anna Piela, "Muslim Women Who Cover Their Faces Find Greater Acceptance Among Coronavirus Masks—'Nobody Is Giving Me Dirty Looks,'" *The Conversation*, April 10, 2020.

10. We primarily build on a theorization of addressivity in the work of Nathan Stormer.

11. Stormer's project is historiographic while ours emphasizes active place-making efforts. However, we are both concerned with the way rhetoric "occupies time" and how remembering and forgetting "are functions inherent to discursive praxis that acclimatize rhetoric to time and space.... performing the present as a figurative event." Nathan Stormer, "Recursivity: A Working Paper on Rhetoric and *Mnesis*," *Quarterly Journal of Speech* 99 (2013): 30.

12. Patrick Cloos, "The Racialization of U.S. Public Health: A Paradox of the Modern State," *Cultural Studies ↔ Critical Methodologies* 15, no. 5 (2015): 380.

13. Jennifer Malkowski and Lisa Melonçon, "The Rhetoric of Public Health for RHM Scholarship and Beyond," *Rhetoric of Health & Medicine* 2, no. 2 (2019): iii.

14. Rail and Jette, "Reflections on Biopedagogies," 328.

15. Rail and Jette, "Reflections on Biopedagogies," 328.

16. Rail and Jette, "Reflections on Biopedagogies," 329.

17. Richard Rothstein, *The Color of Law: A Forgotten History of How Our Government Segregated America* (New York: Liveright Publishing Corporation, 2017): 17–38; David R. Williams and Selina A. Mohammed, "Racism and Health I: Pathways and Scientific Evidence," *American Behavioral Scientist* 57, no. 8 (2013): 1157.

18. Emphasis ours. US Department of Health & Human Services. *2020 Update on the Action Plan to Reduce Racial and Ethnic Health Disparities*, 2020, 12.

19. Ted Schrecker and Clare Bambra, *How Politics Makes Us Sick: Neoliberal Epidemics* (New York: Palgrave Macmillan, 2015).

20. Rail and Jette, "Reflections on Biopedagogies."

21. Cloos, "Racialization of U.S. Public Health"; John Sankofa and Wendy L. Johnson-Taylor, "News Coverage of Diet-Related Health Disparities Experienced by Black Americans: A Steady Diet of Misinformation," *Journal of Nutrition Education and Behavior* 39, no. 2

(2007): S41–S44.
22. Andrew Ricketts, "Masking While Black Could Be More Dangerous Than the Alternative: Walking through the World Becomes Even More Fraught," *Level*, April 2020.
23. Zakiyyah Iman Jackson, *Becoming Human: Matter and Meaning in an Antiblack World* (New York: New York University Press, 2020), 3.
24. Kidada E. Williams and Diana Johnstone, *They Left Great Marks on Me: African American Testimonies of Racial Violence from Emancipation to World War I* (New York: New York University Press, 2012), 9.
25. Dwight A. McBride, *Impossible Witnesses: Truth, Abolitionism, and Slave Testimony* (New York: New York University Press, 2001); Williams and Johnstone, *They Left*.
26. Joe R. Feagin, "Documenting the Costs of Slavery, Segregation, and Contemporary Racism: Why Reparations Are in Order for African Americans," *Harvard Blackletter Law Journal* 20 (2004): 49.
27. Ronald L. Jackson II, *Scripting the Black Masculine Body: Identity, Discourse, and Racial Politics in Popular Media* (Albany: SUNY Press, 2006).
28. Tracy Jan, "Two Black Men Say They Were Kicked Out of Walmart for Wearing Protective Masks. Others Worry It Will Happen to Them," *Washington Post*, April 9, 2020.
29. Charles A. Gallagher, "Miscounting Race: Explaining Whites' Misperceptions of Racial Group Size," *Sociological Perspectives* 46, no. 3 (2003): 381–96.
30. Abril Harris and Ndidiamaka Amutah-Onukagha, "Under the Radar: Strategies Used by Black Mothers to Prepare Their Sons for Potential Police Interactions," *Journal of Black Psychology* 45, no. 6–7 (2019): 439–53.
31. The practice of putting on a metaphorical mask has been used to describe the performative alterations made by Black folks as they traverse predominantly Black and white spaces. While demonstrative of embodied performance, the mask metaphor presumes an authentic state of being beneath the mask. Instead, we point to each embodied performance as entangled within the dynamics present. See Darrell Hudson et al., "Surviving the White Space: Perspectives on How Middle-Class Black Men Navigate Cultural Racism," *Ethnic and Racial Studies* (2020): 1–19; Frantz Fanon, *Black Skin, White Masks*, ed. Charles Lam Markmann (New York: Grove Press, 1967).
32. Dawn Marie Dow, *Mothering While Black: Boundaries and Burdens of Middle-Class Parenthood* (Berkeley: University of California Press, 2019); Harris and Amutah-Onukagha, "Under the Radar," 439–53.
33. Tracy Jan, "Two Black Men."
34. Derrick Bryson Taylor, "For Black Men, Fear That Masks Will Invite Racial Profiling," *The New York Times*. April 14, 2020. Taylor, "For Black Men."

35. Patricia Hill Collins, *Black Sexual Politics: African Americans, Gender, and The New Racism* (London: Routledge, 2004).
36. Abby L. Ferber, "The Construction of Black Masculinity: White Supremacy Now and Then," *Journal of Sport and Social Issues* 31, no. 1 (2007): 11–24.
37. Charles F. Coleman Jr., "Eric Garner: Tall, Dark and Threatening," *Ebony*, July 16, 2019.
38. Neil Hester and Kurt Gray, "For Black Men, Being Tall Increases Threat Stereotyping and Police Stops," *Proceedings of the National Academy of Sciences* 115, no. 11 (2018): 2714.
39. Hester and Gray, "For Black Men."
40. Taylor, "For Black Men."
41. Kiese Laymon (@KieseLaymon), Twitter post, April 3, 2020, https://twitter.com/KieseLaymon/status/1246223090352349184.
42. Usha Lee McFarling, "'Which Death Do They Choose?' Many Black Men Fear Wearing a Mask More Than the Coronavirus," *STAT*, June 3, 2020.
43. Manning, "When Grief," 567.
44. Rachel R. Hardeman, Eduardo M. Medina, and Rhea W. Boyd, "Stolen Breaths," *New England Journal of Medicine* 383, no. 3 (2020): 198.
45. T. J. Tallie, "Asymptomatic Lethality: Cooper, COVID-19, and the Potential for Black Death," *Nursing Clio*, June 8, 2020.
46. Remembering always entails forgetting other memories that were not selected. Stormer, "Recursivity," 35.
47. Stormer, "Recursivity," 41.
48. Stormer, "Recursivity," 39.
49. Kiese Laymon (@KieseLaymon), Twitter post, April 3, 2020, https://twitter.com/KieseLaymon/status/1246223090352349184.
50. Stacy L. Lorenz and Rod Murray, "'Goodbye to the Gangstas': The NBA Dress Code, Ray Emery, and the Policing of Blackness in Basketball and Hockey," *Journal of Sport and Social Issues* 38, no. 1 (2014): 23–50.
51. Amelia Thomson-DeVeaux and Likhitha Butchireddygari, "For Black Americans, Wearing A Mask Comes with Complicated Anxieties," *FiveThirtyEight*, June 30, 2020, https://fivethirtyeight.com/features/for-black-americans-wearing-a-mask-comes-with-complicated-anxieties/.
52. Thomson-DeVeaux and Butchireddygari, "For Black Americans."
53. Thomson-DeVeaux and Butchireddygari, "For Black Americans."
54. Elijah Anderson, "The White Space," *Sociology of Race and Ethnicity* 1, no. 1 (2015): 10–12.
55. Williams and Johnstone, *They Left*. James W. Loewen, *Sundown Towns: A Hidden Dimension of American Racism* (La Vergne, TN: New Press, 2018). Ersula J. Ore, *Lynching:*

Violence, Rhetoric, and American Identity (Jackson: University Press of Mississippi, 2019).
56. Nathalie Baptiste, "The Dangers of Covering Your Face While Black," *Mother Jones*, April 27, 2020.
57. Anderson, "White Space."
58. Angela Stroud, "Good Guys with Guns: Hegemonic Masculinity and Concealed Handguns," *Gender and Society* 26, no. 2 (2012): 216–38.
59. Baptiste, "Dangers of Covering."
60. Stroud, "Good Guys."
61. Anderson, "White Space."
62. Rail and Jette, "Reflections on Biopedagogies," 330.
63. Baptiste, "Dangers of Covering."
64. Gabriel Felix, "Wearing a Face Mask Helps Protect Me Against Covid-19, but Not Against Racism," *STAT*, 2020.
65. Maria R. Lowe, Angela Stroud, and Alice Nguyen, "Who Looks Suspicious? Racialized Surveillance in a Predominantly White Neighborhood," *Social Currents* 4, no. 1 (2016): 34–50.
66. Felix, "Wearing a Face Mask."
67. Rashawn Ray, "Black People Don't Exercise in My Neighborhood: Perceived Racial Composition and Leisure-Time Physical Activity among Middle Class Blacks and Whites," *Social Science Research* 66 (August 2017): 42–57.
68. Felix, "Wearing a Face Mask."

Covid and Disability

Tactical Responses to Normative Vaccine Communication in Appalachia

Julie Gerdes, Priyanka Ganguly, and Luana Shafer

WE WANT TO START WITH A DISCLAIMER: NONE OF US IS FROM THE GEOgraphic communities that we write of here. We all have different relationships to the identity of "disabled," and we have limited familiarity with the towns and local health systems where our study took place.

Nevertheless, when this project started, we felt that we had some experience and expertise, as rhetoricians of health, to offer ongoing pandemic communication efforts. As we received funding to implement Covid communication research in November 2020, it had become clear that vaccines were going to be where we could have the most value-add as rhetoricians of health interested in inclusive, accessible communication. This work began with an innocent call to collaborators across campus. Was there interest in partnering with rhetoricians around Covid vaccine communication? Oh, and by the way, we have a small internal grant to do this. Counterparts from public health connected us to health districts, who immediately came back, asking, "Can we do focus groups?!" And we were off to the races.

In December 2020, we met for the first time with two adjacent health departments that straddle the border of Appalachia. Together, these departments include twelve counties and independent cities in the same state. On a joint call with collaborators from the university's public health department and the local health districts, we chatted about anticipated challenges of the upcoming vaccine rollout and about their priorities for outreach. One colleague mentioned that there had been some focus groups around communication materials in the state capital, lamenting that feedback from people with disabilities in the state was negative. People did not feel like their realities were represented or well considered. As rhetoricians engaged in social justice research, we were not necessarily surprised. We wanted to see how people in the area who identified as disabled viewed vaccines in relation to official vaccination campaign messages.

Appalachian residence and experiences are complex and varied, at times sharing qualities with other rural or regional scholarship and, at others, unique to communities in the region. A 1982 Appalachian studies reflection piece states, "An adequate regional studies approach must be a hybrid. It should be firmly rooted in the life of the particular region it serves as well as aware of the context in which that region exists."[1] We agree, offering theoretical reflections on the experiences of people with disabilities in the region while also acknowledging that these are localized and impacted by varying degrees of economic, racial, and societal privilege. We recognize this geographic context as one that implicates and mediates but does not exclusively define identity. Our work seeks to locate acts of discursive privileging of able-bodiedness while acknowledging the diversity in which people experience those acts. For people with physical disabilities in the region, the hilly landscape is a metaphor for access to specialized care with its long, windy, and rocky roads.

The Appalachian Regional Commission (ARC) defines the Appalachian region as covering 420 counties in thirteen states running from New York to Northern Mississippi. The region is bound, in part, by its connection to the Appalachian Mountains, which have shaped its cultural history. However, exact mapping of the region is historically tied to the promise of economic and colonial exploitation. In addition to its mark as part of Europeans' westward colonial expansion, the region was redefined following the Civil War. The regional boundary eventually became what it is today with the creation of the ARC under the Appalachian Regional Development Act of 1965, which marked Appalachia as a "special territory of federal intervention," expanding from ten to thirteen states as "a sure way to broaden potential congressional support for regional policies."[2]

In Appalachia, people are more likely to face disability issues in all domains, such as vision; cognitive, mobility, self-care, and independent living, compared to people outside Appalachia. Analyses of the distribution of federal disability insurance benefits since the late 1960s have mapped regions receiving high benefits on to areas with high concentrations of jobs in physical labor. These areas cover most of

Appalachia and the rural South in what has been deemed the "Disability Belt," as well as pockets of the West in areas like eastern Washington state.[3]

Appalachian studies, an interdisciplinary field rooted in understanding regional representations, traditionally focused on the marginalization of the region and the discipline but not necessarily within the region. However, the field has increasingly taken up identity issues and intersectional research. Intersectionality importantly owes its theoretical foundations to Black women including Kimberlé Williams Crenshaw, bell hooks, and (before the term was popularized) Sojourner Truth.[4] The concept now helps scholars across disciplines in the social sciences and humanities, including Appalachian and public health studies, draw attention to methods and modes of analysis that address the reality of multiple marginalization. In her intersectional research on gender, race, and sexuality in Appalachia, Anna Rachel Terman pulls on Appalachian studies scholars Barbara Ellen Smith and Stephen L. Fisher to warn against place-based identity or conflating place with "community."[5] Nevertheless, scholarship on medicine and health disparities tend to isolate Appalachian healthcare as largely rural and uniform; Appalachia has been labeled as a socially and economically disadvantaged part of the United States despite the fact that Appalachian residents have been linked to regional, national, and global markets before the industrial transformation of the region.[6]

One example of emergent attention to intersectional Appalachian scholarship is that of increasing acknowledgment of "Affrilachian" experiences. The term "Affrilachian" was coined by Black Appalachian poets-resident Frank X. Walker and taken up by writers and creators of the region in the 1990s as a way to push against the stereotype of Appalachia as white, rural, and poor.[7] While stereotypes of race in the region have erased the experiences of non-white residents, stereotypes of health and education in the region have depicted a disproportionate amount of intellectual disability, portraying the Appalachian "hillbilly" as not only poor and white but also dumb, slow, lazy, and out of touch. Our hope in this chapter is to push against these stereotypes.

In fact, we suggest that vaccine uptake in the region is actually tied to rigorous intellectualism and to a push back against historic public health messaging that perpetuates negative stereotypes of disability rather than addressing root causes of access to quality technical information and care-centered providers. Vaccination rates are historically low across disease profiles, and the case of Covid vaccines has been no different. In a February–March 2020 survey study with adults over the age of thirty-five in Appalachia, 27 percent of respondents reported they were "extremely unlikely" to get the Covid vaccine compared to a national average of 15 percent at the time.[8] In that study, trust in healthcare was a key concept and an indicator of vaccine readiness.

We take up Heidi Y. Lawrence's material exigency approach to investigating vaccine discourse, understanding the intersection of disability with vaccination as an important space to explore perspectives outside of denialism.[9] Like Lawrence, we wish to interrogate dated anti- or denialist rhetoric around vaccination and argue that unvaccinated does not mean anti-vaccination. We approach this task through the lens of epistemic violence, a term developed by Gayatri Spivak and further defined by Black feminist scholar Kristie Dotson as "a failure of an audience to communicatively reciprocate, either intentionally or unintentionally, in linguistic exchanges owning to pernicious ignorance."[10] We ultimately argue that tropes that ignore the material exigencies of the Covid vaccine, from its side effects and newness to its promise for the return to romantic prepandemic practices, inflicts epistemic violence on people with disabilities.

Community service boards, nonprofits, and individual advocates work to address access to care and medical commodities for people with disabilities. Nevertheless, local news, billboards, and public clinics developed by and with health departments have played a large role in the pandemic communications response. In this chapter, we rhetorically analyze official institutional vaccine campaigns alongside focus group discussions with people with disabilities to understand institutional tropes of vaccine safety and appeals to normalcy as epistemically violent responses to rhetorical exigencies that emerge at the intersection of disability and the Covid vaccine.

Disability Studies, Technical Communication, and Rhetoric

Literature on disability studies and rhetoric tend to focus on either accessibility in technical communication or on confronting ableist language, with technical communicators acknowledging that its practices have historically constructed normalizing discourses.[11] James Wilson writes, "Disability studies provides a unique site from which to critically examine the assumptions of medicine and science and their interrelated and mutually reinforcing discourses. Medical science pathologizes disability as impairment and defect."[12] This positioning is seen throughout public health discourse in general and in vaccine campaigns in specific. We discuss this later in the chapter.

The term "normal" has historically marginalized people with disabilities, when normal requires "accessibility accommodations" to allow for rest or inclusion in daily activities. The US healthcare system, including policymaking, public health messaging, medical resource allocation, and the individual-oriented medical model, relies on the ableist notion of a so-called normal perspective.[13] Ableism, or "an orientation that considers physical deviation from a presupposed norm as a lack," creates "a system of discrimination that rhetorically invents and employs the idea of a 'normal body.'"[14] Through this rhetorical invention, any deviation from "normal" marks people as disabled, and people labeled disabled are treated as inferior. In this power dynamic, "normal" people are privileged, and rhetorically generated non-normal people are oppressed.

The rhetorical and epistemic violence of normalcy extends to white supremacy. For instance, David M. Peña-Guzmán and Joel Michael Reynolds write that through "epistemic schemas," or information-filtering mechanisms, networks of information might be prioritized while other information gets downgraded based on the context or situation. They write that racism is an epistemic schema that bleeds into "all sorts of knowing activities."[15] Epistemic schemas based on body-, gender-, or racial-systems are often implicit rather than explicit, rendering us unaware of the influence they have on societal modes of knowing that reinforce harmful stereotypes and stigmatization. Racism in medicine almost always involves some sort of prejudice and stigma, which also holds true for ableism. Ableism, like racism, is understood as an epistemic schema that fosters "epistemic ignorance rooted in privilege and prejudice on the part of healthcare providers."[16]

People with disabilities are one of the largest, yet under-recognized, health disparity groups.[17] One of the many barriers to quality healthcare that public health literature reports is the pervasive use of normalizing language in doctor-patient interactions.[18] Providers that are reluctant to listen to or respect the disabled community align to a healthcare system that follows the traditional medical model of ability in which a disability is considered "an objective medical condition in need of treatment or rehabilitation."[19] The alternative social model that views disability as arising from the social and built environment might offer practical solutions by integrating community perspectives.

Technical communication is a field well-positioned to study ableism in health services and medical commodity issues using social and humanistic models that interrogate the use of language. For instance, James Cherney found that stereotypes around "non-normal" bodies get reified in technical and medical communication. According to his work, any level of disability can work to exclude people in situations deemed relevant. This ableist notion "represents an underestimated concept by many healthcare workers and policy makers in evaluating the equity of service provision to patients with disabilities."[20]

In the introduction to her edited collection *Rhetorical Accessibility: At the Intersection of Technical Communication and Disability Studies*, Lisa Meloncon calls out theoretical foundations and an interest in discourse as ties that bound the fields of rhetorically centered technical communication and disability studies. She goes one step further, though, articulating the fields' shared interest in a programmatic approach to improving accessibility.[21] Here, we tend to this concern, understanding language about vaccines as an access issue with serious consequences. We see the relationship between language and vaccination to be as much about access to information based on an ethic of care and empowerment as it is about access to physical vaccines and clinical sites.

Vaccine Rhetorics

Vaccine communication experts have used rhetoric to understand underlying complexities in vaccine debates, importantly moving beyond binary stances that are common in media discourse. In *Vaccine Rhetorics*, Heidi Lawrence uses the lens of material exigency to understand the nature of vaccine controversy, explaining that "vaccines shape, constrain, and configure human action."[22] She writes that material exigencies—of disease, eradication, injury, and the unknown—can help ontologize discordant vaccine discourse as more than just denialist and instead as a response to real phenomena in health and medicine that are both physical and cultural.[23] We take up this view, as have other rhetoricians. For instance, one group of international scholars recently argued that a rhetorically modified exigence "is especially the case for those that are not necessarily ardent vaccine skeptics or conspiracy believers, but have second thoughts about, for instance, the possible side effects of a newly introduced vaccine."[24]

A material-rhetorical lens "makes the operations of material objects knowable, revealing the 'imperfections marked by urgency' of the rhetorical situation and making them open to modification."[25] We are able to conceptualize the different perceptions of what we consider the risks, benefits, safety, and harm of vaccines by viewing vaccine hesitancy as "material enactments of the body," as opposed to social constructs. This helps us move away from the pro-/anti-vaccine binary and allows rhetoricians to respond to and acknowledge the "multiplicities of realities" created by various medical interventions and policies.

We, as do Veronica Joyner and Heidi Y. Lawrence in their chapter in this volume, push this argument farther to suggest that vaccine readiness among marginalized communities is rhetorically different from that of people who occupy privileged social positions. In the case of people with disabilities, exigence must account not only for accessibility to the material requirements of a vaccine such as transportation, accessible clinic sites, and trained providers but also inclusive communication about the vaccine. We suggest that disability opens a space in vaccination decision-making that is separate from denialism. Moreover, attending to a material exigency lens methodologically opens up space that is particularly important for ethically examining the experiences of people in non-normative bodies, or bodies that have been deemed unruly by hegemonic medical systems, as the material exigencies of medical safety, side effects, and medical authority carry particularly high stakes in the context of physical and intellectual disability.

We take up a contextual, material approach and analyze disability within vaccines and vaccine hesitancy as an important space in which to explore perspectives outside of denialism. While we heard some vaccine rejection from participants, the far more saturated wait-and-see mentality provides critical insight into alternative vaccine rhetorics—those that simultaneously oppose injections and support science.

Methods

This project used a hybrid methodology for data collection and analysis, combining critical rhetorical analysis with focus groups. The combination of rhetorical analysis and empirical research improved our overall understanding of felt rhetorical effects. That is, we could test hypotheses from our rhetorical analysis in real time with real audiences.

Our rhetorical analysis focused on materials developed for a statewide campaign and rolled out to local health districts. We confirmed with colleagues in the health districts that these were the materials they intended to promote on social and print media and that there were no materials targeted at people with disabilities in the corpus of official government materials. Therefore, we focused on general vaccine promotion designs that participants might encounter on local and state social media channels, on billboards, and in posters at local municipal or clinical offices.

We collected 103 communication artifacts from between August 2020 and June 2021. As we progressed in the project and messages began to shift, we continued to collect and update our repository of materials, revising questions posed to focus group participants, so that participants in early March responded to one set of artifacts, and participants in June reviewed similar but perhaps not the same documents. For instance, when the vaccine was already available to the general public, we no longer focused on prioritization rhetorics, but we continued to show materials on side effects for the duration of focus group meetings.

We reviewed artifacts in our repository against the following inclusion criteria: (a) text length under three hundred words or three minutes if audiovisual; (b) publication date between January 1 and June 15, 2021 (when focus group participants would have been recently exposed to them); (c) focus on vaccine-specific messages; (d) authorship from CDC or a health authority in the state; and (e) intended for a public audience as part of a mass media campaign, including social media shareables, public service announcements, and public-facing infographics and excluding lengthy fact sheets or town hall meeting recordings. Two of us reviewed all materials against the inclusion criteria, and if there was a discrepancy, the third team member made the final call. In all, we ended up with thirty-six materials that met inclusion criteria.

After collective exploratory coding on a small subset of eight artifacts, we used NVivo to code remaining materials and to better understand what rhetorics undergirded the health department's messages about vaccines. Coding these materials helped us not only tailor our focus group discussion questions but also see where there was overlap in artifacts' messaging and in participants' concerns. Conversely, it helped us see where there were vastly divergent areas of concern, especially in comparing NVivo codes between artifacts and transcripts, which we intentionally kept separate.

For the empirical research portion of the project, we collaborated with two local health departments. Initially conceptualized as a survey study, we quickly shifted plans to accommodate the health departments' preference for focus groups. This preference is becoming a norm in community and public health research, particularly formative research, as a result of an increasing understanding of health as socially constructed and because of the ability of focus groups to elicit experience, beliefs, and opinions among and with community insiders.[26] Between March and June 2020, we conducted five focus groups on Zoom. We worked with local community service boards to share information about our study with their clients, and we recruited participants into an electronic survey consisting of three sections:

1. basic demographic data, including eligibility screening questions;
2. brief questions about vaccine and vaccine communication perceptions, including a question asking participants to react to a state health campaign material; and
3. contact and availability information to enroll in a focus group.

The survey took, on average, seven minutes and forty-nine seconds for this group to complete. We were recruiting from other populations, and nineteen people out of seventy-two respondents answered, "Yes, physical disability" and/or "Yes, mental disability" to the question "Do you experience any physical or mental disabilities" in the recruitment survey. Of these nineteen, English was the primary home language for all, ten experienced a physical disability alone, five experienced mental disability alone, and four reported physical and mental disability together. Of those nineteen, five answered, "No, I would get it today" to the question, "Do you have any reservations about taking one of the Covid vaccines" and were thus excluded from the study, and one more answered, "No" to agreement to be contacted to participate in a focus group. Four were lost during the scheduling process. In many cases, scheduling required multiple follow-ups. For two participants, our efforts resulted in conducting one-on-one interviews. The other three focus groups included two, three, and three participants.

Overall, the ten participants we reached represented five of the twelve counties in our health districts, seven were white, two were Black or African American, and one was Latinx or Hispanic. Four participants classified their home as rural, four as suburban, and two as urban. Additionally, four were members of a formal faith community and six were not. See Appendix A for a breakdown of responses to demographic questions that participants answered. While this was not a representative sample, we found that it largely mirrored demographics in the area.

We encountered a few challenges with recruitment, which we surmise were a combination of technical and social factors. For one, we conducted focus groups a year into the pandemic, when many of our colleagues and friends were complaining of Zoom fatigue. We had IRB approval to conduct in-person focus groups, which we thought would be important for reaching people where they were and through existing networks such as routine house visits or in-person services. However, community partners had halted all in-person services during this phase of the pandemic. In scheduling, we found that one or two people said that they were open to in-person meetings, but these respondents ultimately chose to access the study through phone calls or Zoom. As such, our study inadvertently privileged active internet users.

Another major factor that influenced our recruitment was the fear of stigma that an environment of public health channels pushing vaccines had created. It turns out that people who are not vaccinated do not particularly want to jump up and discuss vaccines. In some cases, we received emails from interested participants who expressed an urgency in getting their stories out and combating the perception that they were "anti-vax." Given that this urgency to debunk the anti-vax and anti-science arguments that emerged in recruitment as well as in the context of focus group meetings, we believe that labeling the study as a "vaccine communication" study and including nonvaccination status as an eligibility requirement reinforced a fear of antagonism in the recruitment phase.

Last, we understand this fear of antagonism as, in part, a direct offshoot of historic institutional and academic ableism and racism. In fact, "participant trust in research and research institutions is one of the most, if not the most, significant factors associated with research participation."[27] We understand medical mistrust and distrust in research as a product of historic and systematic oppression that leads to disproportionate inclusion of marginalized participants in research, particularly on health-related topics.[28] As such, recruitment strategies for our time-sensitive project might have projected an extractive tone that reinforced distrust.

Other challenges concerned the nature of Zoom focus groups. In the first focus group, only one participant opted to use their microphone, which dominated the conversation despite the facilitator's efforts to read chat responses out loud and to periodically turn to the chat. In this context, conversational cadence was nearly impossible, and there were some awkward pauses as we waited for the chat to catch up. We learned from this and began encouraging the use of microphones or phone lines moving forward. In some cases, doing this resulted in participant disclosure of issues such as poor connectivity in their rural home and as calling in from an essential workplace with a lot of background noise. This contextual information gave us insight into participants' lives throughout the pandemic, which seemingly included juggling medical appointments with the cancellation of home visits, going into work at daycares and schools, and maintaining connection without reliable internet connectivity.

Despite the challenges, we found that this pilot work was incredibly meaningful in illuminating the unique challenges of communicating public health messages during an outbreak while also highlighting aspects of marginalizing public health rhetorics that persist during nonpandemic times. Methodologically, we learned first-hand the challenge and need for ethical and accessible research design, and we have adjusted our methods moving forward in follow-up studies.

We cleaned Zoom transcripts, removing all personally identifying information and inserting chat comments chronologically. We then used NVivo for Mac to open code transcripts. After independent coding sessions, we normed our results, combining codes to develop a comprehensive set of parent codes that help answer the research question, "How do people with disabilities on the border of Appalachia experience vaccine communication?"

Findings: Vaccine Campaign Rhetorics

Covid vaccine communication in the United States shifted quickly from "wait your turn" when supply was high to "return to normal" as supply outweighed demand. These tropes have quickly rotated through various official and unofficial channels alongside a slew of additional arguments for vaccination.

In our material analysis, we located two themes that relate directly to focus group findings: (1) Getting vaccinated is safe; and (2) Getting vaccinated will allow us to get back to normal. In the larger ecosystem of the vaccine campaign, these tropes emerged repeatedly, but generally speaking, safety was a consistent theme over the span of initial communications development in 2020 through summer 2021, and the "back to normal" trope emerged more prominently in April 2021 with campaigns labeled "It's our shot" and the "Hope" campaign.

Although few materials directly referenced the safety of the vaccines, those about side effects provided little definition of risk (see figure 1), or only referenced safety in passing, like in a fact sheet on vaccines for adolescents from May 2020 (see figure 2). Messages from "It's our shot" and "Hope" campaigns focused almost exclusively on benefits, such as safe worship, sporting, or family gathering. In these cases, safety was absent or implicit. While we applaud campaign designers for not following the

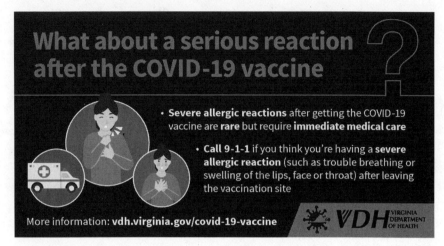

FIGURE 1. Social media artifact about vaccine reaction with vague references to serious reactions. Courtesy of the Virginia Department of Health.

lead of other communicators to overemphasize "safe and effective," we are concerned with the absence of references to clinical trial data.

The "It's our shot" campaign, published in early April 2021, featured racially diverse families around a dinner table that included people of multiple generations with text like "Let's get back to what matters" and an emphasis on the fact that vaccines are free of charge. These scenes were closely shot, with intergenerational connections portrayed through indoor dining scenes and older individuals shown meeting outside (see figure 3).

The Hope Campaign, published in early June 2021, similarly emphasized family and close community. Four social media shareables and three short videos feature family members and close friends reuniting after a year of separation. The highly emotional ads claim that these reunions are "only a vaccine away" (See figure 4). As opposed to earlier materials that used vector images to depict anonymous cartoon characters, both the "it's our shot" and "Hope" campaigns used real actors in photographs and video content.

When examined in focus group responses, participants were tactical in responding to ableist assumptions of safety and normalcy. Our use of the term "tactical" nods to Miles Kimball's take of Michel De Certeau's definitions on institutional strategies and individual tactics in technical communication. Kimball

FIGURE 2. Fact sheet referencing safety as an absolute value. Courtesy of the Virginia Department of Health.

FIGURE 3. "It's our shot" campaign features close family and friends. Courtesy of the Virginia Department of Health.

writes, "Individuals use tactics to survive and to come as close to achieving their purposes as possible."[29] Many scholars have since taken up this analytical framework, as evidenced by the 2017 special issue of *Technical Communication Quarterly* aptly titled "tactical technical communication" and guest edited by Kimball himself. These scholars study extra-institutional tactics to circumvent official technical guidance and instead, become temporary experts in a range of technical fields through unofficial means such as YouTube videos. For instance, Avery C. Edenfield, Steve Holmes, and Jared S. Colton's work explores the use of user-generated online instructions for administering hormone therapy (or DIY HRT) among transgender patients.[30] In doing so, they not only fill a gap left by

FIGURE 4. "Hope" campaign highlights benefits of vaccination without allusion to risk. Courtesy of the Virginia Department of Health.

institutional health care systems but they also queer forms of tactical technical communication by highlighting their stances as participatory, decentralized, and on the margins.

The concept of individual tactics is useful in describing consumers of public health information in our study. These information consumers, we argue, use a health literacy that is built on personal and medical histories of their bodies as well as consultation from trusted providers and access to clinical trial data to maneuver around poorly defined institutional concepts of safety and to redefine normalcy.

Vaccines Are Safe

Rhetorical Construction of an Absolute Safety

Claims about safety in vaccine campaigns were highly vague, as authors used terms like "rare" and "serious" without defining them or including references to clinical trial results. As a vehicle for one-way communication, these artifacts were able to evade specifics. Moreover, the campaign materials treated safety as an absolute quality—something that was or was not.

"Safe," however, is not an absolute characteristic, and referring to it as such can circumvent potential discussions of relative risk that are important for people considering medical interventions like vaccination. Under US Law, CFR 860.7 (d) (1), the US Food and Drug Administration uses a relative definition of safety to make recommendations for the public. The regulation states, "there is reasonable assurance that a device is safe when it can be determined, based upon valid scientific evidence, that the probable benefits to health from use of the device for its intended uses and conditions of use, when accompanied by adequate directions and warnings against unsafe use, outweigh any probable risks." This definition, listed under Title 21 for the FDA, is the basis on which health communicators can reliably support an epideictic rhetoric of drug safety. In definition, however, safety is a relative term, one that is based on clinical trials aimed at weighing risks relative to one another (in this case, of vaccination versus infection). Throughout regulations, and even in health communication literature about vaccines, safety is positioned as weighted against a substance's potential harm.[31]

Nevertheless, in the transition from FDA decisions to health communication, safety becomes an absolute term, and one that requires no further couching in data relative to potential harm. Harm is eliminated completely. In our sample, the term *safe* was emphasized as an absolute term through visual techniques of bolding, increased contrast, and font size. When side effects or adverse reactions were mentioned, even those were met with vagueness, downplaying the individual's agency to question a decision that the FDA had already made.

The logic that the work has been done for people by the government does not necessarily work with people with disabilities, particularly in the context of a preventive measure. The focus on safety and effectiveness, without specific evidence, and particularly in an authority/patient dynamic, is inherently ableist. People with disabilities have been told their whole lives that activities or health interventions that are safe for the "general population" (quotes to acknowledge the illusion of said entity), but not for them.

Negotiating a Relative Safety

In focus groups, participants discussed wanting to see data, in turn questioning the use of safety as an absolute. Instead, they rhetorically positioned safety as a negotiation of relative magnitudes. Safer than previous medical interventions, including standard vaccines? Safer than not getting vaccinated if they didn't leave the house? Participants turned to their own medical literacy and research to tactically investigate personal safety.

One person who had decided to ultimately get vaccinated said, "I looked up the company and the vaccines and read as much as I could about it and decided that it was something that I was willing to take the risk and weigh the risks and the benefits." Another directly shifted the use of "safe" to a relative one, referring to "safety" of the vaccine compared to infection. They said, "If it came down to it [I would get the vaccine]. If I was to go back to work or do anything that was in the public, I would definitely get vaccinated. Just I feel like it's the safer route. Your chances will be better."

Routinely and consistently reframing safety as a relative term could resituate agency so that officials are asking consumers of vaccine and other infectious disease prevention information to consider their relationship with risks and benefits. While potentially flattening the agency of FDA recommendations on the surface, this repositioning could actually bring patients into the decision-making fold. In the current construction of safety as an absolute term, those who do not vaccinate are viewed as noncompliant, a framework that we saw as mandates rolled out. Moreover, people who want vaccines but have legitimate fears were not being given information in a way that feels translatable for them.

One participant who had several amputations after sudden blood loss to their extremities lamented,

> Well, I'm managing [the risk of Covid infection] by sort of living in a house. Yes, I understand risk benefit ratios, and obviously Covid is a very dangerous disease. And I don't, I'm not sure I would survive Covid after what I have been through, but I am not sure that I would not be one of those small, small, small percentage of people that could have a negative reaction to the vaccine. And there's no one that

can tell me whether I will or not. So that's, that's troubling. No, there's no science to help me choose.

Eventually, this person turned to a specialist that they had worked with after several ableist and fatphobic encounters with general providers. She said, "In the past week, I reached out to someone who cared for me while I was in the hospital and gravely ill. And I explained to her nursing staff that I would just like to do a telehealth meeting with her to talk about these concerns. So, she is someone that I think could really understand my position and maybe be able to educate me further on whether or not I should try to take the vaccine."

While many participants cited the CDC or other official institutions as sources of information, they still expressed concern over not having enough information. One person with a mental disability who was also a first responder said, "I understand that experts say I shouldn't be concerned, but I'm just the type of person that gets concerned about those things . . . So, I just, I tried to move forward with the knowledge that's out there." As a first responder, this person was considerably fearful of Covid-19 infection and grateful that most of her life outside of work could be done remotely. They said, "I'm very, very, very, very apprehensive about things changing. I feel pretty settled in the fact that I can self-protect because I only am with my family. And that's pretty much how I'll stay at this moment, but I will be very apprehensive when I have to return to face-to-face contact with others." They indicated that most of their community was not practicing safe guidelines and attributed this to the rural nature of where they live, saying "people are just different here." They managed to practice both self-protection and an "ignorance is bliss" mentality in response to their fears.

In our study, the management of one's condition went hand-in-hand with their relative feeling of safety. They sought out myriad information sources, from trusted specialists to original clinical trial data reports, to self-educate their own position relative to the vaccine. As they did this, they also practiced cautious personal protection behaviors that did not require the level of material interface with the body as an injection.

Back to Normal

The idea that vaccines will help us, collectively, get back to normal has been reiterated across national news media and vaccine campaigns alike. From a behavioral economics lens, this trope is meant to incentivize and encourage, as surely people who have been "trapped" in their homes for over a year want to go back to the way things used to be. Here, we introduce the promise of *normalcy* as not only a marginalizing term but also a material exigency in itself. Just as vaccine safety has real lived consequences, so too are the lived realities of staying home. While participants did not outright suggest that they were delaying vaccination in order to stay home longer, many who had been able to stay home during the pandemic did express fears over an impending shift from pandemic practices back to prepandemic norms as a result of mass vaccination.

In the "Hope" campaign, materials avoid the term "normal" by focusing instead on prepandemic activities that are "only a vaccine away." The implicit argument is that vaccines enable a "return to" the Before Days. In fact, the web description of the Hope Campaign Toolkit reads, "With the hope to return to a sense of normalcy, the Hope Campaign encourages vaccinations as a route to return to the things we miss most in life." This campaign was developed because of what a health authority we interviewed referenced as a high demand. She stated, "At that time, people were saying that getting back to normal, I think it was like 75%, said that that was the number one motivator." At the time of the interview in early summer 2021, she stated that Virginia was past that point, with most residents feeling that "things are kind of back to normal and that's a lot of people's opinions." Of course, things changed again as the virus mutated.

A "return to normal" might work well for behavioral economists in a neoliberal framework. But in the context of a country built on white supremacy and ableism, the term becomes another tool for epistemic violence. In her essay, "Can the Subaltern Speak?," Spivak defines epistemic violence as silencing marginalized groups through the colonial privileging of Western knowledge and subsequent disappearance of local, experiential knowledge.[32] The term *epistemic violence* has since been used to reference the harm caused by a hyperfocus on normative ways of knowing.[33] The term *normal* becomes doubly violent for Black disabled Appalachians whose prepandemic experiences may include both medical and racial discrimination. As vaccination rates go up, we hope that mandates and popular discourse do not discount the justifiable hesitation that marginalized people have based on a myriad of health-related reasons as well as the historic positioning of their health as an othering factor. We hope, moreover, that a health equity lens is applied to vaccine messaging as vaccine supply increases globally beyond the United States.

Christopher A. Riddle suggests that people who are at greater risk of harm from a public health crisis like the outbreak of an infectious disease experience double vulnerability: first, from a "person-affecting way" as a person with a physical body that is at risk of harm, and second, in a "personhood-affecting way," or as a person at risk of having their value in society questioned. He writes, "Relatively healthy individuals who do not view themselves to be subject to person-vulnerability often diminish the negative effects of a public health crisis on the basis that it will only harm the subset of the population that is person-vulnerable."[34] We apply this idea to the rhetoric of normalcy, suggesting that people who view themselves as healthy and able-bodied doubly harm those who experience person-vulnerability, neglecting their needs to continue isolation and to reshape postpandemic life activities to be more accessible.

Focus group participants did not explicitly problematize "normal" but rather referred to their preference for staying home, a lifestyle that has been disparaged in contemporary high-production culture. Perhaps because of our national focus on productivity and socialization, participants' stance on vaccines was very much one that asked community members "out there" to get vaccinated. One person said, "You know, I wish more people would get vaccinated to reduce that risk. It took us four months to get my mom vaccinated . . . I kept trying to drill that [the pandemic wasn't over] through her head and then getting through to her the importance of protecting other people, protecting us, you know, and that she needed to do this. And then finally, well, Dolly got to her." This participant said that their mother was keen to socialize and gather, suggesting that it was her lifestyle that was at odds with the participant's preference to stay home.

Other participants shared lamentations about how difficult the pandemic was for family members, contrasting the previous story with one of positive familial practices. One person said, "My son, he's just been, it was a great deal of stress for him. He took off for six months from work because he was afraid of getting his grandparents, my grandma, my parents live with us, he was afraid of getting his grandparents sick or getting me sick. And, you know, that wasn't something that he could carry." While this participant praised their family member's caution relative to Covid risk, they worried about his ability to participate in his essential job. Because active employment is heralded as a norm for able-bodied publics, taking time off was a considerable burden for the son of a disabled participant.

Health norms in the disabled community, however, do not inherently focus on employment and instead prioritize safety, comfort, and well-being over productivity and socialization. Similar to the tactics employed in considering safety, participants responded to normalizing social and employment practices by staying home as much as they could.

For instance, one participant said that they were not particularly concerned about Covid infection at the time of the focus group, "because I practice safety measures as much as possible. I always wear a mask and wash my hands and I don't really have any direct contact with anybody... I mean close contact."

Similarly, another participant with a physical disability commented, "Because of my [condition], I basically have been almost completely home bound for... when all this was coming out. Other people went to the store for me and stuff." These tactical responses resist a normal that is hierarchical and instead suggest that "normal" is nuanced and contextual despite larger employment and entertainment systems that apply virtue to activities that increase Covid risk.

Discussion

Vaccine discourse, like all discourse in health and medicine, has a powerful responsibility. Commonplaces can be manipulated by anti-science extremists as much as they can be used for widespread vaccination. Vaccine discourse can also be complicit in ableism, despite public health expert's best intentions for inclusion. Our intention is not to take a stance on vaccination itself but rather to illuminate those moments in which there is friction between marginalized consumers of health information and public health stewards of this messaging.

This study had several limitations. Our sample size was small. We also believe, in retrospect, that limiting responses to those who had not been vaccinated during this time period limited our opportunities for rich conversations by perpetuating a pro/anti-vaccine or a vaccine hesitancy framework during recruitment. Moreover, the timing of vaccine distribution alongside our recruitment efforts meant that some folks decided to get vaccinated between the time they signed up for the study and the time they joined a focus group. Similarly, communication artifacts were constantly changing, and we chose to keep up with the changing issues at hand (for instance, focusing on prioritization and "wait your turn" messaging first and then on community responsibility once demand no longer outweighed supply). Doing so meant some inconsistencies in protocols.

This study also offered several opportunities. Perhaps most importantly were the connections between our English department and public health districts. During recruitment efforts (e.g., at vaccine clinics or through conversations with local public service entities), we were often questioned about our disciplinary home. Highlighting the value-add of a rhetorical approach to public health was valuable for us, and, we think, for public health departments. In fact, when coding artifacts during one of our group meetings, a public health student who was present looked on with fascination, eventually saying, "I never thought to look at metaphors in vaccine messaging, but, you know, that makes a lot of sense!" These small exchanges re-energized us to continue pursuing interdisciplinary connections and infusing a new lens into existing social science approaches to disease communication.

We suggest that rhetoricians of health and medicine who are interested in engaging with real-time public health practice be ready to articulate their strengths and value-adds in existing programming. Learning the jargon of public health by engaging in volunteer or consulting opportunities and by reading literature published in public health venues is a good first step, and practicing methods that are common to the field will help rhetorical scholars find common ground. Public health departments operate on limited budgets, so find ways that you can support their objectives with your human resources.

Last, we want to share some recommendations for communicating Covid vaccine information among people with disabilities or chronic medical conditions. Some of these feel obvious but are worth restating, as we continue to see normalizing discourse in public health messages. First, we suggest that authorities develop accessible means of sharing relevant clinical trial data as they emerge. Even social media shareables might include specific data points when making vague claims about safety and effectiveness. While Dolly Parton was referenced by a participant as a cultural influencer for her mother without disabilities, people in our study largely wanted reliable scientific biomaterial information from trusted sources, including the CDC and specialized care providers.

Health informants might include detailed information on side effects, even if they are statistically rare, rather than dismissing adverse or serious reactions as uncommon. In communicating side effects and adverse reactions, they should consider influenza vaccine analogies, which were heralded as useful to deliberation among people who have experienced past negative effects from the flu vaccine. Rather than dismissing these analogies as a rhetorical fallacy, articulating clearly the differences between vaccine mechanics and effects could prove to be a useful communication tool.

NOTES

1. Steve Fisher, Jim Foster, and Mary Harnish, "From Nonsense to Good Sense: A Collective Reflection on Appalachia and Appalachian Studies," *Appalachian Journal* 9, no. 2/3 (1982): 151.
2. William Schumann "Introduction," in *Appalachia Revisited: New Perspectives on Place, Tradition, and Progress*, ed. William Schumann and Rebecca Adkins Fletcher (Lexington: University Press of Kentucky, 2016).
3. John L. McCoy and Kerry Weems, "Disabled-Worker Beneficiaries and Disabled SSI Recipients: A Profile of Demographic and Program Characteristics," Soc. Sec. Bull. 52 (1989), 16; Jacob Schmulowitz and Henry David Lynn, "Insured and Disabled Workers Under the Social Security Disability Program: Characteristics and Benefit Payments, 1957–1963," by Jacob Schmulowitz and Henry D. Lynn. No. 11. U.S. Government Printing Office, 1966.
4. Kimberlé Williams Crenshaw, "Demarginalizing The Intersection of Race and Sex: A Black Feminist Critique of Antidiscrimination Doctrine, Feminist Theory and Antiracist Politics," in *Feminist Legal Theory: Foundations*, ed. D. Kelly Weisbert (Philadelphia: Temple University Press, 1989), 383–95; bell hooks, *Feminist Theory: From Margin to Center* (Las Vegas: Pluto Press, 2000); Antonio Duran and Susan R. Jones, "Intersectionality," in *Encyclopedia of Critical Whiteness Studies in Education* (Leiden, The Netherlands: Brill, 2020), 310–20.
5. Anna Rachel Terman, "Intersections of Appalachian identity," *Appalachia Revisited: New Perspectives on Place, Tradition, and Progress* (2016): 73–88; John Gaventa, "Appalachian Studies in Global Context: Reflections on the Beginnings—Challenges for the Future," *Journal of Appalachian Studies* 8, no. 1 (2002): 84.
6. Sandra Lee Barney, *Authorized to Heal: Gender, Class, and the Transformation of Medicine in Appalachia, 1880–1930* (Chapel Hill: University of North Carolina Press, 2000); Gopal K. Singh, Michael D. Kogan, and Rebecca T. Slifkin, "Widening Disparities in Infant Mortality and Life Expectancy Between Appalachia and the Rest of the United States, 1990–2013," *Health Affairs* 36, no. 8 (2017): 1423–32.
7. Kathryn Trauth Taylor "Naming Affrilachia: Toward Rhetorical Ecologies of Identity Performance in Appalachia," *Enculturation* 10 (June 2011).
8. Michelle Rockwell et al., "Trust in Healthcare and Trust in Science Predict Readiness to Receive the Covid Vaccine in Appalachia," *Annals of Family Medicine COVID-19 Collection* (2021).
9. Heidi Yoston Lawrence, *Vaccine Rhetorics* (Columbus: Ohio State University Press, 2020).

10. Gayatri Chakravorty Spivak, "Can the Subaltern Speak?," *Die Philosophin* 14, no. 27 (2003): 42–58; Kristie Dotson, "Tracking Epistemic Violence, Tracking Practices of Silencing," *Hypatia* 26, no. 2 (2011): 242.
11. Jason Palmeri, "Disability Studies, Cultural Analysis, and the Critical Practice of Technical Communication Pedagogy," *Technical Communication Quarterly* 15, no. 1 (2006): 49–65.
12. James C. Wilson, "Making Disability Visible: How Disability Studies Might Transform the Medical and Science Writing Classroom," *Technical Communication Quarterly* 9, no. 2 (2009): 151.
13. Emily Brooks, "'Don't Be a Knucklehead': Moralizing Disability in New Jersey's Pandemic Response and Rhetoric," *Disability Studies Quarterly* 41, no. 3 (2021); Nicola Panocchia et al., "Covid-19 Pandemic, The Scarcity of Medical Resources, Community-Centred Medicine and Discrimination Against Persons with Disabilities," *Journal of Medical Ethics* 47, no. 6 (2021): 362–66; Dianne Sabat et al., "Community Engagement in Health Care: An Approach to Improve Health Care Access for People with Disabilities," *Disability Studies Quarterly* 37, no. 3 (2017).
14. James L. Cherney, *Ableist Rhetoric: How We Know, Value, and See Disability* (University Park: Penn State University Press, 2019), 8.
15. David M. Peña-Guzmán and Joel Michael Reynolds, "The Harm of Ableism: Medical Error and Epistemic Injustice," *Kennedy Institute of Ethics Journal* 29, no. 3 (2019): 205–42, 210.
16. Peña-Guzmán and Reynolds, "Harm of Ableism," 210.
17. Maya Rowland et al., "Health Outcome Disparities Among Subgroups of People with Disabilities: A Scoping Review," *Disability and Health Journal* 7, no. 2 (2014): 136–50.
18. Maya M. McDoom, Elisa Koppelman, and Mari-Lynn Drainoni, "Barriers to Accessible Health Care for Medicaid Eligible People with Disabilities: A Comparative Analysis," *Journal of Disability Policy Studies* 25, no. 3 (2014): 154–63.
19. Thomas P. Dirth and Nyla R. Branscombe, "Disability Models Affect Disability Policy Support through Awareness of Structural Discrimination," *Journal of Social Issues* 73, no. 2 (2017): 413–42.
20. Panocchia et al., "Covid-19 Pandemic," 362.
21. Lisa Melonçon, *Rhetorical Accessability: At the Intersection of Technical Communication and Disability Studies* (New YorkRoutledge, 2014), 5.
22. Lawrence, *Vaccine Rhetorics*, 17.
23. Lawrence, *Vaccine Rhetorics*, 122.
24. Øyvind Ihlen, Margalit Toledano, and Sine Nørholm Just, "Using Rhetorical Situations to Examine and Improve Vaccination Communication," *Frontiers in Communication* 6

(June 2021), 3.
25. Lawrence, *Vaccine Rhetorics*, 122.
26. Nicolette I. Teufel-Shone and Sheralyn Williams, "Focus Groups in Small Communities," *Preventing Chronic Disease* 7, no. 3 (2010); Li Ping Wong, "Focus Group Discussion: A Tool for Health and Medical Research," *Singapore Medical Journal* 49, no. 3 (2008): 256–60.
27. Margaret Smirnoff et al., "A Paradigm for Understanding Trust and Mistrust in Medical Research: The Community VOICES Study," *AJOB Empirical Bioethics* 9, no. 1 (2018): 39.
28. Ivy K. Ho, Taylor A. Sheldon, and Elliott Botelho, "Medical Mistrust Among Women with Intersecting Marginalized Identities: A Scoping Review," *Ethnicity & Health* (2021): 1–19; Smirnoff et. al., "Paradigm for Understanding"; Lillie D. Williamson and Cabral A. Bigman, "A Systematic Review of Medical Mistrust Measures," *Patient Education and Counseling* 101, no. 10 (2018): 1786–94.
29. Miles A. Kimball, "Cars, Culture, and Tactical Technical Communication," *Technical Communication Quarterly* 15, no. 1 (2006): 71.
30. Avery C. Edenfield, Steve Holmes, and Jared S. Colton, "Queering Tactical Technical Communication," *Technical Communication Quarterly* 28, no. 3 (2019): 177–91.
31. Xiaoli Nan, Bo Xie, and Kelly Madden, "Acceptability of the H1N1 Vaccine Among Older Adults: The Interplay of Message Framing and Perceived Vaccine Safety and Efficacy," *Health Communication* 27, no. 6 (2012): 559–68.
32. Spivak, "Can the Subaltern Speak?"
33. Anon Ymous et al., "'I am Just Terrified of My Future'—Epistemic Violence in Disability Related Technology Research," *Extended Abstracts of the 2020 CHI Conference on Human Factors in Computing Systems* (April 2020); Viviane Namaste, "Undoing Theory: The "Transgender Question" and the Epistemic Violence of Anglo-American Feminist Theory," *Hypatia* 24, no. 3 (2009): 11–32; Santiago Castro-Gómez and Desiree A. Martin, "The Social Sciences, Epistemic Violence, and the Problem of the 'Invention of the Other,'" *Nepantla: Views from South* 3, no. 2 (2002): 269–85.
34. Christopher A. Riddle, "Vulnerability, Disability, and Public Health Crises," *Public Health Ethics* (2021): 164.

Covid and Doubt

An Emergent Structure of Feeling

Jeffrey A. Bennett

SCENE ONE: IN APRIL 2021, DR. ANTHONY FAUCI CRUSHED THE DREAMS OF countless Americans when he announced that, despite his fully vaccinated status, he would not be eating in restaurants. For well over a year, those who had been trapped in their homes due to Covid had pinned their hopes on new mRNA vaccines that might permit them to safely return to routine habits like dining out and grocery shopping. Fauci's cautious calculation instigated a collective groan from those desperate to escape the confines of their living spaces and the anxiety that accompanied months of isolation and dread. When Fauci went public with his decision the vaccines were being touted as scientific miracles with efficacy rates as high as 95 percent. Despite this success, only a quarter of Americans had been vaccinated when Fauci implored further restraint. With the pandemic still raging and the vast majority of people still needing shots, Fauci was performatively embodying the preventative approach he hoped others would adopt. Rather than embrace his circumspect perspective, however, this stance raised questions from those across the political spectrum: what was the point of being vaccinated if people were not able to be in public?

Scene Two: In late July 2021, the Centers for Disease Control and Prevention (CDC) fixated on the July 4 celebrations that took place in Provincetown,

Massachusetts. Nearly sixty thousand people showed up in the seaside town for Independence Day and subsequent LGBT events such as Bear Week, but had their plans stifled by rain, which forced many of them inside. As a result, an estimated 469 positive Covid diagnoses stemmed from the gatherings and the vast majority—upward of 75 percent—were found in those who were vaccinated.[1] Although only four vaccinated people were hospitalized and none died, the event led the CDC to revise its mask guidance policies and recommend that all people, regardless of vaccination status, wear face coverings indoors. This high-profile event garnered an impressive amount of media attention, though the facts were often parsed and unclear. Writing for the *New York Times*, Apoorva Mandavilli explained, "Even if breakthrough infections are rare, the new data suggest the vaccinated *may be* contributing to increases in new infections—although *probably* to a far lesser degree than the unvaccinated."[2] These ambiguous declarations contributed to confusion about the dangers of the Delta variant but also enabled a campaign of disinformation about the extent of the infections and the shortcomings of the vaccine.

Scene Three: In mid-August 2021, representatives from Facebook reported that the most popular post on their platform from January to March of that year was an article that cast doubt on the effectiveness of the Covid vaccines.[3] The company, under increased pressure to be more transparent about its role in political affairs in the wake of the January 6 Capitol insurrection, released the news on a Saturday night, which allowed them to feign openness about their practices while simultaneously curtailing negative press. The article in question was taken from the *South Florida Sun Sentinel* and detailed the demise of a doctor who had died two weeks after taking one of the vaccines. For users already skeptical of inoculations, this report reinforced a preconceived bias about the hazards of the technology. Perhaps more important for those invested in conspiracies was that the medical examiner's office never conclusively stated whether the vaccine played a role in the physician's death. Even as the post was widely derided as spreading misinformation, an undercurrent of doubt about the vaccines held tight and allowed fringe voices to influence easily exploited readers.

These three scenarios are indicative of the doubt that has settled upon the US imaginary during the global Covid pandemic. This affective malaise of doubt, wherein every message seems to carry a rhetorical remainder about the unknown, has only intensified as the pandemic has lingered. The ubiquity of this doubt can be found lurking in almost every facet of life: in healthcare, education, religion, politics, news media, civil society, and interpersonal relationships. The Trump administration's politicization of institutions such as the CDC in the throes of the pandemic negatively transformed America's relationship with official sites of information and citizens' ability to generate meanings from that data. It is not an overstatement to suggest that many people now call into question the most rudimentary aspects of their bodies, social networks, and cultural practices. These doubts were compounded by the relentless campaign to downplay the severity of the pandemic at every turn by a significant segment of the population. On any given day, we can locate doubts about the long-lasting effects of the vaccines, the habits of our friends and families, the political leanings of our neighbors, and our faith in institutions whose mission it is to keep us well. On the Right, there remains a strong undercurrent of skepticism that Covid is a threat, that the vaccines are effective, or that the virus is actually a product of nature and not some science experiment gone awry. Many on the Left continue to have concerns about the flimsiness of mask policies, the ramifications of Covid for children, and the uncomfortable sense that we will never rid ourselves of the political animus that allowed this crisis to persist. The pervasiveness of doubt has become a defining quality of the pandemic.

As I write this in June 2022, the public transcript of the Covid pandemic in the United States has shifted from being an alarming global catastrophe to something treated as a public health nuisance underwritten by risk tolerance and chance. Over one million Americans have died from Covid, and worldwide that number is encroaching on the six-and-a-half million mark. This story, as the introduction to this volume points out, is assuredly not over. It is still too early to tell if the vaccines will protect people from all of the coronavirus's evolutionary possibilities, if Covid will become an endemic disease, or how frequently boosters may be required. In this chapter, I explore the looming, affective character of doubt and its omnipresence in US culture. I am not interested in correcting every piece of misinformation about the virus, its variants, or the vaccines. There is only so much space. Rather, I wish to probe the rhetorical parameters of doubt and its boundless presence in public discussions of the pandemic. I argue that prevalent discourses of choice undergird this doubt, which undermine attempts to streamline collective narratives about Covid's reach. The lasting uncertainty that has exacted itself into our daily lives is sure to impose itself for years to come and, as a result, we must learn to more efficiently manage our relationship to doubt in an era of radical indeterminacy.

Doubt and Medicine

Doubt has long acted as the constitutive outside of myriad rhetorical situations. The field's genealogical roots in persuasion, with its emphasis on Aristotelian proofs and means-centered appeals, points to an unstated recalcitrance that a person must overcome to effectively communicate. Entire genres of rhetoric, including forensic argument, might suggest assumed forms of doubt that must be assessed and transcended in order for a communicator to be successful. As the discipline has evolved, it has explored doubt in many outlets, even when doubt itself may not be a central component of analysis. Ideas that include skepticism, cynicism, conspiracy theories, evidence analysis, risk assessment, crisis management, and uncertainty reduction all engage the rhetorical dynamics presented by doubt. Scholars such as Scott Baker have argued that rhetorical theory itself has shifted the epistemological grounds of modern empiricism and been a leader in the doubts raised about the Enlightenment project.[4] In this way, doubt consumes the discipline.

I argue that the doubt that has sedimented during the Covid crisis is best understood as a "structure of feeling" that is affectually discerning but whose sensorial character is still emerging. Raymond Williams famously articulated the terms *structure* and *feeling* to give presence to the ways sensibilities and patterns of thought surface during specific historical periods. He contended that the method underlining the phrase "is as firm and definite as 'structure' suggests, yet it operates in the most delicate and least tangible parts of our activity."[5] In this way, the structure of feeling that accompanies any era is inherently rhetorical and can be found in the negotiation among official discourses and their vernacular interlocutors. Sean Matthews contends that a structure of feeling presents itself "in moments of transition, of change, and is evident in formal shifts in artistic practice."[6] And while this chapter focuses most explicitly on public health, the heuristic is useful insofar as it facilitates the consideration of "new and emergent elements" in our social formations.[7] Doubt has long played an important role in the realms of medicine, politics, and public health but the concept is finding new life as misinformation circulates voraciously on social media. Criticism is imperative during these moments of emergence because otherwise indiscernible sensibilities can be simultaneously encroaching and fleeting. Any person living through the pandemic could list the many doubts that preoccupy their thoughts, but there is no guaranteeing that these feelings will be communicable a decade from now. In order to approximate this ever-changing notion of culture, we must understand how doubt has played a role in medicine and how it is manifesting today. Importantly, as Williams stressed repeatedly, we can never definitively list every example that falls under the broad umbrella of a structure of feeling about particular phenomena, but looking to representative anecdotes can clarify the conditions that people experience.

Elaine Scarry's proposition about the cultural disavowal of pain is perhaps the most famous refrain about doubt in the humanities. In her book *The Body in Pain*, Scarry contended that "to have great pain is to have certainty; to hear that another person has pain is to have doubt."[8] Medicine was one of the many institutional spaces privileged by Scarry in her groundbreaking study. And while that text is now decades old, the sphere of medicine has continued to be a significant site of investigation when contemplating the parameters of doubt. For instance, physicians regularly grapple with incomplete or inaccurate data, and learning how to productively utilize doubt can lead to better diagnoses, treatments, and outcomes. At other times, doubt among healthcare workers has more troublesome effects, including reiterating biases and prejudices about marginalized communities. Numerous studies, for example, point out that physicians regularly dismiss the pain being felt by Black patients. One study found that medical students believed African Americans were less sensitive to pain, a view that follows decades-old stereotypes not grounded in reality.[9] This unreflective performance of doubt is not contained to the examination room but has compounding residual effects. Because of such treatment, as Veronica Joyner and Heidi Y. Lawrence outline in this volume, people of color might understandably doubt medicine's investment in their health and invariably those experiences inform how they approach healthcare.

Nonetheless, doubt is, in many ways, an essential element of medical practices. Physicians may rightfully withhold judgment about a problem until they collect a useful amount of physical evidence, run tests, or are persuaded by patients that a problem exists. But this structural feature of medicine comes with sometimes unforeseen consequences. Take, for instance, the phenomenon of hypochondria.[10] In its most basic definition, hypochondria connotes the persistent and excessive fear that one has, will develop, or will encounter, a disease or illness. So strong are these feelings that people often experience somatic symptoms that correspond to the disease they believe themselves to have. About 2–5 percent of people live with some form of hypochondria, and to address that wide umbrella the condition has been renamed "illness anxiety disorder" in the DSM. In some worst-case scenarios, people who live with hypochondria find that facets of their lives, including personal relationships, are negatively affected by the condition. Most important for this study is that hypochondria is not simply a product of individual psychosis but a structural problem that is created by medical encounters.

Scholars who investigate the rhetoric of hypochondria find that the form of medical discourse is the central organizing mechanism for these feelings. Because medical providers can never offer sweeping guarantees about the potential risk of infection or the possibilities of disease, patients appropriate the rhetorical remainders of diagnoses to internalize the idea that they may be unwell. As Arthur Kleinman notes, "The hypochondriac's persistent fear is based not on the certainty of a delusion but on the profound uncertainty of persistent doubt."[11] The person experiencing hypochondria is able to intuitively surmise that any variable could upend the assurances given by healthcare workers.[12] In this way, hypochondria is a paranoid predisposition that shifts how a person interprets and makes meaning of their positionality in the world. Such manifestations do not rest as an ontological state of being but a performative interruption that constantly demands reassessment of the most basic sensations. Arthur Frank refers to this as "embodied paranoia," and contends that the difficulty of such a state of mind is "not knowing what to fear most, and then feeling guilty about this very uncertainty."[13] In some ways, this makes perfect sense when we examine vernacular appropriations of medicine. As Frank writes, "Disease is all too effective as a journalistic metaphor for social problems—crime, poverty, drug use, inflation,—because disease metaphors tap the intuitive connection between internal threats to the body and external threats. Embodied paranoia reflects a blurring of internal and external: everything has potential to threaten."[14] This is evinced in the Covid era, in which individual surveillance is complicated by the invariability of the coronavirus. Many of us have uttered now familiar refrains such as, "Is it a cold, allergies, or Covid?" Any slight change in one's body suddenly becomes an indicator that danger might be lurking.

I want to emphasize that I am not making a one-to-one comparison between those who have justifiable fears about Covid and hypochondria. Rather, I use the example of hypochondria as a heuristic to think about the ways the structure of medical knowledge itself mirrors the discourse that permits doubt to materialize. Official messaging from government entities such as the CDC have sometimes inadvertently furthered this preponderance of doubt by giving incompatible, or even contradictory, information.[15] The rhetorical indeterminacy of official discourses has fractured tidy understandings of the pandemic's temporality and our agency in overcoming the novel coronavirus. This structure of feeling that pertains specifically to doubt is already being taken up, under different names, by scholars such as Francis Beer and

Robert Hariman. They suggest that Covid is not simply an epidemiological crisis, but an epistemological crisis as well.[16] They label this emerging attitude a "catastrophic epistemology" wherein knowledge itself is one of the casualties. If Eve Sedgwick was correct in her contention that paranoia is highly anticipatory of future events, we will likely be saddled with such doubts for years to come.[17] The perpetual deferrals of certainty that stem from medicine are perhaps scientifically justified but sometimes have the effect of equivocating risk behaviors and catalyzing feelings of uncertainty.

Risk and Doubt

The doubts that haunt the contemporary social landscape are perhaps best exemplified in the embodied risks one is willing to accept during the Covid era. Risks are not simply empirical phenomena. Rather, risks are inherently rhetorical because they bring into being the very dangers they warn us about. Ulrich Beck famously noted that risk is "a systematic way of dealing with hazards and insecurities induced and introduced by modernization itself."[18] These ideological constructs have become especially tenuous in the throes of a pandemic. Risks are not simply viruses or vaccine side effects but lurk in the ways we build grocery stores, the presumptions we carry about personal liberty, the deficiencies of the healthcare system, and the ways we approach the climate crisis. Each of these is an effect of modernization that constitutes the ways we encounter and negotiate risks. For this reason, Debra Lupton reminds us that risks are value-laden judgments about events or possibilities that are recurrently managed in situ. The pandemic has illustrated that the social construction of risk is impossible to separate from our gradually ingrained sentiments about doubt.

The idea of risk has been slowly reconfigured in modern times by bureaucratic entities, such as health insurance companies, as a set of individualized decisions rather than a constellation of collective practices. Lupton argues that individuals are increasingly foisted with the responsibility of avoiding or minimizing the impact of risks, even when conditions rest outside their ability to do so. As a result, "risk has become more privatized and linked ever more closely to the concept of the entrepreneurial subject, calling into question the very notion of social rights."[19] This was exemplified by an announcement by CDC director Rochelle Walensky in May 2021, following the agency's relaxing of mask mandates, when she proclaimed, "Your health is in your hands." Walensky forwarded this neoliberal mantra, which seemed to have little persuasive effect, rather than accentuate the necessity of addressing the pandemic on a systemic level.[20] People simply continued practicing what they had been doing. Walensky was certainly not alone in such thinking but such a laissez-faire approach to public health is easily repudiated. As Marina Levina has suggested in this volume and elsewhere, people who work in low-wage jobs or who depend on kinship networks not grounded in the heterosexual imaginary can never fully adopt such an individualistic perspective.[21] If a worker needs healthcare to survive, for example, the dastardly overlords of capitalism force them into risk scenarios. Individuals are inevitably scapegoated for making "bad" choices and then are positioned as the sole proprietors of their fate while those in power are excused from poor policy decisions that might keep people alive. For instance, those in education who work in states without vaccine or mask mandates do not *really* have a choice over their risks because they usually cannot choose the rooms or buildings that they teach in, set caps on enrollments, request that students wear masks, or even talk about Covid.

Given the lack of agency people have over their proximity to risk, it is not surprising that many have dramatically increased gestures of self-surveillance during the pandemic. Scientists are still parsing the coronavirus's effects, including the ramifications of so-called long Covid, and this indeterminacy has only functioned to compound public feelings of doubt. Take this singular example from Twitter that illustrates the unusual ways people are imagining ideas about risk and doubt. This particular user relayed that it took an extended length of time for her to be diagnosed with a disease that put her at high risk for Covid and that others might want to be equally cautious. It's a somatic cautionary tale:

> Just wanna say that many folks don't know if they're high risk for covid. It took me a couple or more years to be diagnosed. There's a limit to what we know about our health and ability when calculating 'personal risk.' And anyway, the better question is what's the communal risk?

This user makes a fine point, and I am not calling into question the extent to which she or others are actually at risk. But the post suggests that all of us should have degrees of doubt about the permeability of our bodies when taking risks, not just in regard to the pandemic but to those things that might potentially be lurking inside of us. While the democratization of information about disease and illness on social media can be beneficial, it also acts as a wellspring of doubt.

The user's warning resonates with a string of pandemic writing that foresees danger around every corner. Risk is not just an external threat that must be managed—sometimes the call appears to be coming from inside the house. For example, an essay published in the online magazine *Elemental* told the story of fourteen men in March 1969 who went to spend the remainder of the year in Antarctica.[22] Sometime in July of that year, one of the men began to develop a respiratory cold and eight of his colleagues were also suddenly sick. Scientists were haunted by one daunting question: where could the virus have come from four months after they left the mainland? After analyzing numerous sites and objects where the virus might have lurked, such as handkerchiefs, it was decided that it might have simply lived in the human body unexpectedly. This story acted as an interpretive lens for reading Covid—a present-day allegory that the body itself contains the very potential to commit harm. *The New Yorker*, *Medium*, and *The Atlantic* also published essays that contended the body itself might harbor a concealed threat.[23] The trope of the unknown became even more pronounced after the vaccines were predictably shown not to be 100 percent effective at keeping the coronavirus at bay.

The indeterminacy of medical risks and the doubts they initiate are certainly not a new phenomenon. Elsewhere, I have argued that one of the main reasons for the slow up-take of pre-exposure prophylaxis (PrEP) among gay men is the narrative of doubt that is cast on the medication.[24] As with the Covid vaccines, PrEP can never be said to be 100 percent foolproof. The HIV-prevention medication has been shown to be as high as 99 percent effective in warding off infection but the small sliver of a possibility of transmission allows detractors to argue against its adoption. To be sure, both PrEP and at least two of the Covid vaccines are more effective than widely embraced technologies such as birth control pills. But the narrative remainder that tends to accompany scientific discourse reinforces the very doubts that are held by detractors to start. It is a discourse that mirrors the logic and practices of hypochondria mentioned earlier and has been resurrected with the introduction of new mRNA vaccines.

Vaccines, Risk, Doubt

The relay between risk and doubt has been especially prominent in narratives about the efficacy of newly developed mRNA vaccines. Public health officials have long fought to inoculate large swaths of people from infectious diseases and those efforts have frequently been met with degrees of resistance, skepticism, and hesitation. In fact, many people go as far as suggesting the vaccines actually *cause* disease rather than treat it. That both the Moderna and Pfizer vaccine sparked side effects in some people led many opponents to eschew the vaccines altogether and take their chances with Covid. For example, anti-vaxxers latched onto the idea that the Covid vaccine was causing large outbreaks of myocarditis, a heart condition that had sprung up in a handful of vaccine recipients. But such theories have proven repeatedly to be false. As Smriti Mallapaty wrote in *Nature,* "In one study of more than 5 million people who had received the Pfizer–BioNTech COVID-19 vaccine, 136 developed myocarditis. The other study, of more than 2.5 million people who received the shot, identified just 54 cases of myocarditis."[25] And while vaccine refusers might insist that they are simply giving people all the data they need to make an "informed decision," the picture they paint is rarely accurate. Far from a mere medical concern, these gestures emanate from cultural scripts that are readily familiar. As Eula Biss has observed, "Believing that vaccination causes devastating diseases allows us to tell ourselves what we already know: what heals may harm and the sum of science is not always progress."[26]

The narrative conflicts that arise over vaccines reproduce the tension between the privatization of risk and its actual, collective character. Throughout the pandemic, we have been bombarded with messages that emphasize individual choices in relation to risk calculation, social distancing, and vaccination. But the bigger picture is assuredly more complicated. Lawrence reminds us that vaccines are often imposed on people, so controversies arise because risk may not be a personal decision but a compulsory directive.[27] Vaccines are given to healthy adults and to children, which does not make the persuasive task of healthcare providers any easier. Mandatory vaccination policies put the needs of the whole over that of the individual, which renders vaccination inherently social and political, not simply private or scientific. Of course, all bodies are chimeric compositions of the cultural flows that they reside in. But those aspects of culture that we give presence to directly impact the interpretive lenses used to make risks intelligible. I have had acquaintances tell me that Covid is a matter of fate: "If it's going to happen, it's going to happen." Counterintuitively, such an approach is also based in doubt: despite safety measures, anything could happen at any time. This modified approach to "everything happens for a reason" is as fatalistic as it is hopeful. It is predeterminism dressed as casualism.

A vaccine denier might rightfully point out that any of the available Covid treatments are not wholly effective. While most vaccines have been shown to significantly decrease the harms associated with Covid, there is no guaranteeing that they will prohibit the transmission of the virus. As more cases of infection are reported, those who remain most suspicious of the vaccine will find reason to oppose it. Rather than give emphasis to the complications that might be avoided with the vaccine, detractors offer an intense focus on those cases where infection *might* occur. This rhetorical sleight of hand, wherein ambiguity is saturated with negative affect to suspend the capacity for judgment, highlights the movement from uncertainty, wherein one contemplates situational uncertainties for developing strategies to address risk, to doubt.[28] These tensions over vaccination are especially popular in media narratives about the pandemic because conflict-driven stories and lingering questions about effects present opportunities for coverage that drive ratings. The question of "what comes next" exploits a lack of narrative closure and the desire to collect evermore information about vaccines, even if that means presenting partial information, false equivalences, or sensationalistic headlines. To further explain this, I turn back to Provincetown and the doubts that outbreak fostered.

Provincetown and the Outbreak Narrative

The Provincetown outbreak was framed repeatedly as a cautionary tale about premature celebrations, letting one's guard down, and the limits of the vaccines to inhibit transmission of the virus. After sixteen months of shelter-in-place orders and social distancing, the new vaccines offered people the opportunity to circulate freely outside the confines of their homes. But the festiveness brought by summer 2021 was positioned as too excessive to reasonably contain the coronavirus. As one reporter put it, "People crowded into pools, restaurants, and bars. After a year of canceled celebrations, people were understandably excited to drink, revel and relax under the relative security of a highly vaccinated population."[29] Another outlet observed a "prepandemic thrum" and commented on the "conga lines, drag brunches, and a pervasive, joyous sense of relief."[30] One man who traveled to P-town from New York reflected, "I was definitely going into it with a mindset of, this is all behind us, we're just going into a super-fun, amazing weekend."[31] The promise of a less restrictive summer gave folks a sense that hope was on the horizon and that the longest year of the twenty-first century might finally be behind us.

The Provincetown outbreak was particularly striking because not a single coronavirus case had been reported in Barnstable County for the entire month of June.[32] Massachusetts had vaccination rates above the national average and Provincetown rested around 95 percent of permanent residents. This remarkable achievement was contrasted against the rise of the Delta variant, which constituted about 90 percent of the P-town infections and significantly shifted the public narrative about Covid. For this reason, one infectious disease specialist called the Provincetown outbreak a "watershed moment" in the life of the pandemic and a "reality check on what the vaccines can do but also what some of their limitations are."[33] Boston's National Public Radio (NPR) outlet put it bluntly: the "outbreak stemming out of Provincetown is casting doubt on the vaccine's ability to halt transmission of the Delta variant of the coronavirus."[34] Such bold proclamations should be taken with a grain of salt. From an epidemiological perspective, there were so many vaccinated people in the resort town that it was not surprising that rates of infection were high among those who had received shots. In this way, the Provincetown outbreak had the negative consequence of producing hyperbolic and partial information about Covid and the potential for community spread. This focus came not only from the somewhat allegorical nature of the event but also because of reactions from organizations such as the CDC. The government agency was so alarmed by the outbreak that it revised its masking policies and this (perhaps inadvertently) accelerated false claims about the vaccine. CDC Director Walensky said in a statement, "This finding is concerning and was a pivotal discovery leading to CDC's updated mask recommendation... The masking recommendation was updated to ensure the vaccinated public would not unknowingly transmit virus to others."[35] Walensky's press release gave fodder to media operatives who were invested in novel angles on the trajectory of the coronavirus and the sensational coverage that came from alluding to unsafe behaviors among gay men.

As a result, both the government agency and several media outlets further obscured public understanding of who was safe, who was prone to infection, and who might transmit the virus. As one doctor noted, "reducing risk to zero was never on the menu" and that data from Provincetown had "accelerated the (inaccurate and poorly messaged) narrative" that both vaccinated and unvaccinated individuals were equally contagious.[36] Anecdotally, this misinformation had serious effects. In a conversation with one acquaintance, for example, I was told that 75 percent of the people *hospitalized* were vaccinated, a clear misunderstanding (or willful distortion) of how events unfolded. Regardless, the outbreak raised questions about whether vaccinated people could spread the virus to others who had received the shots. Perhaps more than any other feature of the stories, it was this one that tended to present doubt in its most explicit form. For example, one news story seemed to offer contradictory information in the space of a couple of paragraphs. Citing one CDC study, the report conveyed to readers that "vaccinated individuals carried as much virus in their noses as unvaccinated people."[37] But shortly after, the same write-up remarked, "While the data suggests that vaccinated people can spread the disease, the extent to which they contribute is not yet clear." And while a discerning reader might be able to make distinctions between the amount of viral load being carried and its possibility for infection, the story seemed to offer a staunch assessment of the possibility of infection and then raised doubts about its own proclamation.

These reports also fortified notions about individual choice over the more politically controversial suggestion that vaccines should be compulsory. Provincetown board of health chair Stephen Katsurinis commented that, "I think now people have to start to make their own decisions about their risk tolerance ... I'm not comfortable saying there's a right or wrong choice. There's your choice."[38] This emphasis on personal decision-making was highlighted in later parts of this same report that noted the different vaccination and travel decisions some gay men had made. The trope could also be found in the experiences of a retired couple who said they had to choose between being in public and surviving. It is impossible to discern all of the effects that might emanate from stories that give presence to personal choice. The form of these narratives—featuring public events and private spaces that helped to spread coronavirus–muddies the complexities of this case study. But this equivocation without a difference also points to a noteworthy absence of action: few people called for universal inoculations as a result of the P-town outbreak. Despite a clear communal effort on the part of LGBT people, subtle notions of individual choice often held.

On that note, media coverage of the outbreak produced a deep fixation on the queer cultures at the center of this story. Reporters consistently turned to the famous Tea Dance that happens at the Boat Slip, the Circuit Week festivities held in P-town, and Bear Week. And while there is little denying that queer communities were at the heart of these events, casual references about this epidemic were sure to raise an eyebrow for readers with any remote knowledge of HIV/AIDS history. For example, the *Washington Post* commented that there "was no 'patient zero' in Provincetown, according to experts who studied the virus's spread, and no single superspreader event."[39] Although "patient zero" is a term used in vernacular conversations about public health, it found its strongest footing during the AIDS crisis when a French Canadian flight attendant named Gaëtan Dugas was intentionally misidentified as the source of HIV in queer circles on the American coasts.[40] That outbreak myth presented Dugas as a boogeyman and reinforced predatory stereotypes about gay men and their insatiable quest for sex. According to this tale, casual acquaintances could not be trusted and the possibilities of infection loomed large for those who were not cautious. Other historical parallels were echoed in articles that described a noticeable pattern about viral spread: "all gay men with an average age of 30 to 35, many of whom had seen a doctor for other reasons, like flu symptoms or sexually transmitted infections, not suspecting the coronavirus."[41] Indeed, even references to gay men testing "positive" carried a semiotic excess that was not easily contained by the context of the outbreak. Reports also stated that it was impossible to determine the vaccination status of all those who traveled to P-town but the crowd appeared to be "unusually health-conscious." Writing for the *Washington Post*, Hannah Knowles stated, "It helped that the gay community in particular, scarred by the HIV/AIDS epidemic, was hypervigilant and proactive when it came to public health measures like testing."[42] AIDS history was marshalled as the very reason the coronavirus could ultimately be defeated.

Whereas much pandemic coverage focused on the doubt produced by strangers in the polity, the queer tourists here were enshrined as an exemplar of communal effort. This was true not only for vaccines, but also for contact tracing and testing. A reporter for the *New York Times* relayed that an infectious disease specialist had "praised the community's meticulous contact tracing ... for helping them to understand the scope of the outbreak."[43] That same story went on to quote Rick Murray, the manager of a beachside inn who has been HIV-positive for thirty-seven years and who analogized the pandemic to the AIDS crisis. He told the *Times*, "When the AIDS epidemic came, we took care of our own, and we will take care of our own now."[44] NPR ran a feature on Michael Donnelly, a gay data scientist from New York who had been publishing independent data on the Covid pandemic and was able to document over fifty breakthrough cases coming out of Provincetown well before the CDC was assessing data about the events. One official at the agency remarked that the contact tracing done by the gay community provided "a testament to the power of citizens engaging with the scientific process."[45] In this way, the queer community became a stand-in for the voice of reason and science. The *Washington Post* noted that some people were feeling frustrated and a sense of whiplash after the CDC offered updated guidance on masks. But one queer performer casually noted, "I'm not mad that the rules changed because the virus changed."[46] Donnelly confidently backed up these ideas by observing: "The norms of the gay community say: share your medical history, share your risks with other people so that they can be responsible and take care of themselves as well ... that came with years of practice within the community, particularly around HIV and AIDS."[47] Of course, this has not necessarily always been a community norm. Sexual shame and stigma still haunt many people and new technologies such as PrEP have led some to find the expectations of sharing sexual history to be intrusive and unnecessary. Still, reporters found novel ways to laud the queer community by pointing to social media posts that urged friends to get screened for the coronavirus and the hundreds of people who waited in long lines to get tested each day.[48]

The lesson that should have been communicated clearly and without hesitation was that the vaccines worked. Without the vaccine, many more people would have caught Covid, suffered complications, or died. Recent data suggest that unvaccinated people are eleven times more likely to die from Covid than their unvaccinated counterparts.[49] Even in early reports, there were studies that found unvaccinated people were twice as likely to be infected as vaccinated people.[50] The many moving parts of this case study, however, seemed to lend an air of doubt and uncertainty about vaccines and the protection that they so clearly offered.

Breakthrough Infection and the Mounting Crisis of Doubt

Doubt's place in the American imaginary is structured both by the actions of institutions that have struggled to make the pandemic narratively intelligible and the negotiation of those effects by people who experience uncertainty at every turn. The more imperative question that confronts us is: What do we do with these extremities of uncertainty? How do we revive a sense of assurance when communicating about science? How do we productively direct doubt when there is no way of avoiding its ubiquity? The opening scenes at the start of this essay are cultural touchstones, for sure, but they also point toward long-standing issues that we will grapple with for years to come. Fauci's precaution signals the ongoing necessity of educating publics about the nuances of evolving public health strategies. The P-town example highlights the intersection of cultural and medical scripts—and that what is given presence will steer policy and media narratives. The Facebook debacle illustrates the need to regulate social media platforms and more aggressively retort intentionally misleading information. Each of these points to a structure of feeling that has emerged forcefully during the pandemic, even though this pattern of thought has been coming into its own for a very long time.

Of course, doubt need not be an entirely problematic construct and having a critical eye—especially toward misinformation—can ultimately be fruitful. Giving further attention to the uncertainty that stifles public health must be explicitly taken up to expand the possibilities for keeping people safe. To start, we must robustly engage community concerns in the hope that doubt can in fact be generative. This is clearly a challenging endeavor but not one without precedent. Jennifer Malkowski encourages scholars to turn to the relational dynamics of health to think through the import of community wellbeing. She writes, "When it comes to disease management, communicating with others openly and earnestly about prevention options is an ideal public health practice, one that requires individuals to understand how their own health status intersects with the statuses of others."[51] This is certainly no easy task. One of the most difficult aspects of attempting to persuade people to get vaccinated is that there are simply different reasons people elect to inoculate or not. For some people, there is a genuine lack of access that prevents them from getting a shot. For others, Covid is still not a threat despite its ravenous body count. For still others, there may be attempts to avoid adverse side effects and not miss work. There may be a lack of trust in the vaccines or a lack of confidence in institutions.[52] Despite these drawbacks, Malkowski is correct that difficult conversations must be had in order to best administer health directives. A concept like individual choice is decidedly limited, and attempting to persuade people that notions of risk are best understood communally must happen gradually over time. The Provincetown outbreak is an excellent example of this communal protection but one that must be narrated properly and without the sensationalism that accompanied many popular media reports.

Scholars must also rethink how we communicate about science and medicine by giving additional focus to their rhetorical composition. Many people insist that science is simply ever evolving and that we must embrace the ambiguity that tends to accompany its dynamic nature. I do not dispute that science necessarily changes as it incorporates more variables and evidence into its formulations. But I'm also uncertain that such an approach provides for effective public health messaging. Without clear, declarative communication, confusion sets in. Public health officials and educators would do well to offer more explicit focus to the ways technologies such as vaccines are brought to life. Arguing that vaccines are akin to an umbrella, rather than a forcefield, for example, can set public expectations about an inoculation's capabilities and limitations.

Such exercises might seem futile when we contemplate the major structural problems that confront the nation. As I write this in June 2022, doubt continues to define our political, cultural, and economic reality. And while there is little space to address all of these, I see two that are especially pertinent to this chapter. First, in the United States, our institutions are being tested in unprecedented ways and serious questions remain about their ability to hold, especially in the face of another global crisis. The antidemocratic movement that has taken hold in the wake of the Trump administration has illustrated a profound disregard for verifiable facts and political truths. These authoritarian impulses, coupled with disastrous neoliberal policy decisions, will continue to propel a profound sense of doubt about the world we are living in. On a different note, we are just beginning to understand the dynamics of "long Covid" and its mass disabling effects. There will be those who doubt the existence of this perplexing, still evolving syndrome. And there will be just as many people, if not more, who persistently doubt their own wellness and the degree to which Covid may be lingering in their bodies in damaging and insidious ways. And, to be sure, the autocratic gestures outlined above would only hasten the spread of long Covid and its mysterious consequences.

I continue to be perplexed by the possibilities that lie ahead. Will Covid become endemic or will its variants evolve into something even more lethal? Will mask use remain a precautionary measure in the coming years or will we abandon them altogether? The uncertainty that has underlined the pandemic will likely produce few answers in the short term. What will remain a constant, at least for the foreseeable future, is the doubt that envelopes our world and the ongoing necessity to manage it as we plow ahead into the unknown.

NOTES

1. The original count of infections was 469, but that number eventually climbed to over one thousand as the virus spread away from the resort town.
2. Apoorva Mandavilli, "Vaccinated People May Spread the Virus, Though Rarely, CDC Reports," *New York Times* July 30, 2021. Emphases mine.
3. Elizabeth Dwoskin, "Facebook says Post that Cast Doubt on Covid Vaccine was Most Popular on the Platform from January through March," *Washington Post*, August 21, 2021.
4. Scott Baker, "Reflection, Doubt, and the Place of Rhetoric in Postmodern Social Theory," *Sociological Theory* 8 (1990): 232–45.
5. Raymond Williams, *The Long Revolution* (New York: Columbia University Press, 1961), 48.
6. Sean Matthews, "Change and Theory in Raymond Williams's Structure of Feeling," *Pretexts: Literary and Cultural Studies* 10 (2001): 186.
7. Matthews, "Change and Theory," 189.

8. Elaine Scarry, *The Body in Pain: The Making and Unmaking of the World* (London: Oxford University Press, 1987).
9. Fariss Samarrai, "Study Links Disparities in Pain Management to Racial Bias," *UVAToday*, April 4, 2016.
10. For a rhetorical analysis of hypochondria, see Judy Segal, *Health and the Rhetoric of Medicine* (Carbondale: Southern Illinois University Press, 2008), 74–90.
11. Arthur Kleinman, *The Illness Narratives: Suffering, Healing, and the Human Condition* (New York: Basic Books, 1989).
12. Kleinman, *Illness Narratives*.
13. Arthur Frank, *The Wounded Storyteller: Body, Illness, and Ethics* (Chicago: University of Chicago Press, 2013), 174.
14. Frank, *Wounded Storyteller*, 175.
15. See, for example, Zeynep Tufekci, "The CDC Is Still Repeating Its Mistakes," *Atlantic*, April 28, 2021.
16. Francis A. Beer and Robert Hariman, "Learning from the Pandemic: Catastrophic Epistemology," *Social Epistemological Review and Reply Collective* 9 (2020): 19–27.
17. Eve Kosofsky Sedgwick, *Touching Feeling: Affect, Pedagogy, Performativity* (Durham, NC: Duke University Press, 2003): 123–51.
18. Ulrich Beck, *Risk Society: Towards a New Modernity*, trans. Mark Ritter (London: SAGE, 1992), 21.
19. Deborah Lupton, *Risk* (New York: Routledge, 2013), 132.
20. Cecília Tomori et al., "Your Health Is in Your Hands? U.S. CDC COVID-19 Mask Guidance Reveals the Moral Foundations of Public Health," *eClinicalMedicine* 38 (2021): 101071.
21. Marina Levina, "Queering Intimacy, Six Feet Apart," *QED: A Journal in GLBTQ Worldmaking* 7 (2020): 195–200.
22. Roxanne Khamsi, "The Mystery of Why Some People Keep Testing Positive for COVID-19," *Elemental*, July 28, 2020.
23. Carolyn Karmann, "How Did I Catch the Coronavirus?," *New Yorker*, August 7, 2020; Roxanne Khamsi, "The Mystery of Why Some People Keep Testing Positive for COVID-19," *Medium*, July 28, 2020; James Hamblin, "Why Some People Get Sicker than Others," *Atlantic*, April 21, 2020.
24. Jeffrey A. Bennett, "Chronic Citizenship: Community, Choice, and Queer Controversy," in *Biocitizenship: Lively Subjects, Embodied Sociality, and Posthuman Politics*, ed. Kelly Happe, Jenell Johnson, and Marina Levina (New York: New York University Press, 2018), 95–116.

25. Smriti Mallapaty, "Heart-Inflammation Risk from Pfizer COVID Vaccine Is Very Low," *Nature*, October 8, 2021.
26. Eula Biss, *On Immunity: An Inoculation* (Minneapolis: Graywolf Press, 2014), 70–71.
27. Heidi Y. Lawrence, *Vaccine Rhetorics* (Columbus: Ohio State University Press, 2020).
28. Lynda Walsh and Kenneth C. Walker, "Perspectives on Uncertainty for Technical Communication Scholars," *Technical Communication Quarterly* 25 (2016): 71–86.
29. Angus Chen, "Provincetown Data Suggests Vaccines Protect Against Complications, but Not Delta Transmission," *WBUR News*, July 30, 2021.
30. Ellen Barry and Beth Treffeisen, "'It's Nowhere Near Over': A Beach Town's Gust of Freedom, Then a U-turn," *New York Times*, July 31, 2021.
31. Selena Simmons-Duffin, "How a Gay Community Helped the CDC Spot a COVID Outbreak—and Learn More About Delta," *NPR*, August 6, 2021.
32. Hannah Knowles, "How Provincetown, Mass., Stress-Tested the Coronavirus Vaccine with Summer Partying and Delta," *Washington Post*, August 5, 2021.
33. Chen, "Provincetown Data."
34. Chen, "Provincetown Data."
35. Carolyn Johnson, Yasmeen Abutaleb, and Joel Achenbach, "CDC Study Shows Three-fourths of People Infected in Massachusetts Coronavirus Outbreak Were Vaccinated but Few Required Hospitalization," *Washington Post*, July 30, 2021.
36. Knowles, "How Provincetown."
37. Johnson, Abutaleb, and Achenbach, "CDC Study Shows."
38. Knowles, "How Provincetown."
39. Knowles, "How Provincetown."
40. See Priscilla Wald, *Contagious: Cultures, Carriers, and the Outbreak Narrative* (Durham, NC: Duke University Press, 2008), 213–63.
41. Barry and Treffeisen, "'Nowhere Near Over.'"
42. Knowles, "How Provincetown."
43. Barry and Treffeisen, "'Nowhere Near Over.'"
44. Barry and Treffeisen, "'Nowhere Near Over.'"
45. Simmons-Duffin, "How a Gay Community."
46. Knowles, "How Provincetown."
47. Simmons-Duffin, "How a Gay Community."
48. Knowles, "How Provincetown."
49. Vanessa Romo, "Unvaccinated People Are 11 Times More Likely to Die of COVID-19, New Research Finds," *NPR*, September 10, 2021.
50. Johnson, Abutaleb, and Achenbach, "CDC Study Shows."

51. Jennifer A. Malkowski, "The Human Papillomavirus Vaccination: Gendering the Rhetorics of Immunization in Public Health Discourses," in *Bodies in Transition in the Health Humanities: Representations of Corporeality*, ed. Lisa M. DeTora and Stephanie M. Hilger (New York: Routledge, 2019), 94.

52. German Lopez, "The Six Reasons Americans Aren't Getting Vaccinated," *Vox*, June 2, 2021.

Contributors

Michael Aylward is an internist and pediatrician at the University of Minnesota.

Jeffrey A. Bennett is professor and chair of communication studies at Vanderbilt University.

Sara DiCaglio is an assistant professor of English at Texas A&M University.

Priyanka Ganguly is a PhD student in rhetoric and writing at Virginia Tech.

Julie Gerdes is an assistant professor of technical writing and rhetoric at Virginia Tech.

Veronica Joyner is an assistant professor of technical communication at University of Central Florida.

Diane Keeling is an associate professor in communication at the University of San Diego.

Molly Margaret Kessler is an associate professor of writing studies at the University of Minnesota.

Heidi Y. Lawrence is an associate professor of English at George Mason University.

Marina Levina is a professor of communication and film at the University of Memphis.

DiArron M. is a PhD candidate at the University of Memphis.

Jennifer Malkowski is associate professor of communication arts and sciences at California State University, Chico.

Angela Nurse holds a PhD in sociology from Michigan State University and is an assistant professor of sociology at University of San Diego.

Celeste E. Orr is a research associate and part-time professor at the University of Ottawa.

Hailey Nicole Otis is an assistant professor of communication at the University of Maryland, College Park.

Raquel M. Robvais is an instructor of African and African American studies and communication studies at Louisiana State University.

Allison L. Rowland is Maurer Associate Professor of Performance and Communication Arts at St. Lawrence University.

Luana Shafer is a PhD student in rhetoric and writing at Virginia Tech.

Bernard Trappey is an adult and pediatric hospitalist at the University of Minnesota and director of the UMN Center for the Art of Medicine.

Emily Winderman is assistant professor of communication studies at the University of Minnesota, Twin Cities.

Kurt Zemlicka is a senior lecturer in the Department of English at Indiana University, Bloomington.